LIFE CYCLES

Julian Sayarer

LIFE CYCLES

*How One Bike Courier
Circumnavigated the Globe in
169 Days and Broke a World Record*

First published in Great Britain in 2014 by John Blake Publishing Ltd
The paperback edition published in 2023 by

ARCADIA BOOKS
LONDON

Arcadia Books
An imprint of Quercus Editions Limited
Carmelite House
50 Victoria Embankment
London EC4Y 0DZ

An Hachette UK company

A CIP catalogue record for this book is available
from the British Library.

ISBN (MMP) 978 1 52942 846 9
ISBN (Ebook) 978 1 52942 847 6

10 9 8 7 6 5 4 3 2 1

Typeset by Jouve (UK), Milton Keynes
Printed and bound in Great Britain by Clays Ltd, Elcograf S.p.A.

MIX
Paper from
responsible sources
FSC
www.fsc.org FSC® C104740

Papers used by Quercus Books are from well-managed
forests and other responsible sources.

Contents

New Author Preface

For a number of years the dates of departure and return felt like the most important in my calendar. June 10th, December 4th. They represented the day my life began to change forever, and the day I returned home and started trying to pretend that it hadn't. Most circumnavigators I know have a similar relationship with their dates. On December 4th I cycled back up to the cathedral of Rouen, approaching from the west, having left it moving east: 18,049 miles and twenty countries since I first departed for Shanghai and the 83 days it took to get across that Eurasian leg. The circumnavigation in between was later verified by Guinness as a world record of 169 days. I still remember how it felt that final evening, as I neared the city and saw the illuminated cathedral spires, and I couldn't believe that it was over and I really had done what I'd set out to do, and ridden a bicycle all around the world.

It was no random chance that made the Normandy city of Rouen my start and finish. Many if not most touring cyclists are avid readers, and at that age – and to an extent still – I loved the classics above all else. I won't pre-empt the explanations of the book's opening pages, but I chose Rouen for being spiritual home to Gustave Flaubert, foremost among writers who had created a sense of life and adventure that corresponded to that which I found in riding during my twenties. Flaubert had written with eloquence and nonchalance about things that were tearing me up inside, a

23-year-old politics graduate turned London cycle courier watching the financial crisis unfold.

A little under four months since setting out, on the Pacific Coast Highway in Mendocino county, I met a homeless man riding from Washington State to Santa Barbara so as to stay warm through winter. When he asked me to write something, anything, with a marker pen on his yellow raincoat, I scrawled Flaubert's lines from *Madame Bovary*: 'Language is the cracked kettle on which we beat out tunes for dancing bears, all the while longing to move the stars to pity.' The meeting appears in this book, though not this detail of it, and over the years it has felt valuable to record such things, to prevent the memory of the entire trip being reduced to only what is in the book. That sentence and sentiment is still at the heart of my understanding, and ambition, as a writer; the hope of pinning down the magic of human thought and feeling, and to travel as well as I can through the abstract constructions of the written word.

Riding bikes and writing were always the two things that moved my world. Having grown up in an economically and socially depressed town in the Midlands that I'd rather not furnish the cliché by detailing, the bicycle, like books, was responsible for taking me places I could never otherwise have imagined. That Mendocino coast, with a cycling hobo who was a storyteller more skilled than any I've ever met, was one such place. Another, camped beside my bicycle on the Kazakh steppe, watching stars shoot overhead. And riding through Texas nights, where the pumpjacks creaked oil and cotton was baled under floodlights. Antarctic winds pushed me up through New Zealand, and rainforest rubber plantations pressed the reek of latex into humid Malay nights. It was by bicycle that I found the world. Now, having lived so much of it, and struggling to get as high as I used to, I still remember those early days when home in the Midlands was a recent enough memory that I couldn't believe where I'd got to.

In writing terms I still travel faithfully with a notepad, though often also with a book or article in mind. In 2009 – before *Life Cycles* was even in an agent's inbox, before I had the first clue of how to go about becoming a published author – I simply set out knowing I had to see more of the world, that I had to write about it and, beyond that, I hoped one day others would be able to read it too. Sometimes I miss the purity of writing and travelling in that way, where both are just for yourself, with a less structured thought for the results the other side.

I broke the record for a circumnavigation by bicycle, I broke it by a month, and then of course it passed to others. Now the record is back with the same holder I set out to topple in 2009. Second time out he raised a financial war chest of some half a million pounds, and was supported through every mile by an entourage of mechanics, chefs and a masseur in a camper van following behind.

The community of long-distance cyclists remains confused that Guinness have not yet made a category for supported and unsupported rides, in effect ensuring that the record is mostly determined before the start of the race by whoever can raise the most money. Supported rides will lend themselves to higher profiles, bigger sponsorship and – barring the arrival of a superhuman rider – faster times, which I suspect keeps Guinness happy, not having to differentiate between the aided rider on the one hand, and the independent on the other. Both purists and passing fans of touring cycling are in no doubt as to which version holds the true spirit of adventure.

I miss much of the way adventure was, but perhaps so too travel and even the simplicity of life, cliché as it is to remember simpler times. It amazes me that my social media engagement while away those six months were things called 'tweets', sent as text messages from an old phone to a number saved in my contacts. To get the letter *C* I had to press the *1* button three times . . .

---

you remember. I punched out 140 characters to which I could not attach an image or a link, nor did I imagine that possible. My messages from the roadside were like tiny haikus, one a day so as not to erode my minimal budget with overseas SMS, and in a time before the digital world would blend so much with the real, and both became so saturated with our most fleeting thoughts, musings, references.

I had a satellite tracking of my ride, though it was just before the days in which Guinness mandated it, because it was understood that tracking remained a somewhat high-tech and costly option. My own tracking saw me turn round in my saddle as I rode, and every twenty kilometres press an 'OK' button on the tracking device I had strapped by bungee cord to my rear pannier bag. The twenty kilometres were measured independently by the speedometer on my handlebars which – as in the old days – was of course activated by a small magnet attached to a spoke on the front wheel. Now all this seems fantastically low-tech; and then, naturally, fantastically advanced.

Most of all I miss the maps. I miss the maps drawn by petrol-station attendants in Louisiana to get me back – over the railtracks, down along the bayou – to the clearing in which their trailers were set up and where I was welcome to stay the night. I miss the half dozen maps of Europe in my pannier bag that a couple of youngsters from Cambridge, driving to Ulaanbaatar in the Mongolian Rally, offered to take home for me from where we met in Aral, Kazakhstan, to save the pannier space as I wouldn't be needing them again, their jeep had plenty of room, and they could post them back to my address in the UK. They did.

It amazes me that, held in my pocket, on my phone, there could now be all the hundreds of maps I would need to navigate precisely in and out of every single city, from Shanghai to Vancouver. But still, I miss the asking of strangers, and – before technology gave us all of its options – the basic compulsions of *just head south* or *just head east* didn't work too badly, to be honest.

The world I know I found out there, more beautifully than any other way I could have imagined or lived. I rode the world, and I had so much fun in it. I rode to show that adventure didn't have to be corporate or alpha-male or banker-sponsored or joyless. Relative to the big money circumnavigations, comparatively few saw the message that I hoped to send out, but I know that to those who did, it meant something. In many ways the spirit of a true adventure never is nor was a dominant one. Adventure is not common, popular or widely broadcast. The spirit of adventure is kept in the idea that you can find somewhere a seed of something done differently, and no matter how many or few people find it, it means the world to them when they do. I hope that old ride was this seed for some, and it still means the world to me when people tell me so.

Life Cycles was my first book. It's hard to believe it happened at all, still less that others followed. It took a number of them before I got over my reluctance to refer to myself as 'a writer', a title and vocation that had always felt too fantastical and dreamlike.

The ride itself was a circumnavigation, but it was undeniably predominantly in the northern hemisphere, aside from a thousand miles of New Zealand. By accident I cycled through most of the three global powers of the last and coming century – Russia, China and the United States – adding a fourth power if you count the dozen states of the EU I crossed too, at a time when Britain was still in it, and me belonging to a generation who'd never have taken it out.

The borders of Ukraine and Russia were a less contentious thing then, the people either side of them more similar than at many other frontiers I would cross. I learned in both countries '*priamo*' for 'straight on' (the commonest instruction on the long roads into the steppe) and '*Molodets!*', said emphatically and often with a clenched fist, which at the time was obviously a celebration of my efforts but I later learned meant something like 'good man!', said with the enthusiasm of '*bravo*'. Another now-friend from France, who I met later as we both cycled through Kazakhstan, told me the same word had by force of repetition also entered his vocabulary as he went riding through Russia, and I always liked something about the intrinsic nature of both language and travelling cyclists that it was clearly the go-to word in both the Russian and Ukrainian psyche for a passing stranger on a pannier-laden bicycle.

If I rode about one hundred miles a day on average, China was developing at one hundred miles an hour, and the two priorities clashed badly. I remain sad at all that I will have missed as I hurried through, and embarrassed at the way – combined with a young man's writing style and a worldview that saw, but more so *wrote*, a swashbuckling adversity into almost everything – I often depicted the Chinese as strangers, others, and obstacles in my way rather than a people and culture to meet. In truth, the way I wrote China was different – and coarser – than the way I'd lived it, however challenging at times.

The United States left me at first totally and then diminishingly spellbound, but in general the six thousand miles I rode there were my first insight into the torrid dilapidation of that country. I met countless acts of the most generous humanity, but also the broken lives that had fallen out of the bottom of it, and a mainstream culture of large cars, pharmaceutical ads and no-win-no-fee lawyer billboards that showed a country run *without* humanity, despite the abundance of it found at roadsides. If my heritage in Turkey, and books I went on to work on in Palestine and with refugees of US wars, all gave me a natural aversion to the role of the US in the world, the anger I'd feel at the population as a whole – prone to brashness and stupidity and ego – is still tempered by seeing up-close the victims that US power takes for itself at home. I rode in the first year of an Obama presidency, and by the time I hitchhiked through five years later it was just as bad, and perhaps worse.

The record I broke still sits awkwardly with who I am, and when I talk to new people about it, it is only when they ask 'How long did it take?' that I mention speed. The globe-cycling community, many of whom became good friends via the Internet, I often envy for the speed – or relative absence of it – in their rides, and I think back on my own haste, fun as it sometimes was, as a sort of blasphemy against the richness of the world's diversity and hidden secrets. That being said, I had to break that record; for the sake of travel, for the sake of spirit, for the sake of something called adventure.

Looking back I feel consistently like I was angry before it became fashionable to be angry. Before US bourgeoisie had to suffer their embarrassment at Donald Trump as President, and British bourgeoisie theirs at leaving Europe. I was angry because I grew up watching failed lives and a state that turned away from the responsibility of providing either security or opportunity. I grew up close to substance abuse, around racism before I was even aware this strange hostility was called that, to parents giving their all to offset the social and economic insecurity of immigration, before I knew that word either. Once you have grown up close to the difficulties that are embedded in our systems, and once you have felt the panic of seeing a system that doesn't work while others have yet to realise as much, that is a hard thing to unlearn or unsee, and the imperative of change became obvious. If it is odd that the bicycle became my personal means of finding escape and balance in this world, still, I am eternally grateful to it, however unlikely a solution.

These days I am no less angry, but I have learned how to be

calmer with it, and I remain determined. In some ways I wish I could both ride the ride and write this book again. To see that small Kazakh border crossing that is now a major node on Beijing's Belt & Road, sitting at the median point of all Eurasia as it does. To see that again, that would be something.

A second time I would write it, I think, calmer. I would know my limits better, would know where to make the cut; those things age and experience teach you as a writer. Still, I love the purity of *Life Cycles* as I recorded it then. The colossal energy I must have had to both ride and write this story in such a way feels perhaps more remote now, remote enough that I can be proud of the me who did it. I remember I just did what seemed natural at the time, and I saw nothing remarkable in it. It'd be a crime both as a writer, but so too against my younger self, to try to moderate or tame his voice by toning down any sentence that now jumps out at me with a candour that no longer reflects who I am.

At root, I remain forever grateful to the ride and the foundation in humanity that it provided me. Travel of that nature, pedalling yourself through everything and so many chance encounters, affirms the goodness of everyone, and it saves a lot of needless stress or sadness to be able to dispel the idea, fed by media or hearsay, that we as people are not, in our fundamental nature, good. If the world can seem at times a dark or dispiriting place, it is hard to succumb to such a logic when you know that all that world you've known is still out there, just as I found it then.

Julian Sayarer,
November 2022

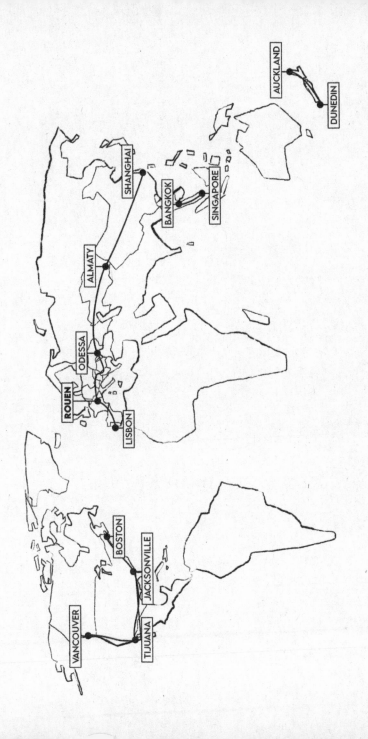

Prologue

It didn't feel good . . . there was no sense of achievement, the idea I was supposed to feel some kind of triumph only made me feel worse about the fact that I didn't. I broke a world record in the hope that it was going to make some difference to the world itself. My ride was the tree, falling in the woods with no one around to hear. One night, soon after my return, I'd accidentally left my phone on, so that next morning the alarm went off and woke me with a start. It grew louder, that same cheerful noise that so recently forced me awake after only 40 minutes' sleep. Cold and wet . . . it demanded I get back on my bike to ride another 150 miles or miss my flight, my finish. And there, in my bed in London, I whimpered at the sound, calmed myself as I realised where I was and that I didn't have to go anywhere.

I shot my mouth off. Still sleep-deprived and shaken, within a fortnight of my return, I'd told everyone exactly what I thought of the previous recordholder. Then more than ever, I couldn't believe how he'd sold it all away. The beauty of the open road, the warmth of human-kind . . . the way he'd slapped a logo on it and sold the whole shebang to whichever bank would pay most. The mild-mannered folk of the cycling community told me I had it wrong, reminded me delicately that he'd done it for charity. That was how I earned myself the moniker of 'angry young man'. They put it my way as some sort of insult, and all the time I racked my brains as to how it was that I was the only one so angry.

I returned to the same job, to the same life as before, and, with visions of the Gobi Desert's outward reaches still blowing through my mind, I went back to picking my way through the potholes and gnarling traffic of London. I thought of all those who had taken me in . . . the Lemoines in Louisiana, Ray over on South Island . . . I tried to piece the world back together, to make sense of the CCTV cameras, the apparently suspicious packages, the strangers who were – *just maybe* – standing too close to me at the cashpoint. I tried to make sense of it all and then, slowly, I stopped trying because the sad truth was it didn't make sense . . . we'd just chosen to live that way.

London swallowed me back in. I watched diggers with their caterpillar tracks crawling across rubble, destructive ballerinas with pirouetting scoops that tore down flats – the same as I'd once watched them do in Xi'an, China – so that I wondered what they did with those who'd once lived there. The deliveries made on my bicycle were all the same, still going to the same offices, the same receptionists scribbling their names impatiently on an electronic screen. One day I turned up at an architectural practice to collect a package going down to an international depot on the Old Kent Road. They handed me a long cardboard tube containing the plans for another structure in glass and steel on the other side of the world. I looked down at the tube in my hand, curious about its final destination, and there it was:

Pudong – Shanghai

Inside of me something heaved, my poor heart gave a lurch, for I'd cycled there, to the airport in Pudong itself . . . 83 days if I remembered right. There I was . . . back in London, my old job, my old bicycle leaning against a wall. I slid the tube into my bag with a sigh, climbed onto my bike and pedalled off. Making my way through the traffic, I watched the chain rumbling below, clinging to the teeth of the cog as they heaved it round, wheels turning and the asphalt moving below, my knees up and down . . . everything just as before, that same scene I'd taken in over so many countless hours, on my way around the world.

I noticed a few changes for my six-month before-and-after. For all that my life remained unaltered, London was a little different. Everyone had started drinking energy drinks, the things advertised all over the place, complete with promises of just how the drinker would feel alive again, and no mention of why it was they all felt so dead to begin with. Sugar was everywhere . . . coffee, yoghurt, you name it and any simple flavour had been made just another way of having dessert. On reception desks and beside doorways, hand sanitisers had made their way over from the US, alcohol-based solutions rising up with a fear of germs, the microscopic creatures that would guiltlessly destroy our lives if we weren't careful. More of London seemed to have taken to cycling, forced into it by unaffordable public transport and long lines of stationary cars. Morning and evening, Lycra-clad commuters would eye me up for a race . . . I left them to it. I rode the Dunwich Dynamo, a night ride of 110 miles, leaving from Hackney in the dusk of a Saturday in late June. Thousands ride it, and you follow the flickering trail of red lights through the lanes and woods of Essex and Suffolk, where candles gutter in jam jars to light the way. With the dawn you reach the sea at Dunwich, you strip, you dive in. On the coach home, all heads tipped to one side with sleep, I heard the girl behind me, talking excitedly to her boyfriend about the record I now held . . .

And he rode 90 miles every day . . . I think his record was 190 days or something . . . it was on TV!

And I smiled slowly . . . didn't even turn my head, so that she'd never have guessed the peculiar story the stranger on the seat in front kept secret. But stop me, that's enough for now, I'm getting ahead of myself, starting at the end. I should tell you how I got here.

The Bicycle

I always rode a bicycle and I always loved that bicycle, it's only as clichéd as it is true. The vehicle of novelists and poets, 'when I see an adult riding a bicycle, I do not despair for the future of mankind', that's how H. G. Wells put it, and I'm just one of many who find in the bicycle a mobile salvation, the ability to propel myself towards my own escape. As a child I rode near to my house, as a teenager I rode away from it, into the countryside, and once I'd hit the countryside it was only ever my ambition to go further. I rode my bicycle to the disused quarry where I played with my brother, to my grandparents' house, 10 miles away, to school, and to the restaurants where I worked as a teenager. Eventually I was riding into neighbouring counties, into rides of 40, 50, 60 and 100 miles, chasing average speeds of 20mph. Occasionally I went too far, ambition beyond ability, so that my mother had to drive out and collect me, exhausted, from roadsides far from home.

I fell in love with the sport, with the Tour de France especially. Head over heels it got me, a sport played out across the roads of Europe, all of it, to the last metre, the most magnificent arena for the most magnificent of theatre. Though they may have their favourites, the crowds that flock to watch that race cheer each and every rider, to applaud the sport itself. The yellow jersey, the *maillot jaune* of the race leader, bears the colour of the Tour, of July sunflower fields beneath the foothills of the Pyrenees. The race begins with a prologue, a time-trial just some 15 kilometres through the streets of the departure town. When David Millar won the prologue in 2000, so leading for the Tour's first stages, he wore the yellow jersey during those days, and, at night, he slept in it. That's what the yellow jersey means, it's an honour, the culmination of fairytales and childhood dreams. Cycling gets stuck inside of you . . . out of my childhood and into my adult years it's been in me. I found it in the lanes of Leicestershire, endeavouring to go so far and so fast my rides finished with the pulse of my heartbeat tucked inside my skull at the base of my brain. That was what I aspired to, the barometer of my commitment, for I wanted one day to wear a yellow jersey, and I had learned that to extend your limits they had, periodically, to be surpassed. I had to get uncomfortable because . . . *oh boy*, did I want to wear a yellow jersey one day. I wanted to get better, to be good enough. I know now, it took time, but today I understand just how good a cyclist I am. Let me tell you, take a deep breath and confess: I am now good enough only to fully appreciate just how average I am, perhaps better than most, but truly piffling compared to the best. I knew it when I was younger too, but back then I could hope I might improve, get faster over time. Nowadays I know. I know that I'll never be fast enough, but I got comfortable with that truth . . . it took a few years, but eventually I came to terms with it. That's just growing up, you give up another dream, find happiness by other means.

Throughout that journey, I suppose the bicycle became my touchstone, my talisman. Of all that will be sold away, please allow that the bicycle be the last thing to remain sacred. I loved cycling through impulse, through instinct, and long before I was cursed to try articulating that feeling with words. Across the miles I've given it a great deal of thought, finally resolved that perhaps for me the bicycle represents some small saviour from mortality, the opportunity to make something greater of myself, to move with such speed and power that a portion of the mind is able to believe in magic, believe we humans are not after all so banal as I must otherwise confront. I love the bicycle like nothing else, the one institution I'm happy to live by, for in it you can feel euphoria.

The Midlands

I grew up in a small town that had been a village when my family first moved there. Every year it grows more, a tumour in some anonymous region of central England. First it got the supermarket, then the housing developments, then a large road bypassing the place entirely, and by the time that was complete, it had lost pretty much everything else anyway. Once you've seen the uglier side of things, you realise just how oblivious half the town is to what's happening. I know the children from *good* families who found their way to heroin . . . houses on respectable streets where passers-by would never guess what went on. Occasionally I go back there, see old faces in new pubs, and they tell me they're clean now, implore me to believe they've started afresh. They're good people, good people like all the rest of us, starting life with the same tender spirit every human does. That's why they turn to drugs, not because they're bad . . . but because, in towns like that, the world offers so little.

It was a series of accidents that took me there, accidents of love, migration, separation. I never belonged in that place, a town in which a brain and talent for education are things to be ashamed of, a class in which even the teacher made jokes out of my Turkish surname. That town figured in my destiny as a place to learn from and leave. Even if I still live with most of the personality I found there – parts of it I like, parts of it I don't – I came to realise you can't change the world for the better without first appreciating just how crummy that world can be. I've been through all of the conventional channels . . . a pre-university year abroad, aged 18, holed up in some Soviet-style guesthouse in a North Vietnamese university. I went there with a thirst to teach people English, help them improve their prospects in life, found instead that my value was no more than a sentence in a prospectus – *the foreign language faculty has native-English-speaking teachers* – and, aside from that, no one needed anything more from me for the rest of the year. Every day I had my make-a-difference heart crushed slowly and, for the first time, I learned the so-called world's poor are doing just fine without us. More than any place I've ever visited, it's our own *developed* world that seems to have in it the greatest need for change.

I returned from Vietnam, enrolled myself at a university in a south-coast town. There I saw the future for the first time, studying alongside the ministers of the next decade, bright-eyed youths who spoke three languages without an intelligent sentence to articulate in any of them. They offered such indictment against the politics that governs us, people who have learned the art of talking without saying a thing, cultivated wardrobes and friendship circles rather than mind or spirit. There I spent three years alongside the most hastily constructed idealisms, values altogether less precious than the salaries people anticipated the other side of graduation.

To Istanbul

My father is Turkish, my mother English, and together they spent the seventies in Istanbul, part of the protest movement against the military, police and government. While at university I realised I could use a bicycle to take me to Turkey . . . 2,000 miles and a month for the journey, learning how to live again as I made my way there. As undertakings go, cycling to new places has always been just enough to provide my life with purpose, yet insufficient to distract me from what that life is supposed to be about. Alone, I swam out into cold Alpine rivers. I swapped stories with my friend as we spit-roasted chicken beside an Italian lake. Strangers took me in and offered me beds, meals, all kinds of humanity that, so I came to realise, is the norm rather than the exception once humans find themselves connected rather than isolated from one another. On humid Albanian evenings, I sweltered in my tent with mosquito swarms waiting outside to devour me. I picked figs from trees hanging over the coastal road in Croatia, ran out of water and croaked on a mountainside in Montenegro. The solitude, the night, the unknown lands that wait for you . . . it was never anything to fear, only a freedom, a simplicity just waiting to be seen as such. What once scared me are those things I came to love most.

On the roads of Europe I discovered who I am, the return home ever the hardest part of the journey. In the wilderness, up in the high places I've found contentment, grown comfortable with the idea that I'm simultaneously special and insignificant. It's hard clinging to that belief back home, in these cities that only ever remind you of the insignificance, condition you to focus on all you would wish to be rather than all you already are. Ours is a forward-loaded life, looking to the weekend, devising the five-year plan, planning the next job, everything a stepping-stone to a better place waiting somewhere down the line. But I don't need to tell you this.

* * *

Aged 23 I finished university . . . exceptional grades, essay prizes, rounds of applause and hard evidence against the ruse that doing well at school will get you somewhere. I was sick of England, sick of Western society, sick of feeling like the only one on our island who recognised or cared about the huge tide of shit coming our way. Within a fortnight of graduation I was cycling east, back towards Istanbul. There I found work as an English teacher, made a supplementary income hashing out uninspiring articles for a business journal, and hesitantly began a new life. For a short time I suppose I must've been content, and yet all too quickly I found myself stagnating. Endless tea-drinking and good food brought great comfort but little satisfaction. I started writing stories that always remained unfinished, evening beers crept into afternoons, and I took up fishing, my sense of purpose drifting off down the Bosphorus.

The expat life was not for me, and, after cycling home to London, I started work as a courier, a bicycle messenger . . . one of those young males I'd seen screaming through traffic with radios strapped to their chests, rolling advertisements for the fantasy of being paid money to cycle. The projected salaries I'd been given soon proved closer to lies than exaggerations, yet I became loyal to the security of being paid each Friday for work tolerable to my soul.

From the city's streets I watched society, trying to see the good in the world around me. I saw the cyclist trapped between a bus and railings, panic-stricken eyes bulging from his face as passers-by stopped to photograph the spectacle. I saw the sticker reading *save our small businesses* in the empty, whitewashed window of the old newsagent who'd put it up too late. There were the Lithuanians, eight in the three-bedroom flat below, so that at night I heard every scream and shout, the sobs and dull, ominous thuds from a couple trying to share the 10 square metres beneath my own.

On the courier circuit I made friends with other riders, though there too I never really fitted in. On the road were men and women every bit the salt of the earth, but people without curiosity, believing life owed them nothing beyond the right to work hard and stay poor. I knew one, an old punk, living in fear of the coming month when the bank would repossess his house, our falling wages no longer enough to meet the mortgage payments. So solemnly he explained how he'd once hoped his house would provide him with a little security in later life. Meanwhile, the newspapers and broadcasters kept me posted on the bigger picture, and I watched the rigmarole, the parliamentary circus acting out some pantomime of legitimacy, a sham bearing no resemblance to the lives people had been born into and lived each day. Televisions had been installed in the offices where I made my deliveries, and each one screened a 24-hour newsreel of murders on the other side of the world, ministerial reports to be forgotten in a week, hypothetical chaos and an unremitting barrage of non-events that led people to believe things were constantly happening when, in fact . . . it all remained resolutely the same.

The Record

In that fashion I felt time passing. It dawned on me there comes an age when an individual ceases to be what they one day hope to achieve, we reach the point whereupon we have become a story, a thing that happened, the bed we made and how we wound up lying in it. I was looking for something, something to do and to believe in, and so I began scratching an itch. It had started in Istanbul, the Cihangir crossroads, where I'd met a couple who were a year into cycling around the world. They'd told me of a Scot, of about my own age, aiming to break a world record for a circumnavigation by bicycle.

Back in London I'd looked him up, and soon after, by chance, scarcely had to look for him at all. The guy was well on his way to minor stardom, a subject for television, advertising and corporate endorsements. Come that time he'd broken the record, ridden 18,000 miles in little over six months, an average of 90 miles daily. The start of my curiosity was the feasibility of the target. Riding leisurely to Istanbul I'd averaged 70 miles a day despite lengthy breakfasts, no thought of haste and sitting in cafés scribbling stories for five hours each afternoon. And yet that alone would never have been enough to tempt me into the pettiness of that dumb record. It was the manner in which the feat had been done that roused my ire, snagged a pathological part of my personality I'm not the least bit proud of.

He was sponsored, up to the eyeballs he was sponsored . . . banks and investment funds all over his chest, a smiling face and a thumbs-up next to a business model that cared nothing for people or for bicycles, only the right numbers in the right columns of a balance sheet. I was well desensitised by then, didn't expect much to be left sacred, but it was the final straw to see the bicycle reduced to no more than a corporate marketing strategy. We had things in common, were not so very different, both in our mid-twenties, both politics graduates. I couldn't fathom how someone of such similar years and education, of the same passion for travelling by bicycle, could come to hold such different priorities.

His pitch was a strong one, a stroke of genius. The financial sector he endorsed was without heart or love, working for only financial gain, and so the undertaking, ostensibly for spiritual gain and the joy of the task, was perfect. Their business wore suits, worked in skyscrapers while he would see those who still lived in huts and dressed in loincloths, all traditional-looking to offset the garish and the modern. Finance wanted to be brave, to be beautiful . . . finance wanted to be adventure. They loved him, were ready to make his whole life easier. They threw money at it . . . he sold . . . and with a smattering of charity thrown in, the banking world purchased a tiny piece of human spirit.

The media went to work, knew exactly how to make a fist of things, commit overkill as if it were understatement. It all offered a glimmer of life, an antidote, the thing that makes people feel better and thereby forget the malady they have contracted. Camera rolling, they put the guy into a laboratory, strapped him to a bike with a hose in his gullet, a monitor upon his disappearing heart. They made him pedal for all he was worth, hard enough to make a light flash and a machine go *ping*! He fell, gasping, from the bike, took off his clothes, climbed into a tank of liquid that would tell him how fat he was or was not. The precise purpose of all this remained unclear. Were his lungs too small, his gut too fat? It didn't matter . . . with flying colours he passed the tests. They fished him out, dried him off, sent him to a scientist of eating, and at a long table man and nutritionist sat alone, one each end and a problem with the lighting, the room filled with shadows. All Moses and Mount Sinai, he had it imparted unto him that he must consume 6,000 calories before midnight each day . . . or risk turning into a pumpkin. He swallowed throat, nodded understanding.

He set off. A narrator told his story, borderline depressive, that voice was miserable, terminally heartbroken and irredeemably bereaved. That tale of 18,000 miles was certainly no happy affair. After all the foreboding preparation, the ride itself was headwinds, broken wheels, miscellaneous misfortune and the voice of that woebegone narrator. After six months of misery, the triumph was complete: he had successfully broken a record no one before him had ever seriously attempted. The documentation was perfect, tutelage for the watching masses, misery followed by happy endings, just like life. For the duration it will all be shit, hardship with a few good sunsets, then more shit . . . and triumph at the last. Just hang in there and die with honour. People wanted fairytales, fairytales with just enough bearing on life to be plausible, and thereafter an escape from everything resembling daily existence. The news of the record was disseminated to the population, and at the end of a hard day's work, the country went home to watch edited versions of one man's emotions in circumnavigating the world, by bicycle, so that millions more would never have to.

To be fair to him, he was no worse than typical, his only crime to say yes to a comfortable life, doing things he loved and being paid for the privilege. I admit it . . . he caught me at a bad time, I'll give him that much. I was desperately searching for some meaning back then, crying out to believe some things in this world remained precious. At a loose end, I was in need of a crusade and, however ridiculous it might sound, a small, embarrassing part of me thought that, in beating him, perhaps I could change the world for the better. I suppose, at the very least, it was a worthwhile quest in which to fail.

In my head the ride gained the proportions of a protest, a demonstration of what humans were capable of and the spirit in which it could be done. I wanted to raise a flag, offer some alternative, prove that a bleeding-heart do-gooder could achieve big things as well as any corporation and their ambassador. I planned my route, cycled between embassies and collected visas for my journey, a British passport enough to get me everywhere but Russia, Kazakhstan, China. I saved on every cost, determined to ask no money from anyone, not to follow that formula of undertaking + charity = donation. That was the mentality I was protesting, the idea of a few plucked heartstrings, a donation of currency and then, hey-presto, business as usual in a social model destined to churn out tragedy after tragedy anyway. The idea that money could remedy our every trouble was part of our problem rather than its solution.

It was a ramshackle affair – things started as they went on – and only a day before departure I was still building my bicycle. The first time I rode it was to the harbour at Newhaven . . . from where I left for Rouen, France. My first destination was to be Shanghai, through Europe, and almost 10,000 miles to the eastern seaboard of China. The route took me towards Turkey on familiar roads, at the Black Sea I would climb north, moving over the Ukraine and a knuckle of Russia before riding every mile of Kazakhstan and then China. From there I took a plane south, riding between Bangkok and Singapore, and thereafter the length of New Zealand's two islands. Landing in Vancouver, I'd leave Canada for the Pacific Coast of the US, which would lead to Mexico. From Tijuana I would pedal to the Atlantic, and then to Boston, New England . . . an American leg eventually totalling some 6,000 miles. From Boston I'd fly to Lisbon, and there begin the sprint to Rouen. The rules demanded I maintain a west–east direction, and cover 18,000 miles. The new record averaged some 93 miles each day, I aimed for a round 100, giving me a target of the world in 180 days.

Truth be told, as I set out I never thought I'd make it . . . not really. I don't know if it was the British class system or Islamic kismet, one way or another I didn't believe such an achievement was the sort of thing that happened to people like me. I thought events outside my control would prevent me breaking that record, that I myself would decide against it before the end, or that the adjudicators would not verify my record even if I were to complete it. I don't know where such fatalism came from, why it was I felt success to be out of reach.

Europe

Day 1 – Cathedral

It started in Rouen, the Cathedral of Rouen. The stained-glass windows Flaubert once gazed upon, that was why I started in Normandy. It was he that I thought of as I rode east, beside the railway tracks winding with me through wet, grey countryside. Flaubert hated the railways, hated the fuss they caused in 1850s' Paris. He couldn't understand the value in scientific progress without moral progress, said the railways simply allowed more people to move around faster and still only be stupid together.

As soon as I start riding it begins . . . the bicycle brings out my fantasist and, even if everything's under complete control, still my mind starts conjuring adventures for me. That first day the clouds moved in and out, drizzling a while before skies clear, everything brightening as colours returned, the fields shining green and gold with that black asphalt snaked between. In my head the road appears as a serpent, some mythical beast half-asleep and too huge to sense my small presence. I ride along the back of that creature without causing a disturbance, watching the surface of its reptilian skin as it changes, gains and sheds platelets, becomes pocked and pitted with age, runs smooth again thereafter. On days waiting in the future, I know the heat will melt the bitumen, make it bubble through the rocks to turn sticky and crackle beneath my passing tyres. Sometimes the serpent sits right up, arches steep and makes me climb out of the saddle to spin the pedals. Other times it works itself into some frenzy over something unbeknownst to me. It tries to throw me off its back, so that I lean down as far as I dare into its writhing twists. Because I'm so small, almost always I outfox the thing. Other times I wear myself out, my mind and legs grow tired . . . and then I remember, it's only a road.

That first day was 10 June 2009. By late afternoon the rain had started to fall from a darkened sky, water dripping from my collar and onto my neck. I passed a cyclist replacing an inner tube with his bicycle upturned at the roadside. There was nothing I could do to help, surrounding him were the tools of a man well prepared . . . but he caught my eye as I passed him, a fist raised in some show of solidarity. Determined for my 100 miles in those first days, head tired and body increasingly cold despite its labours, I rode on. I came to an incline, longer than most that day, shoulders rolling as I pedalled upwards.

Halfway up I felt it, there at the small of my back, a wide palm placed against me and pushing, that man coming into view, a bulbous nose, large beard flecked with drops of rain and riding by me, pushing me forwards as he rolled alongside. He drew level, pulled his hand away as he moved ahead, drew his hand into a clenched fist, fixed a stare upon me, dark eyes behind orange lenses . . . 'Allez!' He hissed it, so sharp, almost like an order. And there, beneath cold, Normandy rain I loved cycling so much, for preserved in that exchange was all the camaraderie the rest of my world seemed willing to give up. The stranger unlocked an entire tide in me with that small act, the community and culture to which it belonged, a thing that could momentarily unite two people who had never previously met and might well have nothing more than a bicycle in common. For the next six months, almost as an omen, I carried that moment with me.

My first night I slept beneath a church doorway, wrapped inside the plastic sheet in which I would later pack my bicycle for flights across the oceans. The wind blew rain into my hideaway, a first resting-point in my six months of adventure, of voluntary hardship. Water dribbled, slid between me and the hard stone that left its imprint against my shoulder and thigh, aching into the coming days.

Day 3 – Champagne – 272 Miles

That same wind moved the clouds away, sky turned blue and heat set down on France. I watched and listened as fighter jets roared above, wondering how long it might take such machines as those to reach Shanghai. The road came to me, decked with all the sounds and smells of the countryside. There comes the manure with its memories of my childhood, the cries of disgust I raised with my brother and sister as we drove into the country and the stench drove into our nostrils. A small windmill purrs against the wind, a clanking of metal coming from the well shaft below, a splash punctuates the silence as water leaps from tap to trough.

I rode through the vineyards of Champagne, line after line of grapes bulging in the shadows of the vines, or else pierced by sunlight so that the veins glow through the fruit itself, assembled like bunches of eyeballs. An old farmer pushes an even older contraption down an aisle of vines, paddleboards spin like waterwheels either side of him, slapping the grapes from their stalks into a giant bucket stowed beneath the handlebars. In the villages, two pensioners stand before stone gates. A pile of branches, a pile of firewood, in the middle a circular saw and the two men . . . white vests, peaked caps, bronze skin dotted by liver warts. The saw spins out a rhythmic pitch as one pile joins the other, as branches become firewood. In the next village a man stands alone, centred against a heavy oak door, braced with black metal straps. Ivy climbs around him. His legs are spread, arms folded, a red shirt and portly stomach tucked into a belt and jeans, large sunglasses over his eyes, a moustache across his mouth, set purposeful as he watches the road. I promise you, that man is watching the road as if it were 1813 and the Napoleonic Army were passing through. Nothing changes . . . all over the world people simply watch the road pass them by.

The hay lifts off the fields, its perfume takes up the breeze as evening falls. Throughout the day I smell myself sweating, secreting hormones, muddying the grimes that sit in the maze of my skin. I start to smell like my grandfather, like hard work and a bonfire on his allotment. Beside an ageing wolfhound that farts all the night through, eyes watch me from a row of rabbit hutches, little thumper on the far left, next in line for the pot as the warmth of the hayloft bids me sleep. Sandrine packs me off next day with a jar of foie gras, this morning three months before she'll email me in China, saying she'd like to send me money. Come evening, I sit with Fabrice, his dog chasing cattle in the field, a hot-air balloon floating across the clear horizon above us, burner tearing on and off as Fabrice talks of the farmhouse beside us. He and his wife saved for 15 years to buy the place, worked on the ruin to make it a home. Their first baby is tucked up in bed behind a window with curtains already drawn. It's strange to think so much goes wrong, in a world where the majority of people desire little more than a house in which to raise a family.

Towards the mountains of the Vosges my route unwound, flat fields concertinaing into forested hills. Under the shadow of the trees I went, through the sweet smell of cut cedar in the lumberyards. Along the road emerge amateur cyclists, slouched over handlebars, turning left and right onto the smaller routes that climb up to steeper gradients. From below I watch them ascend, pick my own way along the river path, a cycling coward with no time for mountains . . . 18,000 miles on as flat a road as could be found. During those first days I felt pressured, hurried as I rattled off my daily hundreds, one after the next. Each one proved easier than the previous, and yet I rushed on in fear of a slow exhaustion, of days when I'd begin to struggle.

Day 7 – Bavaria – 614 Miles

Cherries had fallen from trees, their stones left in tiny gravestones as the juices bled out into dry tarmac. Butterflies fluttered by, whipped up fast on the breeze from my spokes before flying on. A pink sky settled . . . rich, vibrant pink, as if the world were shut inside some boiled sweet, spat out and shining on the pavement of a better place. At night I'd pull into a field, draw the curtains and sleep beneath the falling veils of a willow.

My knees began to hurt, needles stabbing in my tendons, a sharp stinging from the effort of pulling my load up to the hills of the Black Forest. I wore knee-warmers each day until the summer and deserts were well underway. I would pull on those Lycra sheaths to keep the tendons and ligaments warm, less brittle, as my legs wound on. I nursed my joints, pedalled easy gears, lightly span a high cadence until my muscles grew accustomed to what was expected of them, gradually relieved the knees of their burden. Each day, I performed my quotidian mileage, a little more when the urge took me or if conditions were good. I'll talk as little of numbers as possible . . . I wasted enough of my time with them out there on the road. For now, just read it as given: each day . . . 100 miles more. Century after century disappeared behind me.

The temperature grew hot and yet I did my best to cherish all weather, no matter how uncomfortable, knowing eventually I'd find myself longing for those same conditions. In the rain I thought of the deserts of Turfan, in heat I took Massachusetts in November. It was all coming to me, those innumerable pedal turns were breaking me in, wearing down at my groin, placing the first sores upon my inner thighs. I grew a mound of tender flesh, red as the Mars Volta, letting out a tiny scream that eased as the miles passed. With each day I scratched a little more, at my arms, my back, saw skin peel off under my growing nails, a black film collected in slivers. First I began to stink, and then, with time . . . I just stank. In the corners of my eyes each morning was the debris of a previous day's flies and bugs, encrusted and preserved in sleep, a fossil record of the miles travelled. I was becoming a state, a fine mess, all of it familiar to me, and . . . you know what, no other way would I have had it. Washing one's face at a café's basin each morning becomes a ritual fit for an emperor. The cool water, the massage of the soap, the first breath of clean skin. Sure it's embarrassing, trying to sit in a restaurant like a respectable citizen, even as the flies continue to circle, impervious to my wafting hand. My mother would not be proud, I don't doubt it, but still . . . I was returning to a world in which I could be only a body once again, without that cause to police my every passing odour, those embarrassing evidences of our inner animal, those lapses that will shatter the illusions we work so tirelessly to cultivate.

Down to the Danube the road led, the first I saw of a river that once again would take me all the way to Romania's coast upon the Black Sea. Compared to what it becomes, in the south of Germany the Danube is small, its waters clear, moving fast through the rocks and hills that hang above the valley. A herd of cattle trudge along the riverside, the farmer following, staff in hand and a dog at his side, the valley walls filling with shadows as the sun lowers and the tolling of bells echo in silence.

With everything so tranquil, in my head the numbers were starting up, striking up the band and parading through. That evening, though the outside world offered nothing but peace, the numbers began their madness. Statistics, figures, dates and distances had taken over up there, running amok, linking arms and swinging their partners from wall to wall, falling over with laughter and crawling across floorboards. A 4 punched a 7, 2 kissed 3 ... 100 wanted to be 110. How many miles would I ride that night? How many *could* I ride? How many days had already passed? What was average mileage, average mileage under scenario one, two, three. Average mileage with the allocation of a rest day, a mechanical issue, a good day, maximum mileage, increasing distances with enhanced fitness, decreasing distances with increased fatigue? There was no relent, an anxiety that became a panic, shifted south from my head into my heart, a quickening pulse, legs pedalling faster, but recklessly, so that my progress slowed. Numbers can get to be quite an affliction, they suck you in, make you stare at the computer screen counting the miles from your handlebars. Believe me but China feels like a long way to ride a bicycle, once you're besotted with thoughts of bigger numbers accumulated over shorter times, once you lose the love for the process in favour of a destination. Enough already. I get off, walk to the river, grasses tickling at my legs, the sound of cowbells drifting towards me on the wind. Sitting down, I think of the horrors that await such a mindset, the prospect of six months beneath a head run ragged for the sake of that record. My fingers in the water, I look up at the sky ... I see myself, an idiot beneath the clouds. Taking deep breaths, hand upon chest, eyes closed, a decree is passed down. No one's going anywhere, not until sanity prevails, until peace has been restored.

Day 9 – Danube – 979 Miles

In the coming days, I moved over Bavaria, heading towards the Austrian border. The clouds passed, heat returned to the hills along the horizon, rolling like some giant green tablecloth with the crumbs shaken from it after dinner, up and down with cows and wildflowers falling everywhere. I rode under the silhouettes of domed Catholic churches, maypoles with reefs and ribbons streaming from them, the road stitching back and forth through villages moving east.

One evening I found such tender directions waiting at a turning on the lanes of Bavaria, a young boy walking with his mother. She knew roads, he knew English, and so he communicated her directions, skinny arms pointing uphill, a bowl of blond hair falling straight into his eyes, a set of metal braces across smiling teeth. He first relayed the route, and then he said it, so quick and proud, in a voice with the high pitch of youth: '*I'm a cyclist too.*' And to prove as much, he lifted the sleeve of his T-shirt. There on his arm, where a bicep would have been had he not been so thin, was a solid band, a break from pure white to pure bronze, the mark where a Lycra jersey clings tight to the skin, lets no sunlight pass and so stops a suntan in its tracks. I smiled as I saw it, for I'd once worn such a mark all of my own.

The boy told me of his bicycle, that they only let him ride a fixed gear for his training. He looked up at me and paused, his build so slight, voice so delicate and yet determined. 'I'm going to be like Merckx,' he announced, wide-eyed and glowing. 'I'm going to be like Merckx!'

* * *

Passau sits as the last German town upon the Danube, the river wide and ready to cut through Austria, a solitary flat path through a nation of mountains. A break of land juts out into the waters, beneath stone walls from some old fortification. Already the night was advanced as the sky growled a slow rumble, rolling closer above my head. There was a crack, pitchforks, night illuminated, the silhouettes of swings and seesaws beneath the walls of the fortress to which I'd made my way. The storm announced itself by the first pattering of rains on leaves, falling into the river's dark waters. I looked about for shelter, saw only a stone wall and a playground.

I was travelling with a new tent, had never used the thing, now no time to start practising. Moving closer to the wall, I stood under its cover and saw machicolations opening in the stones, dark spaces the size of a man, the sort of opening through which boulders and hot tar were once dropped onto invaders. More lightning struck, shadows of the forest flashing to light as I threw my bags inside the wall, dived in after them. The rain fell, thunder, lightning and the steady drip of water across the entrance to my bolthole. A church bell sounds the passing time, the stone above about half a metre from my head as I curl up in the dry, listen to the storm, and sleep comes.

Riding out next morning the church bells of the previous night sounded more imposing. There were no storm clouds, no thunders, only a mist laid low with drizzle. Unable to climb out of that valley, all day the clouds emptied. The Danube comes with its own cycle path, a constant strip of perfect tarmac that flows without an engine in earshot through 200 miles between Passau and Vienna. That day I had it all to myself, the river rising so that in places the banks had burst into ponds submerging my path. I grew damp, then wet, then sodden and finally, resentful of the conditions, pulled in beneath the glowing orb of a teapot, illuminated above a café awning.

She was warm in her welcome. A middle-aged woman of maternal stature, beady eyes, an apron fastened tight about a well-fed middle, a cheer to the manner in which she bobbed back and forth around the floor of her café, sweeping, mopping and then mopping a second time. As she stood over my table she smiled, untying her apron strings in order to tie them once again, tapping her pen on a notepad, shaking her head, a furrowed brow at the idea I might go back out into the rain. I stayed a couple of hours – maybe the weather will improve, maybe the weather will improve . . . – never such a waste of time as waiting for weather to improve. I drank coffee, ate a sandwich, slices of bread and jam she brought me, the bread growing stale, jam in pouches of plastic. The weather doesn't improve. I drink more coffee. Still no change in the weather. I ask for the bill. She stands over me, says *'und so'* with every thing she does . . . tapping the pen upon the note-pad, *und so*, lots of numbers going down, more than the three numbers you'd expect for coffee, sandwich and stale bread with cheap jam. *Und so* . . . She gives a final, conclusive tap of the pen. 17 euros. *Und so* . . . I've been had. I should've known better than to set foot inside that place, a captive market from the Danube path, menu in a nice typeface and professionally laminated to keep things respectable. You can't argue with a laminated rip-off. We Westerners, who kick up a stink the moment some poor guy in a medina tries to catch us out, walk off outraged at the five dirham by which he inflated the price, righteously sanctimonious about being treated as no more than passing euros to be hoodwinked. Let's hope they never start laminating their prices down in the Third World . . . just watch us fall into line, cower in the face of such officialdom.

Having left London with a budget of approximately 10 euros a day and only overdrafts in reserve, Western Europe, from the pas-tries of France to the restaurants of Bavaria, gave my wallet and willpower a true hammering. I suppose I'd known all along that I set off without enough money, yet I had to leave when I did, know-ing if I didn't the seasons wouldn't favour my route out of London until the following spring. The anxiety of a falling bank balance became a necessary sacrifice for that decision, but I'll say one thing, a lesson inadvertently learned from that predicament. Money buys comforts, buys luxuries, protects you from the need to use your initiative, to survive with a little more independence. With too much money you will only buy things you don't need and fail to savour luxuries you would otherwise enjoy. My finances might have caused me concern on my way around the world, but on balance I'd recommend, if you have it, the luxury of choosing to travel poor.

* * *

Vienna passed next day . . . the golden tiles of Klimt, quiet streets with paint peeling from masonry and the doors of grand apartment buildings. Illuminated bridges spanned Danube canals, glowing red with an arc of light shimmering in the waters, bricks decked in graffiti and other murals. Under the steeples of a gothic church I pulled in, ate a sandwich, and then rode out to the east, over cobbles, the tramlines wide enough to snatch a wheel from underneath you. That was my Vienna, my Alma-Ata, my Xi'an, my Seattle, my sweet San Francisco too. All fell by the wayside, in and out in a meal, just another waypoint along the road. Cities aren't so forgiving for a touring cyclist. They become expensive, leave you nowhere to sleep but hotels, foist on you the tyranny of choice that, without realising it, you came to find you were happy without. The countryside is by far the better home for a bicycle, and yet . . . I'd have liked to spend longer in some of those towns.

Day 13 – Transdanubia – 1,453 Miles

A bright morning, a cold breeze pulls at the river's surface. High grasses flutter beside the inlet of shingle where I stand, waters lapping against me. I strip naked, jig out of my clothes, left in a pile with my soap upon the pebbles. I step out into the Danube, my first wash in five days, waters cold around my ankles and shins, touching the back of my knees as I start to leap, then *whoosh*! Reborn. Clear blue, the current pulls me in, bubbles wriggling upwards from my plunge, grasses waving from the riverbed as I bore a perfect hole in the water. I swim down, breath held as I touch the bottom then drift to the surface, rolling onto my back and floating with sunlight full in my face, clouds through clear sky as I bob upon the water. I watch the remnants of the dusty road as it leaves my skin and heads downstream for the Black Sea. The accumulation of a little dirt is worthwhile when washing it away brings such joy.

Slovakia disappeared in an instant, barely a morning's ride before the flats of Hungary opened ahead. The wind brought back the rain, busy roads replacing the Danube trail, trucks covering me in water as they hurtled by. At lunchtime I found the *real* Hungary . . . roads and meals are always the best way to discover how people actually live, travelling through in my circumnavigation of generalisations.

A supermarket had been built on the Hungarian plains, rising colossal in the distance, surrounded by a flickering sea of the windscreens of those who pilgrim there. It was a French company, the supermarket colonialism by which Western Europe might one day rule the world once more. The shop was so big they could have sold convenience stores in one of the aisles, behind the climbing frames and sit-down lawnmowers. With the help of a map I found food, passed aisle after aisle of fridges, cutting a chill into my wet clothes. I found bread, deep buckets of bread, hundreds of rolls in different shapes, constantly falling from bags upended by staff. A crowd throbs at the bakery trough, stuffing plastic carriers with the largest rolls, reaching through, remonstrating with those who crossed the boundary from competitive queuing to rude. I get in line, wait my turn . . . the queue must be somewhere around here, just a case of finding the end of it, discerning an orderly procession of things. Standing perfectly still, I wait my turn. An old lady puts the heel of her shoe onto my foot, moves in front before I have time to apologise for getting my shoe under her heel. A man, a real mountain of a man, shuffles up, puts my head in his armpit, moves ahead of me to make a little more space. A boy and his sister, holding hands they squeeze through the gaps, but they're only children, not to know any better. Minutes pass, more minutes, and . . . you know what? There isn't a queue anywhere. It is a brawl, a free for all. Minutes of waiting and I'm further from the front than I started. Raised in Britain and queuing in Hungary . . . I never stood a chance.

Giving up on bread, I make my way to a delicatessen selling pizza and hotdogs. I point at pizza. 'Ketchup-chilli-*muzterd-méjonez*?' she yells. Above her head are four large teats, squeezed by her gloved hand. Down splatter sauces. Shuffling on, I move to another window with chicken legs at a price that guarantees those birds have not led happy lives. I gobble down pizza, lukewarm chicken flesh. She gave me too much *méjonez*, but all calories are valuable, so I dip chicken bones into surplus *méjonez*, scoop up a good globule and lick the bone clean, a lollipop of hydrogenated fat. And it's *that*, it's *méjonez* licked from cheap chicken bones . . . that's progress, that's the future, right there at a French multinational in central Hungary.

Day 15 – Transylvania – 1,651 Miles

By the time you reach Serbia, the difference is apparent: you've reached a place substantially removed from the one you left.

Eastern Europe is driving towards you, the cars grow smaller and the men bigger, shoulders hunkered beneath the low roof of the Trabant, knees up and a tiny steering wheel held in large hands just below the jaw.

Bicycles pass, old and rickety things that creak and squeal, rust and wobble, their tyres flat, wheels buckled and mudguards bent, but each one beautiful as the rider goes patiently beside me with a rake or a fork tied to the frame. A man with no legs goes floating silently by in an electric wheelchair, towing a small cart of hay. Women in the black of the Orthodox Church watch my strange spectacle, men observing from over tapered silver moustaches, just a trim above the lip, their eyes behind thick, black-rimmed spectacles, prayer beads rippling through their fingers. I ride on, past fields of sunflowers still shy, their petals flecks of yellow against that green head. The road passes scrapyards of oxidising metals, disfigured hulls and buses upside down, the weight of the chassis crushing the shell into metal sheets that burst apart. Cement factories crumble, flaking grain hoppers and silos stand in ruin as a memorial to industry. Into those open and eternal plains I went, beneath the leaning pylons that form a low, drooping tightrope into the distance, purring with the sound of escaped electricity.

Out there you find few reminders. Come the Serbian countryside the modern world has taken leave, its amenities sparser, all those trimmings we see so frequently back West we are no longer consciously aware of them. Street lighting, signposts, warnings and orders, kerbstones, manhole covers and drains, well-painted lines and arrows on the road's surface. It felt so good to see it all slipping away, moving to a world still left to its own devices, less littered with the hallmarks, the neurotic upkeep of our own.

Each day it changed the more. Moustaches grew, eventually became wide and bushy enough to sweep streets. Skin darkened, darkened the more, and then became the blackest shade of brown you'll ever find. Clothes frayed, became ragged . . . the women shrank, shuffling the roadsides under the burden of a woven bag and a hunchback. Faces watched me from beneath low head-scarves, so that I picked out features from among the growths and the weathering. The rubbish, the litter piles up, becomes land-fill . . . they set fire to it, and smoking plastic covers the land.

You follow that road all the way down to Romania, the white church of Bela Crkva watching over those dividing hills. I'd been to Romania once before, ridden along the valley and thought nothing of it. Since that time I'd spoken to others who had cycled there, been shouted and spat at by angry locals. I did the worst thing anybody can do before travelling anywhere: I listened to other people, took their misgivings on board.

A storm approached. The air cold, the sky a shade of darkness beyond that of just the night. Back over the hill, the silhouetted trees of Serbia were aflame against the setting sun as I sped down to meet the river, lights dotted beneath me in Romania, across the Danube border in Bulgaria. From a field the clinking chains of a tethered horse shook ghostlike, gave way to a shrill braying that flailed in the wind. I passed a small building, only a concrete shell with a cluster of fire inside, smouldering beside the shadow of a man hunched against a wall, arms resting on raised knees, hands swinging from the gallows of his wrists, head hanging forlornly between his legs. A sound comes, from through the darkness I hear a murmur . . . *'Come home quickly, darlin'* . . . *Come home to me.'* I look round. Nothing, nothing but storm clouds stacked up high. The sky cracked, a canvas torn open, lanced right through and thunder trapped furious between those valley walls. The storm came roaring, burst from evening into night.

Next morning I sat outside a supermarket, eating cereal from a cooking pan and reproaching myself for the fears I was fostering. I lectured myself about the decency of folk everywhere, the power of imagination in creating things that were never really there. Romania was only a place like any other. A motor scooter pulls in beside me, a woman hopping from the back and towards the supermarket. The rider looks down at me. He removes his helmet from a round, golden head, bald as a coot, and smiles. Dismounting, he asks if he can use a match, and draws back on a cigarette as we speak some sort of Spanish. His name is Sorin, he squats, we shake hands.

We talk of my bicycle, he calls it *guapa,* says it's beautiful and asks where I'm going. I say China, don't trouble him beyond that. We talk languages, of which he speaks four, his gypsy tongue, Romanian and an Italian and Spanish that overlaps easily with Romanian. I am enjoying that conversation, the abatement of my fears, a smile rising with this evidence of everyday Romanians. We begin to talk Romania.

He hates it. Sorin makes no secret of just how he feels about Romania, a scrunched-up nose and downturned lips, like a child forced to eat sprouts. He likes Romania even less than I do. He wants out, plans to follow me sharpish across the border.

'But where to?'

His eyes fix on me, widen to a smile. He enunciates the words, spreads his palms and fingers as if speaking some holy truth of a promised land, he blows . . .

'For *España!*'

'*España?*'

'*Si* . . . *Pamplona* . . .'

I smile, he smiles, we say something about bulls, put horns made from fingers on our heads and then, joking aside, he straightens, looks at me seriously.

'Good idea . . . *non?*'

'*Si, si* . . . a very good idea!'

Sorin begins counting wages on his fingers. '*Fifteen hundred euros a month!'* just waiting for him in Spain, right on the end of his fingers. 'Only 150 in Romania . . . if you can find a job!'

I haven't the heart to tell him Spain is on the cusp of some pretty impressive figures for economic ruin.

'Romania . . . *España* . . .' Sorin holds up fingers and draws them together. *'One family.'*

I can't bear to tell him the Spanish don't quite see it that way.

Sorin points to the sky. 'God willing, one or two years, I'll be there.'

I don't want to tell him that round about then Spain would be getting worse.

His girlfriend returns from the supermarket. Sorin stands up, leaves me with parting advice.

'Be careful –' a warning finger in the air – 'this land . . . *is full of robbers!'* and he repeats himself, punches a fist to his palm, then grinds the two together, in case I don't understand.

Day 18 – Wallachia – 1,871 Miles

That coast was cooked, long dead the lot of it. The Serbs had done it well, real bonhomie, a humble warmth to the land. Over in the Romanian south they'd taken the poverty thing too far, made it awkward. Romania was something else altogether, the thing with that valley was not lack of wealth so much as its state of disrepair. In its entirety it was ruined, abandoned, a place for which no one seemed any longer to care. There were cranes, docks, boilers, hydraulic presses in the gardens of concrete carcasses that had once been factories, goats scrambling among the ruins, bells chiming at their necks. In the river-setting those factories looked apocalyptic, like innocence torn up by experience, and then experience itself torn down by the free market, green shoots and brambles clawing at concrete pulled back to rubble. It had all failed, the only success stories were the vandals who had smashed through 500 miles of windows, and a government determined never to give up. To their credit, the Romanian Government had always remained primed and ready for another try at failure. I imagined that first hopeful day of opening: the speech, the growth forecasts, the Soviet champagne smashing on the bough of the crane. Four hundred miles later, in the east of Romania, using new money and new forecasts generated with a new -*ism*, there they had built a new port, with new cranes and new colours. It all went to show that ministers, regardless of dogma, are all suckers for cranes.

At precisely that time an election was approaching southern Romania, banners and bunting above the road, orange team versus red, Liberal Democrat versus Social Democrat . . . one of them must win! Orange promised to revitalise and liven up that Danube backwater, the reds would liven up and revitalise it instead. The street, that endless street I rode from Romania's far west to east, was throughout each kilometre covered with posters of politicians eager to make their faces known without ever having to visit that confounded dump. They were the normal fare, universal species . . . side-parted men, looking proud and ready in a suit, ready to continue wearing that suit each and every day until it was time to retire. They'd allowed women in on it too, one looking like she'd maybe earned her spot on that poster, the other with a promise of cleavage for the masses. Up and down the land, people wore T-shirts of orange or red . . . slogans, chosen values and their hopes for the future. At first I thought it must have been passion, election fever, and then in time realised it was only a free T-shirt.

Don't mistake me, Romania may have been shabby, but in my head I was making matters far worse. If you get back from a place what you put into it then I was in trouble, for if I were to get back the smallest fraction of doom and loathing I was projecting upon that land, quite simply I was done for . . . I'd croak. It was an irrational fear, but that was the point, there's no such thing as a rational fear, a rational fear is only a problem. For true fear, the calamity has to be all but impossible and yet potentially devastating. It wasn't the prospect of being beaten and spat on, in that order too, that distressed me so much as the likelihood of it happening along bad roads, while still miserable from my last meal and regretting the next before it had even begun. That was what made things difficult . . . the pleasures of life itself were becoming far less pleasurable. I had to carry bottled water, the food grew medicinal, and doses of rubberised cheese and stale bread were all that would see me through to happier times. Daily visits to the toilet, they too had become arduous, and I was in no doubt the Romanians weren't shitting in the same places they were directing me to. Down the garden path, turn left at the horse . . . cigarette butts, paint cans, broken ceramic, the whole thing an adventure in its own right. I soon opted for the countryside, but there too I was conspired against, for the land was resolutely flat, barely a hill or thicket in sight to crouch behind. The moons of my white buttocks protruded below foliage all too thin, my head protruded above, and the fields teemed with farmers out in force to witness everything. I'd no wish to offend people by the giant wigwams I constructed to conceal what I left behind, tepees full of shit from whence I'd scarper, afraid if I was caught shitting on Romania someone might interpret it symbolically.

From that single skin of houses all along the roadside people watched me. Every house had its own bench out front, adults sitting as the children went about their indefatigable play, postponing that time when they too would sit down on that bench and be done for. All day and into the evening they sat there, feet spread, shuffling in the dust. Into the dust they would stare, stare down at the rock bottom of something, and as far as mournful was concerned, they had mastered the aesthetic down to an art form. Crestfallen, they looked at that road and beyond, leaving you to wonder just what changes it was they'd seen, sitting there in those plastic flip-flops, those thick spectacles. Occasionally they looked up, caught me full in the face. I would offer a wave, they would reject it. I still know nothing more tiring than unrequited hellos.

I don't know what it was the people there saw in me . . . their own poverty and the labours of life, or Romania's failings exposed by the presence of a stranger. Whatever it was, they didn't like it, and throwing a wave to them was like casting stones into the deep. It was exhausting too, for Romania felt like eggshells, swimming underwater with held breath. Maybe it was unwise to adopt all those worries, yet that was exactly what I did, convinced it was just a matter of time before fate caught up with a dose of the hospitality of which others had spoken. So as to prolong that comeuppance, however, I'd resolved to do all in my power to affect airs light and cheerful. In short, I skulked through some 500 miles disguised as a coward. I held every door, thanked every action with a *mulțumesc*, that single word of theirs that I knew. I looked solemn whereupon they did, and entered bars trying to emanate an aura of *here I am, amongst you, trusting, equal men . . . now let us be peaceable*. In reality, this probably translated closer to *please don't hurt me*, and perhaps full of an unpleasant spinelessness too. But so long as they didn't hurt me, I didn't care. At mealtimes I scribbled my stories, sharpening a pencil with my knife. Occasionally I would look up, take in the gathered crowd looking back at me uncertainly. I would grimace a smile, look down to see that I was still clutching my knife.

One thing in particular weighed heavy on my mind. I'd left home without a vaccination in sight and, though unsure of what they looked like, nor any other useful piece of information about them, I'd grown terrified of ticks. The nurse's propaganda had worked a treat … a booklet of giant photos showing magnified insects inserting their needles past follicles and into skin. Those images had not scared me into a £500 vaccination bill but, come Romania, they were all too present in my imagination. The nurse had told me to avoid pig shit and long grass, said the mosquitoes on the shit and ticks waiting in the grass would carry encephalitis, meningitis. Pig shit not being high on my list of attractions, I'd got over the initial blow pretty fast, but camping my way around the world without long grass was a taller order, and her maps showed clearly that Eastern Europe was where ticks began. Before I knew it, my brain would be swelling and I'd be dribbling towards a premature death in excruciating pain.

Ordinarily I'd give such scaremongering pretty short shrift, scorn the money people will pay to be told by someone in a white coat there's nothing left to worry about. Ordinarily I'd parody the idea of ticks lined up at borders with their families, trying in vain to start a new life within the prosperity of the European Union. In those Romanian days, however, my mind was infirm, irrevocably cast, for nothing is quite so contagious as fear, and my thoughts were on a slippery slope. I rolled into the Romanian evening, eyeing up the roadside for the shortest grass, telling myself the lunacy of attempting to avoid long grass all the way to Shanghai, of fearing grasses I had walked in fearlessly three years ago. It was no good. I'd contracted fear.

Before leaving the road, I would pull on trousers, a long-sleeved sweater, tuck in my socks and even then imagine red dots emerging on my wrists and neck. I erected and crawled inside my tent. Things scuttled. I swatted, things dodged … I swatted again, killed them. They jumped. I killed them a second time, wanted nothing but myself left alive inside that tent. Those nights were so marked by tossing, turning, suspected sightings and mishearings, my head torch going on and off, that come the early hours even the cicadas pleaded with me to hush down and go to sleep.

* * *

I came upon Maglavit, a town I'd once heard from a Romanian in Paris was synonymous with being sent to the middle of nowhere. I'd told him the British used Coventry in much the same way. It was my second time in Maglavit, three years earlier I'd cycled through with a friend, the other side of Romanian accession to the European Union. I remembered a man, a border inspector returned home for the evening. He'd found us the coldest beers from the bottom of the fridge, sent his son to fetch cheese and cucumber, packed us off with a bag of tomatoes, refused all money.

Three years later, I pulled up at the same café, prepared to ask after the man, Ion Smoccu. It was one of those moments hard to believe, a first moment of fate in a journey that eventually grew full of such magical coincidence, evidence of Mark Twain's words: 'The difference between fiction and nonfiction is that fiction must be believable.' As I stepped off my bicycle, there he was. Ion Smoccu, walking straight towards me. Age hadn't been kind, unusually cruel for just three years, but it was Ion, unmistakably so. He had retired, didn't work the Calafat border any longer, stood tall in his Social Democrat T-shirt and square-cut hair, the same silver chain hanging wide about his neck. We both laugh, slowly nodding our heads against a language barrier as the memory of that evening returns. I raise my hand to hip-height in recollection of his son. He laughs, raises his hand to show the boy has reached his chest.

Another man sits there, speaks English, translates as we drink coffee around a small tabletop. I lean in, ask Ion if life has changed at all . . . 'European Union?' They all laugh, that's a good one, the cyclist has a sense of humour. The man answers for Ion, 'It makes no difference . . . the main problem is always corruption. We got a new road, that's it. Politics starts and stops in Bucharest.'

* * *

Bucharest neared and, where I'd hoped towns would grow towards it, there came no change, just one after another, that single skin of houses along the road. The national colours were everywhere . . . flags, banners of blue-red-yellow, and then more flags at every junction. It's always a sign things are bad when someone encourages you to get excited about the piece of rock beneath you. Through fields of sunflowers I rode, their heads leaning heavy under dark hoods, a yellow dust of fallen petals along the roadside. They spray the crop to kill the flowers early, help the plant put its energy into seeds that will be sold and pressed for oil. Beside the fields were the names of French agricultural corporations, the EU's road built to transport the harvest from Romania, even as farmers all around looked to me so poor and hungry.

The carts with which I shared the road were piled high with hay. Sometimes a driver would pull alongside, grinning and pointing at the open road, the hooves of his horse clipping apace, harness around its head. The man points at me, gestures a race, bells ringing faster as the driver first tugs the reins, then brings down the whip with a crack of air and sudden acceleration. The first time it happened I dropped a gear, cranked harder, only for the cart to career down the road, bells flying, whip landing, landing, landing . . . the poor horse flogged rotten. I watched the silhouette of that man disappear into the distance, standing with legs spread, heaving at the reins as he tried to wrestle his animal onto a straight course. I didn't race after that.

I rode into dusk, beside petrol stations that glow white light and never close, filling-station pumps standing like a stocky matron, one hand on the hip. A woman sweeps the forecourt, birch broom scratching concrete in the silence. I ride by as her back is turned, she never to see the peculiar sight that passes into the night, our lives never again to come any closer. Amid a navy-blue sky with a pink horizon, there ventures a fog from the Danube waters, where men fish in tiny, bobbing canoes. The mist moves out and over the land, only the topmost tufts of grass protruding from it, spirals of pale vapour swarming over tree and thicket. Away from the road, out into the grasses I step, lifting that white quilt of mist. I peer under . . . I sleep beneath its cover.

Day 19 – Oltenița – 2,017 Miles

They pointed to a restaurant with a *Peroni* sign outside, the best bar in town, the only place where you can drink a beer five times the local price. The owners have purchased a pizza oven for the kitchen, use it to produce the one meal in all Romania that I enjoyed . . . not that 'enjoyed' is the right word, you can't enjoy a good meal when you've no idea when the next will come.

A girl sits at the bar, dressed in a light-brown dress that matches her hair, eyes, skin. She's beautiful, stunning, the universal phenomenon. The best-looking girl in a small town who goes about making a local of the best bar in town. She spends her time there, looking beautiful, and eventually shacks up with one of the barmen. His name is Nico, a gentle guy, young, soft features, a warm smile and some English. He asks after my pizza, and I ask after Romania.

'I love my country, *love my country*, but it is strange –' Nico contorts his face, shrugs – 'where you have gypsies, you have problems. Two . . .' He pauses, considers a more generous statistic, 'Five . . . *no* . . . two per cent of gypsies are good. Where there are gypsies, it is bad. The South . . . is bad. I know a guy in Bucharest, a gypsy, a big guy, strong guy, and he begs . . . well, he tries to sell socks . . . but he's a big guy, he could work. It started out good. At parties the gypsies would come, they would play music. This is no longer the way, they don't want to work.' He pauses again. 'I've been to Spain, to Italy, I speak the languages . . . but they don't like me because I'm Romanian. They think all Romanians are gypsies.' He fixes me with a look. 'Romanians are not gypsies!'

I ask about the ruins, the factories I'd seen along the river. Nico replies, his face soft, but sure in his words. 'The South is dead.' He shrugs again, sadness in his eyes. 'They built a tomato factory, to make tinned tomatoes . . . *Dead*. They built a factory to process sheep meat . . . *Dead*. They built a clothes factory . . . *Dead*. They built a chemical factory . . . *Dead*.' And with each death, he wipes the back of his hand through the air, clears the drawing board all over again.

Day 22 – The Ukraine – 2,388 Miles

It passed. Immediately across the border, on Moldovan soil I felt better about it all. Camped among the hills, even the long grasses were no longer so intimidating as they had been a dozen miles earlier. The speed with which I overcame the fear was direct proof of how idiotic it had been. I take full responsibility for my state of mind back there, wouldn't want anyone thinking ill of Romania. Once you've started looking for it, it's easy to find all that is negative in a place, and there's nothing like fear to make you ignore all that is positive.

Moldova was over before it began, less than 50 miles and then

Ukraine. Against stark, gold wheat fields and empty blue skies, the trees beckoned to me. I'd never seen the colour green before that summer in Ukraine ... the leaves they lured me towards their shade, for July neared, and with it true heat was coming. I shimmered among the landscape, the particles of my body expanding and vibrating as I started to lose my previous form, melting steadily into road and horizon. I rode those long, opening highways, passed by the buses, the famous ones from documentaries of the USSR. Coops of hens on top, mattresses, linen baskets, bookshelves, the paintwork with a single stripe of blue or red right through it, bodywork rounded like a wheeled bathtub, porthole windows floating onwards, smoke pouring, engine hatches wedged with coat hangers, tied open with rope to let air into the motor.

The Ukraine is the beginning of the change, the shoreline on which habitations still stand before that endless, open sea. There are fields, endless fields and nothing but fields to drift upon. I rode by fields freshly ploughed, tractors labouring through the soil, thick smoke sputtering from chimneys as they toil. Crows followed after the smoke, a plume of them, jet-black, billowing they hobble ... heel-toe ... through open furrows, beaks jerking upwards against worms that would not let go of the ground. From the earth it all grows golden, stretching to the sky among hedges and trees that hang like garlands about the neck, the fields within their grasp, that fullest of greens against a pale shade of dusty heat.

Mornings were a crossfire of cockerels. Those birds would explode, each neighbour eager to resolve once and for all who was loudest. The roadside became a procession of tiny stores, of tablecloths with jars and punnets of produce and foraging. Women, their heads covered against the heat, sold eggs, or else live chickens, vines of tomatoes, pickings from the trees and bushes, so that the road was lined with baskets of apricots, blackberries, gooseberries and redcurrants. I watched as people shuffled down the road with bushels of firewood and kindling strapped upon their backs. They moved slowly, as human hedgehogs, doubled forwards and recoiling from the road as a truck thundered by too close. All through the Ukraine, you see the signs selling honey beside the highway, painted on an old door or floorboard that waits half a kilometre before the stall itself. As the store nears you see the honey in golden pyramids, jars stacked in formation, the sun refracting through them and a handful of determined bees hovering about the lids. You see chests of drawers, filing cabinets in which the hives are kept, slumped beneath a tree, safe distance from the shelter or caravan in which some entrepreneur waits for passing traffic to stop. At the smaller stalls they fill plastic drinking bottles, half-litres of honey, or else whole litres, the price falling the more you buy.

I stop beside a sign more modest than the rest, the roadside empty. In a field through the trees sits a caravan, propped on bricks beside rows of hives. I make my way forwards, past plastic bottles of honey stacked together, sticky in wooden crates. A man walks out to greet me, his face blemished with one of those discolorations whereby the pigment fails, leaves a beard of bleached skin. He looks forlorn, sick of the sight of honey as he points to a large bottle, holds up seven fingers, points to a small bottle and holds up four. I stroke my chin, honey connoisseur that I am, swine that I am, a man who pays 50 for coffee and stale bread, if only the pricelist has been typed and laminated by owners already turning a profit.

You know what . . . stroking my chin . . . I like the look of your honey, old man, with your sorry mien, your big toe jumping from the hole in its slipper. I like the look of it and yet . . . I just don't think the small bottle is worth four, so I'll give you six for the big one, *how's that?* I point to the big one, wag a disapproving finger at his seven . . . *nonono* . . . offer six fingers.

He doesn't like that, nobody has told him about bargaining as a cheery cultural exchange at which to try your hand when travelling. He starts shouting, white skin turning red, spittle forming at the corner of his mouth, lips snagging on an incisor as he yells at me in Ukrainian, in Russian. He holds out his hands before me, he rocks them, bellowing, thumbs and fingers pressed in an insulted plea for reason. He curses me . . . *Do I look like a rich man?* . . . lays rage all over me before throwing a hand at his caravan, throwing another at the bottle of honey, one more at his bulging eye before throwing both back at his caravan and cursing me to damnation. Roused by the commotion, from the caravan steps a second man, an old fellow with a stung face, mounded and bubbling from a lifetime of beekeeping. He saunters over on a crutch, peers at me from a tiny eye lodged within a large swelling.

The two of them stand there, the first with his chest heaving, breathing deep through the last of the rage, skin turning back to white, toe twitching from the hole in its slipper. The second man looks at me through his deformed and bee-stung face, the three of us in front of that ramshackle caravan, a bee bobbing unawares through the air between us. The Westerner picks up the small bottle of honey that he always planned to buy anyway, for which he always thought four fingers to be a reasonable price.

Day 23 – Bessarabia – 2,498 Miles

The light changed, the air cooled, dimmed to a brooding disquiet. Looking overhead, I saw what lay in store. An almighty roar went up. The cloud emptied.

A storm came to the Ukraine that evening. It moved the sky to black, threw down a hail of premature conkers from the trees and then, once no more conkers would fall, the storms simply threw down the trees instead, tore them up, left shards and branches along roads that sobbed tearfully to the leaves at the gutters. The trees cracked, splintered, and what remained of the trunks was left to point accusingly upwards and back at the clouds, cursing . . . *You did this!* The rain came, the sky opened, it pelted. I jumped from where I had sat, retrieved my bike and raised a sail, eager to catch a tow from favourable winds. The rain turned that road to rivers, muddy waters brown and swirling, a Limpopo of molten chocolate. Cascading down the hills, some two-wheeled amphibian flew down those currents, the roads disappearing, submerged and reduced to only shallow flumes. Sunken potholes gaped at the last second, those fissures I'd seen when the roads were dry, that rut that would snatch at my front wheel, pull it from underneath and spill me from my bike without a thought. Relentless, the storm continued, wrought insanity against the land, as I hurled myself into it. The rain fell, did its worst, and then stopped as swiftly as it had come. From the heat of the road, days of sun locked inside of it, that water evaporated, slow trails of steam winding upwards in the headlamps.

Night came up, the sky pulling on the woollen sweater someone knitted for it a long time ago. A dark navy stripe along the bottom, rising dirty violet, a light blue, and then darkening again, the moon and a few stars dotted among it all, loose threads of cloud dropped here and there as tassels. The air was warm, the night comforting . . . that time of day when all stills and only three shades of white, grey and black remain. Three shades, some outlines and nothing more troubles the eye, the ears obliged to hear so little, those remaining noises calm beside the chaos of a day.

A woman clatters her stepladder, arranging a string of fairy lights on the branch overhead. Her green umbrella glows like a lantern, beneath it sits her humble business: a kettle, instant coffee, sugar, some confectionery, a cardboard sign with titles and prices written upon it. Further down the road there comes a larger stop, the trucks pulled in, grilled meat aromas, refrigerators shining sterile light, that same light that shines out of a drinks cabinet beside every roadside on earth.

I pull in beside a gravestone. The road is full of them, the words ever in silver or gold, Cyrillic characters and a simple depiction of a face. That face is always stoic, always male, a husband or a son, the driver who perished at that stretch of roadside, who the family saw fit to commemorate beside that same road where it all happened. A small candle is burning, burning in a bowl of yellow glass that glows, breathing gently as the wind toys with the flame, choking and then coaxing it back to life. There are flowers, fresh flowers, not the artificial variety normally found, these ones are real, petals curling dry but still alive. I look at the headstone, the stoic face that looks me square in the eyes from beyond the grave. From inside the safety of his tombstone he stares me down, and among the Cyrillic are some numbers, a date. He died only a year ago, a year and two days, which explains the candle, the new flowers. Turning from him, I make my bed and sleep beside his grave, my temporary resting place beside his last. It feels so comforting to sleep beside spirits, to have no fear of the dead, who cannot touch me here.

Day 25 – Kremençuk – 2,606 Miles

Lying on my back, just after dawn, some disturbance catches my attention. There's a movement in the leaves, a twitching of trees, the sound of scuffed feet pushed through long grass, snapping twigs, a shape making its way around my camp, circling me, crouched some distance off but looking directly my way. The footfall nears, a figure appears. Bent over beneath branches he peers at me, eyes shining through the foliage as he continues peering and makes no effort to hide as much. I begin picking myself out of the sleeping bag, grope around at the bottom of my legs to try to pull on my feet. As I stand, the shape comes crashing through the last of the undergrowth to where I lay. His arms spread, hands bared, ducking beneath the final tree and then bursting out before me with loud exclamation.

He is smiling . . . my word, but he is smiling. An old face, like the sun shining through the heel of a loaf of bread, his round, brown head bursts into joy and a mouth erupts, glows as the smile takes over the entirety of his wizened features and his eyes begin to beam. He's dressed in a pair of shorts, sandals and a polo shirt with the liver-spotted plate of his sternum poking from below the collar. He means no harm, that much is for sure, yet I don't understand why he's tracked me down and why he's deriving such excitement from me. He throws his arms up and around as if he can't get over something, wants no more to do with his limbs. Old skin flapping, he grabs me by the hand, pumping at me like a well in a drought. He's ogling my bicycle, and, though it all seems perfectly convivial, I still don't understand . . . not until he points back through the trees and there, propped up on its stand, is his own bicycle.

He's marvelling, shouting Russian like there's no tomorrow. He points at cranks, at wheels, at my *1,2,3,4* bags . . . he counts them, slaps his forehead and then beckons, gestures I must follow. We crunch back through the trees to his bike. He slaps at a large, plastic laundry bag strapped above the back wheel, slaps at the plastic tarpaulin also there. He makes a tent from his hands and then a bed on which he lays his head, closing his eyes a moment in sleep before opening them again excitedly, pointing at his tarpaulin and giving a thumbs-up. Now he moves across the bike, starts pointing at the old-fashioned derailleur arm on the back, the cable shifters mounted on the frame. He slaps at his saddle, then strokes it, and then slaps it again before shouting *'Italia!'* and pointing towards my bike, crunching back through the trees with me following dutifully behind.

He straightens up, wants to talk business. Euphoria subsides, pragmatics . . . he wants particulars. He points at himself . . . 'Anatoly' . . . and I repeat, 'Anatoly.' Then he shakes his head and points at me, repeats . . . 'Anatoly'. 'Anatoly,' I echo. He shakes, sticks a finger right at me, right into my chest . . . 'Anatoly?' 'Julian?' I offer. He cups a hand around his ear. Cottoning on, I point at him . . . 'Anatoly' . . . and point back to myself . . . 'Julian'. He takes my arm, shakes it a second time. Now we're getting somewhere. After licking a finger, he starts speaking Russian very slowly, a word at a time, just in case it's the tempo of it holding me back. He speaks and points, points to the sky and then points to the ground. It sounds like the cadence of a list being given, and among it I hear a 'Smolensk'. I repeat it. He repeats it, only louder, so now there's no mistaking we are talking about Smolensk. Anatoly starts drawing lines in the air, throwing out more place names, pointing to the land beneath us. I go to my pannier and unpack a map. We look at it together, Anatoly's Russian accelerating as he draws big loops starting at Smolensk in Russia, where he makes a ring out of a finger on his left hand, slips it onto the ring finger of his right hand, where he keeps his wife. He had ridden to Belarus, towards Minsk, south to Kiev . . . to Kremençuk, where we stand, and he now rides to Kharkov, to Kharkov where . . . Anatoly raises a fist beside his head and pulls the whistle . . . *choo-choo!* . . . where he catches the train home to Smolensk. He draws numbers on the map now, a straight line and three hoops. *'One thousand . . . 1,000 kilometres!'* he shouts, finger triumphant in the air, his face all aquiver with a smile that swallows his eyes into a pair of puckers. Then he points . . . *listen now . . .*

and starts drawing more numbers, but only two this time, a seven and a two, and he thumps himself on that liver-spotted sternum of his, which thuds like a heavy floorboard, and Anatoly from Smolensk, with his 1,000 kilometres on his old bicycle, sleeping on a plastic sheet under the stars, Anatoly is 72 years old and brimming with the energy of a boy.

He raises his finger again . . . *listen now* . . . points at me, that finger in my chest, he wants my number. I give him a two and a four. *I'm 24* . . . but Anatoly he just howls with laughter, doesn't believe it, clasps a hand to his forehead, covers his mouth, chokes on his tongue and then buries his face in his hands, fingers spread. Anatoly emerges, agape, from behind those hands, stares at me and then tentatively holds up three fingers, points to us both and indeed, he's right . . . he is three times my age. That is enough for him, he can't compose himself afterwards, just keeps giggling away, chest bouncing up and down, head shaking side to side. Once more he looks at my bike, then straightens . . . he's realised something, an intake of breath. I look at him, look at my bike. He's staring at the saddle, the honey-brown leather and wide copper rivets, hammered heads shining in the morning sun. He steps towards it, hesitantly, as if confronted by some true beauty. His eyes and mouth open, he raises his hand, slaps it down to plant the palm upon the saddle and Anatoly lets out a shout of, '*Da! Da! Brooks!*'

That was a sweet bit of history right there, that saddle . . . a company started a century and a half ago in the same backwater of Leicestershire from whence I'd come. And there, in the year 2009, in Kremençuk, Ukraine, standing beneath the trees with 72-year-old Anatoly from Smolensk, and for just one moment the two of us knowing exactly what the other was talking about. Once more he grabs me by the arm, fixes that face upon me a final time, the smile growing warmer and warmer as he shakes my hand, a little slower this time. He turns, walks back through the trees, a parting wave as he pushes his bicycle out of my life forever.

Day 27 – Belgorod Oblast – 2,833 Miles

It was enormous. Russia. A place in which to realise just how you squandered all your superlatives of size back in the Ukraine. You see the trucks coming down the road from five kilometres away . . . thin pipes run above the wheels, trickle water to quell the heat that builds in the tyres. Road signs show cities 1,000 kilometres in the distance. The people are silent. They'd planted trees, two-skin deep, all along the roadside. It was so you couldn't look out, out into the abyss, that endless vast that would creep into your mind and drive you insane. Occasionally at crossroads I would catch a glimpse of that sea I swam in, where I could drown in land long before there came a town in which I might slake my thirst and revitalise. As I rode, I saw squares, off-colour rectangles drawing closer. Houses, habitations . . . I thought I'd made it, that I was saved. And then I neared, and those squares and rectangles were only the spaces between the trees lining still more endless fields. Green, gold, brown and ploughed, black and ashen, the thing that never changed was it would always be only another field. Sometimes, struggling, I would splash on in need of respite. Miles and still more miles would pass before eventually I would find a patch of shade, a covering of leaves thick enough to shield me from those rays. I'd swim over, cling to it, the last flotsam from a spring by then destroyed. For hours at a time I'd stay in those places, clinging to the cool until it was safe to once more take to the waters.

That landscape was a child's painting, the one in which they want to use all the colours. Where rivers ran dry there flowed wild-flowers instead, flumes of yellow and purple hedged against the green grass, the heathers, dots of bluebell, daisy and the pale slippers of a lily. In the mornings that sky sat, milky-white, like the surface of an iced lake. As the sun climbed higher so did the cloud thaw and crack, break apart from the edge of the lake, set adrift, ever smaller and floating loose over the sky. All too seldom, one cloud would float across to block the sun and, as shade passed over, so I would fall momentarily deep in love.

By then I was through with grocery stores, until the end of time the food in those places will be fit for consumption only with spirits of 40 per cent alcohol. For too long my menu had been a growing tragedy. Bad after a day in Romania, after two weeks it becomes soul-crushing. I would buy a kilo of dry sea biscuits at a time, bread already stale, cheese that squeaks as you bite it, margarine ghostly pale. Three-quarters lard, a quarter candle wax, by some ungodly powers it refuses to melt even in the hot sun. I would pay for my goods, a middle-aged woman leaning over a calculator behind the counter. From inside a cabinet my transaction was observed by row upon row of scorched dead fish, scales covered in brown dust that stank out the entire shop. Full of horror, tiny, dry eye sockets gaped at me. I reached a watershed.

For the purposes of riding I divide myself into Brain, Body and Soul, three comrades shacked up in the same mission. Body is the workhorse: pretty dim but real honest, a good spirit, needs care but will work hard for his masters. Brain is a swine: sits up in the office, a chair of padded leather, a desk and nothing but thoughts all day long. Never done a day's graft, never satisfied, he's only such a prick because he's never known happiness himself. He's the fool that tells the Body to cycle past a perfect campsite because we've only ridden 98 miles and 2 more are expected. Soul: rarely puts in an appearance, for the most part makes himself scarce. He sits in an alleyway somewhere, and one at a time he flicks a pack of playing cards into the gutter. Soul rises periodically, carries rights of veto, can tell Brain to shut up and be reasonable, to take it easy and relax before we all end up in an early grave.

Out in those Russian shops Body itself had risen up, didn't like to cause a fuss but really demanded some proper food. The workers were outside the factory gates, threatening strike action and already a picket growing, placards bobbing up and down . . . '*Stop the suffering!*' . . . '*We want Taste!*' A real furore was in the offing as Brain argued there wasn't enough money for luxuries, that we would have to make do until better times. The workers wouldn't tolerate it, threatened a mutiny.

And so I came to join the truck drivers at the roadside, their engines parked hot and sighing outside the restaurants. Meals were ever the same: a plate of buckwheat, a fried egg, a dollop of stew. Always that large woman in an apron, shuffling on tree-trunk ankles beneath the weight of a bucket of cabbages, a priceless scowl just for me. Out in the corridor would be a basin with a tap that constantly dripped. Neither on nor off, it trickled dirt from tired hands but was unable to wash them clean, a grey puddle forever in that white basin. In the rafters the swallows nested above a doorway, a bulge of mud with rows of minutely screeching beaks and white-yellow breasts tucked inside.

The trucks were of a sort not found in Europe, where we have nowhere big enough to put such things, and nowhere distant enough to drive them. The cabins, each the size of a bungalow alone, bear two gargantuan exhaust stacks, chugging like cooling towers as the engine heaves the load. Tankers, shipping crates, wagons of rock or scrap metal . . . those trucks would rear up over my shoulder, roaring and rattling as shadows stretched over me in the form of some terrible foe. When we were heading the same way, I would inhale as they swept by, all too close to my side, and I would exhale as the slipstream of that giant fist in the air picked me up and pulled me on. When they came from the opposite side of the road I had to duck, throw myself towards the ground, flat on the handlebars before they floored me. Orthodox, southpaw, they just punched me backwards with all of the atmosphere they blundered through, each of us vessels on that same sea.

Day 29 – Voronezh – 3,002 Miles

Downtown Voronezh . . . a parade square, Lenin saluting as he makes for the shops. In the windows they're selling exercise bikes, floor-to-ceiling posters in luminescent colours, large numbers advertising the saving to be had as Lenin, all set in stone, strides purposefully towards the automatic doors. Admittedly a touch portly in his waistcoat, arm raised, Lenin points up at the bike he wants in the top window. That's modern Russia . . . statues of Lenin and cut-price exercise bikes, the two get along just fine. People don't need their world to make sense, only a coherent version of events repeated frequently enough, that's the key to good politics.

I opened my wallet, looked in . . . a vortex, not a kopek in sight. I cycled to a bank, a cashpoint, watering hole in a twenty-first-century adventure. In went my plastic, my number, my language, my request. Out came my plastic. That wasn't to plan. In went my plastic, my number, language, request. Out came my plastic. Again and again I tried, moderating my wishes, lower numbers, pleading almost, still no budging. That machine adamant it would give back nothing but the plastic I pushed into its hole. Out comes the telephone, another survivalist tool. It connects . . . I hold . . . *'Yes, sir, your card has been blocked, for your protection . . . somebody tried using it in Russia.'*

* * *

A stern woman stands with one hand on the handle of an industrial-size pizza oven, the other on the cash register. I wait for my food. Over her shoulder is a clock face with horizontal bars of Russia's red-white-blue, around her neck a silver necklace, an ornamental flag fluttering those same colours on the metal. As with any nation prone to believing its past brighter than its future, the Russians had taken up nationalism. It was like every other fervour too, most potent where least warranted, where the winds of change blow cruellest and most seldom. All through Russia it went that way, the air thick with nationalism. It was tattooed on male biceps, stuck in car windscreens, waving from aerials, dangling from the jewellery.

After clearing my plate I walk to the toilet, into the tiled room, a click from a sensor above. *Illumination* . . . light shines off polished walls. Upon the throne, I open the map of Russia, make myself at home, rustling paper, relaxed. A minute later and darkness comes. Pitch black. I know that I'm still sitting on a toilet in Voronezh, but only because I haven't moved. The entire world has disappeared, no light anywhere. This is how death must look. I flutter the map, wave a hand, a click from a sensor, the light returns and there I am again, nothing changed. I study my route towards Kazakhstan, towards Saratov on the Volga River, perhaps two more days. Darkness. Darkness returns, quicker than the first time, nothing in sight. A flutter of the map, a wave of the arms. Nothing doing, won't work. Leaning forwards, I wave arms in the air, a click from a sensor . . . wrong sensor. The machine for hand towels whirs as it unrolls paper. I keep waving, the hand towel dispenser cranking out towel after towel but not a bit of light, nothing at all after a full 30 seconds waving. And right there in Voronezh, I saw the future again . . . pants around your ankles, waving your arms in the darkness, all at the mercy of some technology supposed to make everything easier.

Day 32 – Volga – 3,364 Miles

The road delivered me to Saratov, the old wooden houses falling into splinters beneath the glass and concrete of the new. I cycled up and over the bridge, that half-mile between the east and west bank of the great Volga River. It started there, down past the Volga was where the desert began for me. Everything more remote, more barren, townships made of tin, water towers the largest structures around. A horse watched me fearfully from an unpaved roadside, its front legs chained to hind.

The restaurants grew ramshackle. You reach them at the end of a long gangway, creaking planks crossing above a series of ditches. The planks rattle beneath your feet, some have burst under heavier weights than mine. You pass the outposts of rusting cars, bare flagpoles, punctured lampshades casting punctured shadows as sparrows flutter around sleeping dogs, their heads resting upon rocks. Closer to the middle of nowhere the proprietors grow warmer . . . grandmother after grandmother . . . old women who take a liking to you simply for being another human to look after and feed. On long benches sat the truck drivers who stopped to buy water for their engine radiators and food for their stomachs. We ate at rickety tables, each of us with our separate businesses upon the road. By then I'd learned the passwords that unlocked good meals – *borsch, goulash, macaroni* – and, though the cup of tea would arrive with a fly floating on the surface, and when the wind blew the wrong way the smell of shit wafted from the squat toilet across the tables, still there was a humanity in those places, a real warmth.

The land dried up, turned to dust, that skin of roadside trees a thing of the past. The wind blew hot, like riding down the barrel of a hairdryer. You can't open your mouth, for in an instant your tongue and all the insides below are torched and cracked. At last I removed my knee-warmers, changed my vest for a long-sleeve pull-over of thin merino wool. It let the air pass through, kept a slender shade against my body. I tied a scarf into a turban, soaked it in water each time I left a restaurant.

My nose started to bleed – the thing always had been sensitive – a trickle up behind the sinuses every day for the next three weeks. Dry desert air thinned the blood vessels inside my nose, opening further each time they bled so that the next day's bleeding was harder to prevent. I rode with tissue plugged inside my nostril, and once saturated I'd feel the fresh blood hit against it, dribble back-wards down my throat. The blood would clot upon the paper and, as I removed the plug, once the bleeding had stopped, out would fall a great slug all dressed in scarlet.

* * *

My final day came, my last meal in Russia, the bowl of *borsch* pink before me, scented with dill, a white ball of sour cream floating at the centre, exploding in great clouds as my spoon pierced its side. The place was a little way from the road, drivers stopping, walking slowly to the building, placing roubles on the counter so that the woman behind it draws a bottle of vodka from the freezer, pours a short glass. Each man drinks, and then goes on his way.

I finish my meal, put my feet up and close my eyes. Passing cars occasionally disturb the silence, ripping by on the road, axles rat-tling. The proprietor comes to me, she sits – an old woman, black hair tied back in a flowered scarf and silver hairclips. She has a savings account of gold teeth, dark skin, lips painted the colour of the sunset, green eye-shadow, crescents hanging from each ear beside a face like a brass lantern, engraved with the etchings of age and work, old and worn. I look at her, wonder if she had once been beautiful . . . beautiful in that way everybody is supposed to have been at some point in life. She tells me she's Tartar, I hesitate, and then for the first time on my trip, I spoke Turkish.

My books had told me the languages of the Caucasus were Turkic, though I had expected the similarities to have been overstated. My eyes first opened and then shone as I listened, ears ringing while she counted out my bill in Turkish numbers, told me the tea was free. Suddenly there I was, talking with an old Tartar woman on the edge of the Eurasian steppe. I don't think she recognised the element of chance that allowed us to communicate. In places like that, a house-cum-café 60 miles from the nearest village, the outside world must be a smaller concern, language a given. It's no surprise to have the person in your café speak a language you understand because everyone who ever came that way before him has done so too. In lives like hers, serving *borsch* and vodka without any *world's-your-oyster* tourism Shangri-la, the idea of people wilfully going to a place they don't understand a single word probably wouldn't have made much sense. Why would anyone cycle into a 3,000-mile wasteland, unable to speak a word to the few dozen people who lived there? And so it was that beneath a tin roof surrounded by scrub, the Westerner had a thrill of anthropology, and the Tartar woman had a conversation.

With her fingers she pulls her eyes to slits. She laughs as she says, 'This is what Kazakhs look like.' With playful sadism she laughs again, laughs that there will be no trees, no shade where I'm going. She points to a tiny sapling at the edge of her plot, a twig about a foot in height, two leaves growing from it. 'The trees will be like that . . . There will be only sun where you're going, only the hot sun.' Her face bursts to colour, eyes close behind green curtains, golden teeth shine as she starts to laugh and laugh and laugh still harder at what I'm doing. She leans towards me, speaks Tartar history, tells me of the Mongolian people who worship the sky, a timeless tribe from before the age of nation states. Proudly she speaks . . . 'From China to Russia, we have travelled by our horses.' And then, abruptly she stops. Interrupted. From a bag, hung on the back of her chair, comes a ringing. With a wrinkled hand she picks it out. The old Tartar woman flips open a mobile phone, starts shouting.

* * *

At the Russian border they made me unpack the lot of it, sent me back and forth to offices where I received blank stares and ink-stamps, before being directed to the Kazakh side and one man out of uniform. He wore long shorts, an unbuttoned Hawaiian shirt with a white vest beneath. Large sunglasses gleamed at me from the midst of an olive face with a cheerful smile you wouldn't trust. A phenomenon at crossings worldwide, he knows one word of English . . . 'money'. He uttered it, and I followed to a hut.

After hurrying me in, he bade me shut the door quickly. An air-conditioning unit whirred on to keep those square metres coolest in the whole province. He had a cheap quality to him, friendliness too immediate to mean a thing, radiating the contentment of the man making most money from the least work and in the most comfortable surroundings. He asked how many roubles I will be bringing to him. With pen and paper, I wrote 1,000 and he declined any 10s or 50s more than that. With assurance he entered numbers into a calculator, showed me the screen, pointed at the '3,000' that appeared. He muttered something that made him laugh, unpeeled my thousands from a roll pulled from a breast pocket.

Out of futile principle I challenged his calculation . . . too low . . . though 75 miles of hot sun, without food or water, were on his side as far as the nearest cash machine was concerned. He refused any number other than his 3,000, readied the calculator once again. On it was a wide display screen that he tilted to 45 degrees, inputting another sum equal to 3,000. Pointing at it with a nod, pointing at the brand of calculator with another nod and then, for good measure, to demonstrate his good faith in his figures, he boldly cleared the screen of any shred of history, entered a three and three zeros, also equalling 3,000. Turning the calculator to me, he pointed, smiled some more of that smile you'd never trust as if to say that calculator, as a mere machine, could have no bias . . . why would it lie?

You can't argue with such perfect logic, despatched with such assurance. And so I took my 3,000, waved the smile goodbye . . . and headed into Kazakhstan.

Steppe

Day 34 – Oralsk – 3,681 Miles

For a long time I'd wanted to be there. Kazakhstan and Uyghur, alongside America, were the places I'd hungered for. Everywhere else was just geography on the way to my 18,000 miles. Wands fell, magic fluttered, twinkled down from the sky as the plains rolled out towards a horizon stripped bare. In an instant I was transported, one of those moments when the incredible difference between everywhere you've ever been before and the place you find yourself form some concoction after which the world will never be the same again. Orientalism goes haywire, the most mundane elements of your surroundings become enchanted, spiritual, intriguing beyond all measure. If only we could look at our own world with that same love . . . and if only our own world could still look that way.

In truth it wasn't a bad arrival. After 10 Kazakh minutes there came a fairly good introduction for a fantasist arriving in the lands of Genghis Khan and his horse lords. From out of sight came a rumbling, the earth shaking with an ever-louder violence until, standing on a rise above me, there emerged a long line of horses, a herd the same size as we see cows and sheep back home. They were beautiful creatures . . . long manes, shining coats, such graceful power in them. Those flogged and tethered creatures of Romania and Russia shrunk into pale forms by comparison.

Together they stormed down the hill, a single horse, bigger than all the rest, mounted with a rider as they galloped towards the road, dust kicking into the air behind, a break in their stride as they clambered up to the asphalt, a swarm of muscles streaming over it, back down the opposite bank and onto the plains once again.

The rider saw me, pulled at the reins of rope so that his mount slowed, straightened and turned my way. Towards me he cantered down the road, his body rocking with the step, the other horses slowing, starting to graze. He rose above me, an ageing man, gaunt features, the narrow eyes the Tartar woman said I'd find. Dressed in a thick sweater falling to his lap, covering his skin against the sun, he wore a baseball cap, silver teeth in his smile, and in his hand a stick, a rope tied to it by way of a whip. He pulled up before me, seated on a saddle of no more than heavy carpet, the horse fantastic, standing there braying, stirring, veins full inside its legs, skin glowing as hooves kneaded at the road. The man was followed by a cape of flies, circling, fresh air overturned by the smell of horse, his waiting animals dropping their shit into the field. He looks at me on my bicycle, I look at him on his horse. Nodding, he smiles, 'Where are you going?' I call up, as if the steppe itself has asked me, 'To Oral!' The words snatch from my mouth on the wind . . . they float, drift to him as he looks down, a curious smile as he wishes me a safe journey.

There was little more to it, only a simple exchange, but one held in a different world. He tapped his heels at the flanks of his horse, cantered down from road to plain. He circles his grazing herd, encourages them back to first a run and then a gallop. The land shakes at their departure, that dark mass moving off into the wilderness, dust settling behind them.

* * *

The land out there was flat, though not entirely, for when the world was made fit for humans, stripped of incident and sanitised in readiness for us, so did they take the ogres of the planet and lock them beneath the Caucasus. There, inside the earth, livid and enraged, the ogres had pummelled, kicked and punched at the stone door under which they were trapped. They never broke through, perished below, but not before leaving tiny hills, dimples all over the plains. Those hills rise unannounced, like pointed hats, sudden tors in the flat that climb, peak and then drop.

Up above the wind fell in love with the sun, without condition or caveats. The wind adored the sun for her radiance, her strength, yet she would not indulge such a small admirer from our own world. Each day for all eternity, he resolved to show her his strength and, with all his power, he tears over the lands, east to west, following to her horizon with only a cyclist travelling in the opposite direction for resistance. That steppe was headwind country, and neither man nor nature had constructed any obstacle to disrupt the daily rampage across it.

Staffs of stone were rooted in the earth along the road, painted markers counting off each kilometre . . . *1984, 1867, 1789.* I deliberated, pondering whether this truly was a desert I cycled through. Then, one afternoon, a horse emerged upon the horizon, an odd-shaped creature of peculiar proportions. The silhouette grew a mound on its back, then a hump, and then . . . *lo* . . . it was not a horse at all, but in fact a camel. I stopped in amazement, for camels lived in deserts and if this was a camel then it must have been a desert through which I rode. The scale of it captivated me, the thought that I had left my house in London, taken a boat for 20 miles of the English Channel, began cycling and then, by only the power of my legs, entered into a world where camels stalked the grasses, snarling back as I stood staring beside my bicycle. In Kazakhstan I spent over 2,000 kilometres on a single road with hardly a turning, a gallon of water carried over my back wheel, pannier full of bread and jam, a head full of worst-case scenarios in which my bicycle broke down between settlements. The villages were 100 miles apart, then 150, and eventually 200. Imagine London were only a village, Manchester were another, and now imagine nothing in between upon that single road that joins them. You can see the towns in the distance, a single radio mast stands skinny against the horizon, comes slowly into view from 30 miles away. Kazakhstan is the ninth-biggest country in the world but with a population of just 16 million. I rode through some 3,000 miles of it, find it hard to believe even that many people are living there.

The land delighted in its endless scrub, and among those wastes I found myself smiling, simply smiling, for never have I been so at peace. The steppe was just a mirror, could comfortably represent either stark death or perfect simplicity, and each time, against that landscape so eternal I realised all I saw was in fact only a measure of my own impatience or contentment. Out there I was humbled, so tenderly was I humbled, for I took with me all my earthly weight . . . my cynicism, my fear, my egotism and insecurity . . . and, when we arrived in those wastelands, they saw the world in which they wished to live, so that very soon, all had fled from me.

At dusk I watched settlements from afar, eating a small meal before disappearing back into the road. Trails went, kicked up behind the goats, the horses and bulls being driven back inside the mud walls of the village. A bell would ring from a short tower, and I watched figures sitting lazily on horseback as they rounded up the herd, lines of dust making their way slowly back through the gate from different points on the landscape. Those sunsets in the Caucasus were something else, a tiny, nightly supernova, like a hot ruby sinking to the bottom of a well . . . you could light a candle on them, smouldering in a pink that turned to blood. Peels of black cloud would sit upon the red, leeches sucking that firmament to the last before floating to the tops of the sky, greying, and then melting to join the night.

For a while I'd lie awake, growing certain the stars were breeding overhead. Every night there were more, new stars appearing among the million, white waves of cosmos trailing among them. Sometimes I would stare upwards and imagine the outside universe as nothing but light, the world itself wrapped in a black paper bag with tiny holes, pinpricks all through the walls and roof of our resting place. In those lands there was no need for a tent . . . rain was impossible and the mosquitoes could not survive, the silence too absolute for their wings to hum through. The stillness would play a lyre as I looked up at the sky, resolving to keep my eyes open until a shooting star had passed. In most places I have lived, such a game would have failed entirely, yet out on those plains it comes within five minutes. The tail of that burning rock would take a needle from those scrub thorns, and together they stitched closed my eyelids each night. The scrub sat over me, bathed my forehead as if a warm flannel, soothed me to sleep beneath those acrobatics.

Day 37 – Qarabutaq – 3,847 Miles

The morning moved slowly, my wheels pulled back by wind, the weight of my water, a sense of fear at my small rations. After 45 of the 230 miles to the next town, a rise gave way to a caravan pulled in to a crossroads, smoke lifting from a grill of coals. The setting was dusty, the caravan blue, patched with sheets of rusted metal, steps leading up to a single bed, a rug with a neat row of sandals upon it.

An upturned bottle hangs from the caravan's underside. It

serves as the tap, you unscrew the lid a little and water trickles out, cool from the shade as you wash dust from your hands and face. A tray of coals smoulders as children play. The father walks towards me, smiles, shakes my hand. That was how every greeting went, all through Kazakhstan I was shaking hands, the second hand placed over the grip, eye contact, as if you're really meeting someone. He gestures that I should sit, returns to turning skewers, numbers tattooed across his knuckles. His three young sons switch from game to game, hold bricks of chalk that they throw at the road or use to draw on the caravan. I ask the father if they have soup . . . potatoes . . . rice? Only meat. He barbecues two skewers, brings them to me with salt, tough bread. A boy pours himself a bowl of tea, gazes at me from under the prayer cap on his crown. He looks at me as I eat, looks back to his bowl of tea, watching me from over the rim. With a slow drag he stirs in the sugar, metal chiming ceramic, so that distant church bells begin to ring.

Two dogs lie in the shade beneath the caravan, whistling a sleep that calls me over after eating. I wake only when the pool of dribble under my cheek grows too big to ignore. That old contraption of a home sits above me, the wagon suspended on strips of iron sprung over heavy cartwheels. Beside me is a derelict car, yellow paint peeling away, no wheels, seats disintegrating and replaced by folded newspaper over the wire frame. Occasionally a radio signal made it through, so that the father would come to sit in the driver's seat, listen to music crackling.

The children picked up their rocks of chalk, began copying the words I'd brought with me, that Latin script they'd never seen before. The name of my bicycle, the name of my pannier bags and saddle, written in chalk upon their caravan – *Mavic*, *Ortlieb*, *Brooks*, *Tout Terrain*. I sometimes think of those names, still scrawled in chalk on the side of a caravan in Kazakhstan. I wonder if anyone else went along that road and read them. Lying on my mat, I looked up at the sky . . . clouds floating high above, swimming through the blue. I saw myself then, saw myself as a boy in Leicestershire, cross-legged on a carpet at primary school, learning of the Silk Road. And I could not believe that same body, boy, brain was mine, was me . . . that it had existed there, and was now beneath a caravan on a deserted road in central Asia.

Day 39 – Highway 32 – 4,087 Miles

The road turned bitumen, then rock, and then finally . . . it disappeared. I rode into Purgatory, entered a state of war and had my sins scrubbed down. That road gave me no more than broken tarmac, shingle and soft sand for the worst part of 200 miles. Out in the desert, construction machinery had pulled up every metre of the old road, and though a year later I might have found glorious asphalt, the thought was slim consolation in the July of 2009. Highway 32, just past the town of Qarabutaq.

Already it was set to be demanding. Between the towns of Qarabutaq and Aral were approximately 230 miles, the longest empty road I would encounter in all the world, a plunge due south that people said increased already hot temperatures by 10 degrees. At the halfway point was the town of Yrghyz, though to reach it would require a 30-mile diversion along old roads. As I was never sure whether I'd find a shop in the towns along the main road, I held out little hope for Yrghyz, and would take that diversion only out of desperation. One final calamity made it irrelevant anyway, a cock-up all of my own making. I don't know whether it was the heat or the adventure that had gone to my head, but one way or another I'd taken my eye off the ball, hadn't paid heed to the denominations on the bills remaining in my wallet.

What waited on the road ahead soon became a lesser concern, and it dawned on me that I had almost no money left to buy anything anyway. I should have replenished my wallet in the city of Aqtobe, but instead rode through without a care in the world and no prospective bank until Aral at the earliest. I had perhaps 700 Kazakh tenge to my name, the equivalent of about £2. Life in Kazakhstan is not expensive, but it's not quite that cheap either. And so one morning, with a bag of biscuits, seven litres of water, a heel of bread, a quarter-jar of jam and £2-worth of Kazakh tenge . . . I set about riding 230 miles through the desert.

My bicycle and load were not designed for that. I'd set about the task of 18,000 miles with as little thought for venturing off tarmac as I had for going up hills. My tyres were hard and narrow, the weight I carried pushed my wheels down into the sand, the bicycle slipping out from under me. I'd put down a foot to stop it toppling, start again, hopping along to pick up speed, making to roll my bodyweight with the shifting terrain, shoulders heaving handlebars as time and again the front wheel slipped down a drift of sand and pointed me into a standstill.

I deflated my tyres, let the rubber spread so as not to sink so fast. I span easy gears, backside rooted to saddle to keep traction in the rear wheel, pumping the pedals so that I could accelerate out of each pitfall before it pulled me down. Sometimes I got off and pushed through the rock and debris, other times I persevered with the pedals. The first three hours on that broken road I managed under 12 miles, and yet those three hours, without doubt, were among the finest and most disciplined in all the days I rode. I stopped thinking of the alternative road I might have taken, of the banks in Aqtobe. I banished 'could have' and 'should have' from my vocabulary, did away with the past tense and the future too, for nothing existed beyond 1,000 metres in a kilometre, and however many kilometres before the road surface returned. I did what I've always done in these situations, slipped off into some place between meditation and fantasy.

The camels were pirates, all with blackened faces that spat shadows as they heard me near. Twisting like serpents, necks coiled round to point triangular eyes right my way . . . a chief sauntered up with wilted humps and burnt legs, a bandana about his head and rows of black daggers in his teeth. His nose was pierced with a sheet of scrap metal, fur tattooed by brands, and dark eyes watched in laughter as a sand drift pulled me slowly from my bicycle, knees hitting the frame as I fell. It's cruel when you move as slow as that, so slow the flies catch you, walk around upon your skin until you can take it no more, slapping at yourself to make them fly away at last. And then settle once again.

It was the Devil's land, but I was not alone out there. The same wind that plagued my first week in Kazakhstan became a friend to me there, a reminder from a better place, whipping up dervishes to spin gusts of fresh air towards me. I looked into the desert, at the salt marshes so pure . . . all innocent and white. They called over, bade me sit beside them a while. So sweet came those voices, and very nearly was I seduced, but I knew to sit and rest beneath that sun would destroy me. I watched the salts ripple a gentle applause for my efforts and, though in my heart I was sure that it was a slow, sarcastic clapping they performed, at the time it came to feel so generous, so inviting and sincere. Music rich and exciting trickled to my ears. The sound of a black soul choir, they sang out, whispering that all men were evil, were liars, and yet no matter how dark, the words they came to me so sweet.

Sparingly, I ate my food and drank my water. It was hard, but though needless suffering is folly, I can't help but find a purity in such pilgrimage, a journey whereby the suffering becomes merely a bodily experience you no longer attempt to resist. I find my tranquillity, neither fight nor struggle nor curse, for hardship is less encumbering than frustration, and triumph comes only with peace. You make peace with yourself, with that which defies you, and then silently, without ego or rage, you defeat it . . . you overcome that which caused you pain, make of it a physical travail that cannot trouble the calm inside your mind.

Day 40 – Highway 32 – 4,120 Miles

The word '*café*' was daubed in paint on a metal sheet above a concrete hut. Cardboard covers the windows, a basin is mounted in a dressing table out front, the sort I'd seen all through Kazakhstan. The water is ever murky, but details like that didn't matter . . . it feels so civilising to wash your face and neck, draw a line between endurance and rest. There was always a small bar of soap, a towel still damp from the last man, everyone on all Highway 32 drying his face on that same towel.

A woman appeared, dressed in an apron and looking older than she probably was. Her face was dry, split lips turning to skin and disappearing down her throat, so that the mouth became only a voice ushering me inside. Down a corridor, she led me to a room kept free from light, a vain effort to leave the place a little cooler. Lying down across cushions, I listen to the muffled sound of spitting fat, lifting and falling in a pan beneath the veils of what could only be frying eggs. She brings them to me, pale yellow, four of them, with tea and bread, the first of what became a common meal in those days moving south. I cover them in salt, replace the white crystals forming on my red sweater. Pointing to a bulb in the ceiling, I ask for a light by which to write. She shakes her head, pulls a rag from where it is stuffed into a hole in the wall. A shard of light dives in.

She waits in the shadows of the corridor as I rise to leave, gathering up two bottles of water. I ask the price, watch as dark, shrivelled eyes sparkle with incrimination. It is only an instant, a pause just long enough to show her assessing my value instead of giving me the honest price. She doubles it, opens that dry mouth and hisses a figure through teeth stuck like nails in a parish notice-board containing only bad news. I smile, offer two less than she has asked, all that I can afford. She nods. Outside, I step back to the light ... *my God* ... but that light is blinding, the sun so fierce, once from the sky and twice reflecting off the white earth. You shield your eyes, turn your head away, you squint, come to understand how that woman's face became so cracked, stepping from her darkness into the light each day, face squeezed shut so it doesn't ignite beneath the strength of that sun.

Over the dressing table with the basin, I splash water at my face, wet my scarf and hold water in my mouth before spitting it to explode against the dust. With cupped hands I perform the trick my father taught me as a child. I fill my palms with water, place them against the back of my neck, clefts of my arms, backs of my knees, ankles ... points where the blood runs closest to the skin and cool water draws out the heat. I tie my scarf into a turban ... 300 tenge to my name as I retake the road.

Afternoon came easier than morning, though I don't know if that was the result of better conditions or lower expectations. A surface of road reappeared, if it could be called as much, and I picked my way through the gravel at its side, the centre of the road no more than potholes, drifts of dried mud, craters big enough for whole cars to fall inside. After perhaps 60 miles for the day, in the early evening I came to a dirt road, the fork that would continue to Yrghyz. At the junction was a series of shelters, a small house sunk below the level of the road and constructed from old tyres, wooden boards thrown among them and mud on top. Taking my empty wallet, I walked towards the house. I recognised that I could not make Aral without more money, yet I also knew I could not make it through the night without another meal. The present had to take priority over the future and, beg, borrow or steal, the future could eventually be addressed by whatever means.

Inside an old woman wound a handle on a machine, spinning a wheel that churned beneath a bowl, froth spilling from one spout, milk from the other. A man squatted over bloodied newspaper, a bucket full of skinned limbs. A goat's head, black, horned and solemn, sat beside him as he hacked at bones with a heavy axe. They shooed me outside, pointed to shelters with tables beneath them. Appearing from the dust, small children look my way, standing to stumble towards me from where they had squatted in a pile of straw and mud. Dirt was smudged all round their mouths, confusion in their eyes. They teeter forwards, up to their knees and elbows in the greenish remains of dry manure, an orderly row of mud bricks assembled on a plastic sheet beside their heap of wet dirt. They walk towards me . . . give a sob, a cry . . . then wail as if just informed of the geographical lottery of their birth.

A man emerged, bare-chested, young and stout. We shook hands, head-of-the-family style, romantic poverty nowhere to be seen. Warts grew from his hand like a bunch of grapes dying on the vine, looking worse as I remembered I'd held that very hand with my own. His eyes were boss, one of them looked directly at me, the other peered east towards Shymkent. We negotiated food, an agreement that left me with the uncomfortable thought that I might not have enough to pay my dues. The graduate from London would fall short in his debt to a family at the Yrghyz junction. His children ran about in only T-shirts, my presence no longer a cause for fear as they stood with dry shit up to their knees, one boy still crying with the wind, his mother's breast milk dribbling down his chin. Born in Africa and the dear sprogs would have had A-list celebrities falling over themselves to adopt them, central Asia and they had to make do with me and a bicycle.

I ate my meat quickly, aiming to leave as soon as possible. In every moment I reproached myself for my judgements, my squeamishness . . . and yet I'd been born of a place so very different. We Westerners sense others' economic poverty more acutely than ever they would themselves. Having been bombarded with the idea that happiness comes through possessions, conditioned to obsess over our every appearance and action, it is incomprehensible to us that a man living in a house built from mud and dung opens his eyes each morning, wipes a hand of warts across his face, and goes about his day not the least bit miserable about who he is.

The father sits, licking his fingers at the next table, as I ask my debt. He wants 500 tenge. I have 200, show him as much. He shakes his head, furrows his brow, thinks I've misunderstood . . . thinks I've got more. I have one final hope, and with the Russian border less than 200 miles north, and Russian trucks occasionally passing on the road, so it is that I look hopefully into his cross-eyes and ask . . . '*Roubles?*' He nods, and I hand over all the denominations that the man at the border had refused to exchange. He counts the notes, paper against the tough brown warts of palm and fingertips. He gives me an agreeable nod . . . takes the lot. With a final clasp of that hand I set off, penniless in all currencies of the world, still 100 miles from Aral.

Day 40 – Highway 32 – 4,151 Miles

Now I'll tell you, tell you what scheme I'd been formulating, no shortage of time for weighing up options, assessing the pros and cons of each possibility. I didn't want to steal, nor did I want to start running out on bills. Conscience aside, I didn't fancy my chances of escape on a 100-mile road. What I needed was a single creditor, an angel investor, a white knight . . . but I couldn't ask a peasant to loan me the fortnightly living costs of his entire family, nor did I expect to find anyone else willing to do so.

What I needed to stumble across . . . stranded halfway down Highway 32 . . . was a rich man, a thought not so soft-headed as it might sound. That stretch of non-road was not entirely deserted, and I shared it with two other types of vehicle. First were the trucks, driven by the average working-class Kazakh, and in these I placed no hope. Second, however, were the four-wheel-drive jeeps, the sports utility vehicles from Japan and Germany, vehicle of choice for oligarchs and swines the world over. Ever they'd come at me through the heat, polished against the dust, and no doubting that anyone with a vehicle like that had a few spare tenge on board. Don't get me wrong, I'm not proud of having to size up a scrape like that; asking money from rich people isn't something I aspire to, flouts all of my principles, but you can't eat principles, and what good's a principle when you're collapsed in the wilderness?

As evening falls, my quarry nears. A Mercedes jeep . . . black, gigantic, shining. He picks his way down the road, steering around craters. I drift towards him, breezy and upbeat as he pulls to a halt. He's curious at my white face, my bicycle. He speaks clearly, not the tribal dialects I'd been drifting in and out of, his was a plain Kazakh, overlapping nicely with my Turkish. He leans out, a hairy forearm on the door panel, side-parting swept over Mongolian features, a khaki shirt unbuttoned, wafting the collar at the heat as he opens the window with a release of cold air.

We talk about where I'm from . . . going . . . how's Kazakhstan? How much further is the road like this? Eighty kilometres, he tells me. Not exactly good news but the uncertainty of when it would end was part of what fatigued me. To think in 50 miles more I'd be pedalling normally, that is a boost, a definite goal. Slowly we get down to business. 'Have you had problems?' 'Problems!? . . . My word (!) . . . Not at all, Kazakh people very kind, Kazakhstan beautiful, food nice.' Ah yes, which reminds me, some food . . . I do have one problem, now you mention it, one *small* problem. I reach into a pocket, pull out my purse, unzip it to reveal a dead fly and a single kopek in the universal tongue for '*I have no money*'. He rolls his eyes, as if this is all he ever hears from youngsters. He reaches over his shoulder, unzips a leather purse, pulls a note of 5,000 tenge from a clutch of 5,000s. Just shy of £20 and between two fingers it comes towards me, that papery plastic, that shade of blue and those three wonderful zeros waiting behind the five.

I take hold of it . . . like a dangling rope as you fall from a cliff. The driver has disdain on his face, no warmth in that gesture, a trace of obligation perhaps, but foremost an affirmation of his own wealth, the power it left him. I don't mean to be ungrateful . . . really I don't . . . he saved me right there, but I've been given money a few times in my travels and that was the ugliest, the most sneering. I suppose, of the occasions people have given me money, that was the only time I ever had to ask for it.

Over and over I thank him, he offers me a second note, doubles the sum, real nonchalant, like it's nothing to him. I refuse, one hand waved in the air and the other gratefully on my breast. I ask where his house is, his address. *Almaty . . . Almaty!?* I'm going there! What street!? I'll come myself, give you back this money. He shakes his head, stony-faced. *Keep it!* I insist . . . go into my pannier, find a pen, paper. I'm coming to Almaty, I want to give you this back, I only need it because there is no bank until Aral and it's taking a long time to get there. I *have* to give you this back!

I hand him the pen, insisting, my honour dependent on that address. He rolls his eyes, writes down an address in Almaty, writes a name. 'Alisherr, my son . . . speaks English . . . his phone number.'

Day 41 – Aral – 4,197 Miles

At the cash machine in Aral, my bank protects me from somebody trying to access funds in Kazakhstan . . . two hours until my card unlocks. I rode out of that small city, once a fishing port, until the Soviet Union dammed the rivers that fed the Aral Sea, decided the water would be better used farming cotton. The sea raced away . . . disappeared, the shoreline galloping 30 miles inland, fish floating to the salty surface, dead as the livelihoods of all those fishermen. In the wake of the waters you now find only a salty residue of chemicals used to grow the cotton, and temperatures colder in winter and hotter in summer. Stark winds blow over the land in a toxic dust, killing crops the families I'd met along the road would once have grown, leaving them at the mercy of world food prices . . . peasants competing with bankers for their basic meals.

My spokes broke. They'd made it through Highway 32 only for a pair to explode shortly afterwards. I was sitting in a café, a bowl of *laghman* in front of me, that soup of thick noodles they served all through Kazakhstan. Beside me my bicycle waited upside down, the rear wheel stripped, new spokes ready to go in. From the next table, one in a gathering of gentlemen turns my way. 'And what are you doing in the middle of this godforsaken desert?'

Slowly I turned to him. Turned slowly back to my upturned bicycle with its naked wheel. Good question. I tell him of my journey, of the record, he laughs. There were six of them at the table, businessmen from Qyzylorda, all piled into a jeep and driving towards Aqtobe. Brothers and cousins, their grandfather had died in Qyzylorda, had to be buried in his home village, the men driving north for the ceremony. I asked about the road ahead, if there were more cafés waiting.

'I think yes, 80 kilometres east is a crossroads. There is a café there.'

I loved that about Kazakhstan, the way that *a crossroads . . . 80 kilometres east* was as complicated as directions needed to get.

'And the climate, the temperature . . . does the desert change?' I was eager for information, to be told it would be getting easier.

'Soon, past Qyzylorda, the country changes. It is hard to believe that it is the same place . . . there are trees, hills and rivers . . .' He paused. 'A bit like paradise.'

'I don't believe you!'

He laughed again. 'I only lie three times a day. This morning I already told three lies to my wife, so now I am telling the truth!'

My broken spokes made way for their replacements, leaving me to adjust tensions and bring the wheel back into line. Asking for the bill, I watch as the waitress shakes her head at me. I ask again for the bill. Head shakes. Flustered, I ask once more, make an abacus of my palm and slide fingers. She smiles, brushes her hands together . . . *all done* . . . points to the table, now empty, where the men had sat. She nods at me, a short smile of understanding.

* * *

I'd expected the improved conditions of weather and geography but hadn't quite allowed myself to believe in them. The steppe was so hot all possibility of cool weather had left my head, and yet along Kazakhstan's southern reaches there lifted the folds of earth that rise to culminate, hundreds of miles south, in the ranges of the Himalayas. Occasionally you feel it on the breeze, winds that reach you with a memory of snow-capped mountains passing over your skin.

Rivers flow from those peaks, snow melting or falling all the year round. Even if such water remained a long way from me, the land, though always living quietly within the scrub, became more noticeably alive as I joined the Silk Road. Habitations had grown from that old freight line, left behind as Marco Polo made his way out of Persia and continued east for China. You could always tell when a town was coming out of the desert, for the land would turn green, gently at first, then vibrant, with crops growing up beside the road. It was the opposite of Europe, where towns are the greens of countryside turning the grey of concrete. In Kazakhstan, towns turned green because there was water in the ground, and so humans had been permitted by nature to exist there. It was that simple. I watched a flock of sheep clambering over each other beneath a large tree, following the shadow of the leaves as sun moved over sky. The watermelon harvest was newly in and, with a pile of rind around me, I felt my troubles were finally over, a slice of melon in my mouth, my feet in a shallow stream.

My mood relaxed, nosebleeds drying up at last as I passed through 45 days on the road, a quarter of my 18,000 behind me. There had been no sign I couldn't ride a century each day without tiring and, truth be told . . . I was riding well within myself, mindful I kept my powder dry until closer to Shanghai. My hygiene deteriorated as ever. Without a wash since Russia I neared rock bottom, a chastening experience to stand beside a stack of cow shit upon the road, watching despondently as the flies left it to settle instead upon me. Eventually I came across a river, said a prayer of thanks, picked through the rushes and jumped into those waters running through the steppe. There I washed, swam, sang . . . then stood with the current rushing around my knees, mud between my toes and tiny fish tickling as they nibbled at my skin.

I was happy there, making my way through a scarcity of resources that provided enough for life's essentials but not the abundance that leads humans to create things nobody ever needed. Evenings were best of all, those roadside cafés where time grew so generous, so slow and gentle, as if the hours themselves were exhausted from the day now over. Everything passes, but in kindly fashion, so that nobody cared for anything more than the plates of food before them. Those were the greatest of meals in the greatest of restaurants, run by a mother with her young daughter. Outside I'd sit with the woman and her child, with the three truck drivers who had also stopped. We sit cross-legged, leaning on cushions, drinking tea and discussing the road beneath the light of a single bulb. Mosquitoes arrive with dusk, a whirring commences and we begin to swat at arms and shoulders. The mother fetches a bowl of old dusty logs, moves to the centre of the clearing and, with the bowl at her feet, lights inside it a small fire, smothering it immediately with leaves and grass. She stands over plumes of white smoke, wafting a rug that sets white clouds billowing from her feet. 'She is a shaman,' jokes one of the truck drivers, and to the sound of laughter, smoke spreads its scent across the dusk, and mosquitoes retreat.

I watch one final mosquito sitting on my wrist, so that in the light of the bulb I see my blood entering the creature. Slowly its abdomen turns red, rising like a thermometer in a patient's mouth. My hand comes down . . . lands with a splatter.

Day 51 – Almaty – 5,273 Miles

Qyzylorda, Shymkent and Taraz all slipped behind. Traffic was growing as Almaty appeared, Kazakhstan's largest city just 200 miles from China. I once asked why the capital had been moved inland to the centre of the desert in Astana. The answer came back, short, blunt – *'In case the Chinese move the border.'*

I telephoned Alisherr, son of my creditor out on Highway 32. His English good, he told me of a café where I could get an espresso, said he'd meet me there. A single coffee helped me loiter the hour before he arrived, high prices in some mock-French establishment where Kazakhs reminded me of a poverty I hadn't felt since my last delivery to Mayfair. Alisherr pulled up in a large, Japanese coupe, shining like the lenses of the Italian sunglasses on top of his head. He walked towards me, we shook hands, kissed both cheeks, and he ordered an expensive drink he scarcely sipped.

It was a weight off my mind, settling my debt there relieved me of a burden . . . my own man again. Alisherr was a nice guy, my own age, straight-cut black hair, his skin slightly pitted from teenage acne. He waved his collar against the heat, just as his father had done out in the desert, explained that his father's job was overseeing reconstruction of the Kazakh road network, which explained why he'd known, to the kilometre, how far until the surface of Highway 32 resumed.

We talked Kazakhstan. Alisherr explained his intention to study in America, joked that he'd miss Kazakh traditions like eating lots and falling asleep in the afternoons. In truth, it was all quite cursory. Alisherr was a nice guy, no doubting it . . . his dad *had* saved my skin but, as far as daily life went, I had as much in common with him as I would your average Etonian. Sometimes I wonder what would happen if Westerners knew that millions of people in the 'poor' countries live in greater comfort than they'll ever know.

My bicycle pump lost, my spare tubes all gone, when Alisherr asked if I needed anything, a bike shop was my only request. He led the way slowly in his car towards a bike shop. On arrival he translated my questions about the pump, about valves and the diameters of inner tubes they sold. None of it was cheap, the discovery of gas and oil beneath the Kazakh desert has made the city of Almaty expensive. Businesses have flocked to tap the boom markets, opened offices with rents, living costs and prices lifting accordingly. Western bicycles in Kazakhstan were something of a luxury too, toys for the rich, so that 30 pounds of tenge would leave my wallet for a not-very-good pump. I walked back to my bicycle, wallet waiting for me, hiding scared in a pannier. As I considered the 12 deliveries back in London that I'd one day make to pay for that pump, a shadow appeared beside me. Alisherr walked up, a smile about his round face, full of warmth, glowing, so that I wondered what he'd found in a bike shop that had made him so content. My eyes lowered, settled on an armful of pump and tubes held out in front of him, extended my way.

'*These are for you, from the people of Kazakhstan.*'

* * *

The heat, exhaustion, or perhaps the fermented camel's milk shared with a farmer in his yurt, I don't know what it was that got me, but soon after Almaty I was being kicked, thumped, beaten this way and that as I vomited into a toilet. As I lay deathly still on the sofa of a roadside restaurant, my head began moving, turning slow circles. The world was spinning, forehead scalding, nausea rose from stomach to throat to toilet bowl within little more than five minutes.

Delicately into the evening, I pressed gingerly at the pedals for 15 miles. My body was weak, head ever hotter, a simmering paranoia that finally I'd been bitten by a tick, meningitis was upon me and here was the beginning of the end. The world became sinister . . . up ahead loomed snowless mountains, grey and angry they appeared, spreading downwards from on high, coming at me from vast slopes without colour or movement. I watched them watching me, peering down their falling noses, hundreds of kilometres in both directions so that each time I glanced over my shoulder they were always present, nothing but still, hideously and ominously still. The noise of the trains too, that sound I'd always listened to at night with such reassuring comfort. In the past the clackety-clack of the trains had come to my fantasy as the chopping axes and the marching feet of dwarves felling the trees for the railway sleepers. That night, lying in a dry trench where a river must some-times run, I heard the *clackety-clack* of the train just out of sight. It burst through the night, and in my head I imagined the soldiers of some brutal army, that *clackety-clack* the furious sound of spears beaten on shields as they gathered below the rise and readied to charge.

Even with my head beginning to smoulder in the grass, so the rest of my body began to freeze and shiver. However many sweat-ers I pulled on, all warmth had gone, and yet I knew my body was already quite warm enough, ablaze, the beginnings of a fever shiv-ering within me, teasing out sweats I could not feel through tingling skin. The warmer I dressed, the more I'd sweat and, with the next town still 50 miles down the road, I hadn't enough water to lose much in such a way. Somewhere close I heard a donkey bray . . . heaving slowly up to speed, wound tighter and tighter until eventually there came a crack, the creature exploding in cries that filled the night.

It's around about then that the detachment of my brain and body really begins. Brain, sitting clear-headed and comfortable upstairs, realises the blind panic that has taken Body, starts to nur-ture his loyal friend, tells him what to do. I took the scarf that I'd worn as a turban, folded it into a cloth and allowed myself enough water to dampen the material, then placed it across my forehead. I lay on my back, head cooling, body weary with fever and closed eyes starting to sting. Brain takes Body, takes him away from it all . . . starts to imagine better places. I see bare feet padding up a spiral of carpeted stairs, pressing gently on the hard skin of the sole as Brain leads Body up to the tower.

A door was bolted shut, lengths of oak with metal straps across them, a circular ring for a handle. Slowly, one by one the bolts slid with the sound of metal gliding over metal. Two pale shadows, one hunched over, step delicately into a small room, a row of shelves along one wall. Waiting there were small, bulbous bottles of potion, corked and glowing so that red, orange and green swirled among the darkness. Shut within thick glass, tiny bubbles of air were trapped where the bottles had first been blown. All around sit half-empty demijohns, drawers left open with scrolls protruding from them, jars containing dried flowers and forgotten oddments. Brain ushers Body forwards, encourages him to pick a moment, a memory or a comfort with which to escape. Slowly, uncertainly . . . up steps the hunkered shape, Brain urging him on as Body opens a jar, unscrews the lid, sips at a memory. And there he was, playing with the catapult on the allotment, beneath a wigwam trellis of runner beans flowering all red, taking shots at the old watering can. Body straightens, strengthens . . . moments took him, and one after the next, Body relived passages of better times, and fell to sleeping.

Next morning I woke, rubbed my head back to a life that opened with a dull thud. I allowed myself enough water to wet my palm, cooled my eyes and washed the sleep away. I got to my bicycle, the one priority to ride 50 miles and get water. That done, I had no concern for what would happen next. For all I cared, the world could end. My body ached, bones brittle, so that it felt as though my wrists were snapping as I unscrewed the lids from my water bottles, let the last drips fall against my dry throat.

The wind was with me that day, travelling on towards my rest. At the roadside I gazed into an empty bottle . . . the pursed lips of the breeze blowing across the neck, bringing forth a slow, ringing song.

Day 53 – Korgas – 5,486 Miles

The coming days passed slowly, my body recovering with sleep and water, while I continued squeezing 100-mile days from it. Those grey mountains turned to block my path, forcing me to scale hills and plateaux. The road was new, lined in concrete barriers painted red and yellow to show who'd stumped up the cash for fresh tarmac, easing the journey of the Chinese trucks that passed me by. In time I came to the rear of a line of traffic, the typical feature of borders everywhere. At the head of the queue, striped barriers were lowered across the Korgas checkpoint, soldiers stony-faced behind their guns. I walk up to a soldier . . . point past him at China, his shaking head and drawn lips confirming my bad feeling. A second soldier comes up with a brighter nature, a pocket diary held open. He points to a date that would have been Monday morning, scribbles '9:00am' on a page. The time was six in the evening. The Friday evening.

The weekend passed, shacked up in a small restaurant run by a husband and wife. He came out to meet me as I trudged by, accepting my fate sullenly. As he shook my hand, he started saying something I didn't understand. '*He-rb . . . Lo-is . . .*' Pointing back towards his home, to my bicycle, lowering his palms to indicate I should stay where I was while he went inside. '*He-rb . . . Lo-is . . .*' he repeats as he returns, unfolding paper with his hand, turning to stand beside me and opening a map of Kazakhstan, paper worn and tearing at its creases. He traced his finger out into the clear blue of the Caspian Sea, where in biro was written a message in English:

Thank you for letting us stay at your house with our bikes, we are
very grateful – Herb and Lois

He was an old man, his face full of folds as he smiled, pointed at
me, at *Herb and Lois* in the Caspian, at the closed border . . . at my
bicycle. Laughing at the predicament, he slapped his hand across
my back, waved me inside. That bolthole on the cusp of China
became a welcoming place along my road. I scribbled away at my
little stories, talked to the man's wife as she asked questions of
what I was writing, where I was from and going to. I'd stand
quietly in their doorway, watching the line of trucks lengthen as
Monday neared, cargos covered with canvasses that rippled with
the winds. The husband would splash water across the hard earth
outside, dampening the dust to stop it from lifting up and blowing
into the house. In one of our faltering conversations he showed me
his unstamped passport, the picture of his aged face, cracked like
the earth . . . and I saw there a date of birth only 49 years before.

I slept profusely. That was the thing I did most of, hoping to
recover my strength towards full health. That place taught me a lot
about sleep, a real education in slumber. I had to be exhausted, the
sleep had to be determined to take me or else it was no good, I'd
just lie awake fidgeting. The house was hot, disgustingly so even in
the shade, yet I had to cover my skin with a sheet to stop the flies
from feasting on me. If I slept on my front, I was too hot, so that
I'd be kept awake by sweat sliding under my arms and down my
sides. On my back, I was exposed, with flies drinking in my nostrils, from my lips and eyelids. It helped to arrange myself with one
hand draped over my face, like a scarecrow, to perturb the flies just
a little, and so that I had to do nothing more energetic than wiggle
fingers when they descended anyway. Eventually I came to enjoy
the sensation of flies foraging through my leg hairs and around my
ankles, for that meant they were at least nowhere near my face.

Afterwards I'd lie with eyes half-open, watching as the truck drivers and locals played games of cards, the loser of each round obliged to hold still as the other players flicked him hard upon the forehead, stern taps and laughter drifting towards me.

When Monday morning came, we hugged our goodbyes and I joined Herb and Lois in the Caspian Sea of their old map. I said everything that needs to be said for all Kazakhstan . . . words for the next people that find themselves at the Korgas crossing.

You are in a wonderful place, with wonderful people.

China

Day 55 – Uyghur – 5,486 Miles

They put you in the back of a minibus, drive you through a kilo-metre of no-man's-land, bodies pressed together, elbows on knees, a stranger's breath warm on the back of your neck. The door slides open, a man climbs in, wearing a white coat and holding a plastic wand that shines red light against the foreheads he points it at, checking for high temperatures and signs of dissent. I squirm as the thing came snaking towards me, snarl as China reads my brain.

We pile out of the minibus into the immigration terminal. The staff wear white coats, white gloves and elasticated surgical masks snapped around the backs of their heads. There are posters all over the room . . . images of picnics, basketball games and construction sites, all of it full with happy times for all. I was prepared for it. A year in Vietnam had left me good and ready for what China would be like. The Vietnamese and Chinese have a thousand-year history of animosity and war. You come to learn that the less any two nations like one another, the more they tend to have in common.

They give me a form to complete. *'In the last week, have you had any symptoms of diarrhoea?'* Five times a day, half-hourly, regular as the trains. *'Fever or temperature?'* Fearing the explosion of my head . . . if that counted? *'Headaches?'* Especially in the afternoons.

'*Drowsiness?*' Most noticeable in the mornings. '*Aching joints or muscles?*' Every day for two months. Imagining quarantine, solitary confinement in a secure Chinese hospital, I tick a resounding *No* beside each ailment, a *Yes* for '*the above information is true and correct*'. I proceed to the next stage, pass a water cooler, stop to refill my bottle. A white coat appears, a mask snaps. 'Only for workers,' he scowls. I step away. Another man appears, speaks English, no mask, black hair cut with a ruler and spirit level, a loud, uncomfortable laugh to punctuate each sentence and set you at ease. He asks where I'm going, asks why, how long, do I have money? He joins me . . . sits, softens, gets informal:

'What is your name?'

I answer, asking his.

'My name is Johnson,' says the Chinese man.

Impatient, I ask why I'm waiting. He straightens up, speaks in hushed tones, 'Don't be afraid . . .' Johnson points to the man from the water cooler, 'He is my chief.'

'You like him?'

Johnson nods.

'Why?'

'Because he is kind and warm-hearted.'

An intermediate-level answer from Lesson Three: How to Talk about Friends. Johnson pauses, softly serious. 'Tell the truth now,' he says, 'do you have any political views?'

'Me?' I stammer, pointing to my chest. 'Political views?' I go puppy-eyed, shake my head, make the most of being left alone with Johnson. Something's troubling me. 'Is everything OK in the region . . . in Uyghur?'

I'd heard riots had taken place. Johnson giggles, starts laughing . . . a real kid, nothing but giggles . . . draws his neck into his shoulders so as not to hear. This will be my first meeting with the reality that

Chinese officials are less grown up than Chinese children. As if these people immature as they grow older and especially once they ascend to minor authority. I don't dispute the exceptions to this rule, nor the idiocies of Western equivalents, but each nation has its traditional absurdities and that's one of China's. These guys behave with too much decorum where it is unnecessary and none where a straight answer would be nice. Johnson kept right on giggling to himself, put a fingertip to his lips, like someone who knows a secret but is more interested in letting everyone know he has that secret than properly keeping it.

'In Xinjiang . . . of course everything is OK. It is very peaceful here.'

He giggles some more, turns his head away with a grin.

* * *

Uyghur Autonomous Region, Tibetan Autonomous Region, Mongolian Autonomous Region, Kazakh Autonomous Region . . . They've got 'autonomy' all over western China, the result of that 1949 land grab that will slip slowly into the accepted facts of history. 'Autonomy' in China reminded me of the word 'Great', back in the West – Great Depressions, Great Wars, Plagues and Fires – all those events of dubious magnificence called 'great' by those who get through unscathed and are left in charge of naming history. Up in the Northwest, the Beijing Government has given people the freedom to call themselves autonomous and be doomed in all other ways.

Uyghur, as far as the West is concerned, is 'the other Tibet'. We have only the stamina for one moral outrage at a time, our public opinion incapable of being equally moved by two such similar abuses. If the Uyghur region is Muslim and the Tibetan region Buddhist, dressed all cuddly in their orange robes . . . the truth is a Buddhist wins every time. For decades, Muslims in Uyghur have been fighting for political freedom in lands once their own. As the saying goes, 'One man's terrorist is another man's freedom fighter', only not, alas, where Muslims are concerned, for a Muslim freedom fighter . . . try as he might . . . is still only a terrorist, especially since sunrise on 12 September 2001. The Beijing Government go on screwing the Muslim Northwest just as they've done since 1949, only now they deliver it as 'cooperation in the war against terrorism'. The Government fund the schools of ethnic Han – the 'true' Chinese race – they incentivise Han migration from elsewhere in China. The profits from oil and minerals mined beneath the Uyghur earth are repatriated to companies in Beijing, ethnic Han given jobs at the expense of Uyghur locals. Make no mistake . . . the Chinese plan is to breed them out. Naming the region 'Xinjiang' rather than Uyghur, making the names Mandarin – Urumçi to Wulumuqi, Korgas to Huocheng – is part of a process of cultural extermination that, if only they cared enough to know, would set your average liberal tingling on the injustice glans.

The newspapers in Almaty had written of the riots. A car bomb detonates in Urumçi, people fighting the police, Han shops with their windows smashed through. An uprising had drawn attention to the problem from as far afield as London, which just goes to show that violence solves nothing. The Chinese . . . excuse my language, but China doesn't fuck around where political protest is concerned. My mobile phone stopped working. At first I thought it was the signal dying out among the coming desert, and then, when I saw Chinese people using their phones, I realised the authorities had simply blocked all foreign phones across a 1,000-mile province. The military had set up checkpoints at each settlement, special forces dressed in black uniforms with machine guns. In a couple of towns I tried to use the Internet, to tell the outside world that I was fine. No good . . . in every town and every city until Gansu . . . it had all been shut down. A thousand miles, the equivalent of London to Rome . . . the Government just flick a switch, turn the Internet clean-off. It was in this climate, after one search of my bags and two X-rays of my bicycle, that I entered China.

Day 55 – Sayram Hu – 5,571 Miles

The temperature cooled as I gained altitude, making my way towards the peaks that hold China at bay. Yurts appeared, and though Kazakhs had proudly shown me ceremonial yurts in the gardens of concrete homes, as the altitude grew, in the hills of Uyghur you see people still living the lives of their ancestors. Homes of animal hide, faint smoke spirals making their way out the roof and into the sky. Shepherds drove livestock in and out of trucks along the dusty road. I saw white dots, clustered flocks of sheep still higher up the mountains over me. A young boy on a short mule sauntered past, old panniers across the animal's haunches, the boy waving the nine tails of a leather whip by way of hello.

Among the traditional and China had arrived with gusto in Uyghur. Throughout the valley the aspirations of the nation cast concrete shadows, the echoes of explosions rumbling as Beijing's road-building policy marched upwards. Those yurts and shepherds might well have been timeless but the outside world sure was not, and henceforth those people will graze sheep beneath the concrete columns of modern China and its highways. The mountain was on its last legs, rivers of mud all bleeding to death. The Chinese set to make it tame, riddled with tunnels and holes as if no more than a wedge of Swiss cheese. The existing road was a decent route around the contours of the slopes yet, for the new construction, they'd blown open the mountain, built clean over it . . . because they could, because the power was theirs to command.

Cranes protruded from the forest, above trees and into clouds, a score of them erecting concrete stilts, two at a time to bear the bridge across the valley. At the base of a pillar, mounted on a concrete cube the size of a tower block, I looked up to the very top, top, *top* . . . head tipping so far onto my neck that I grew dizzy and toppled backwards onto my heels. Dangling from the tops of those columns were men on ropes, spilling buckets of sparks overboard as they welded open steel. So this, I thought . . . *this* is what you do with the profits from a billion microwaves and electric toothbrushes. There were work camps all the way up, tents of bamboo poles with tarpaulins tied to them, pulling in the wind, blustery homes to which the gangs returned once they'd finished banging, digging, exploding and lacing the steel shell ready for the concrete. Men and women sat feet to feet, two lines of thirty workers apiece, lengths of steel rod and large pliers between them so that together they knitted frames over which the concrete would be poured and set.

Little triangular flags lined the route, all colours of the rainbow, a reminder to workers that this, beneath the smoke of readying asphalt, was just one gigantic party, the event no more than a cake stall at the church fête. There were posters too, posters 15 metres high, men in red overalls, beaming smiles as they shook hands with a beaming man in a suit and hard hat, everybody beneath a Chinese flag making them beam all the more. It had a sensitive side too, development with compassion, for among the plant machinery and dynamited rock a whole hill had been given over to hanzi, written in white pebbles . . . enough surplus labour for an English translation on a second hillside to be seen by only one English speaker. 'HAPPINESS – PROSPERITY,' it read. The Chinese were covering all bases . . . liked a bit of happiness but wouldn't baulk at cash either.

I was scared, it was daunting all right, riding up that

mountain, the colossal power of China all about, the whole thing almost enough to make me glad the Government wanted to renew Britain's nuclear deterrent . . . not that that would count for much against China. During the Cold War, Mao had proclaimed that 200 million Chinese would always survive, ready to build the socialist dream from the ashes of even a nuclear holocaust. Seeing the way that road went up . . . it had been no idle boast. I found a nation that will never be manhandled again in our lifetime.

* * *

I rounded the final bend, the top of the climb and the land flattening again. There I stopped, stunned. Suddenly before me was water, waves kissing shore. I recalled my map, that lake . . . Sayram Hu . . . 3,000 metres up, visible as a tiny dot on even a map of the world. All the way to the far mountains it spread, the lake fading where they hemmed in its distant shore, the cradle of those summits filled only with silence and the slowly moving waters. Up there was a purity, a crushing peace upon the yurts, where plain flags beat from a single stick in the ground, and red ribbons fluttered from the neck of a precious bull or horse. Around the lake's basin were bursts of forest, upon islands the silhouettes and tiled roofs of pagodas. The whole scene shone with silence, radiated the light–dark of a blinding sun slipping through holes in heavy cloud, piercing the lake, diving into the waters as the tide kissed still at the shore. Dismounting, I walked down to the water, over sparse grass and smooth white shingle. I knelt, drank from the lake . . . water so recently snow, so that for the first time in weeks I felt cold, hands frozen to the bone. Gazing into those deep, clear waters, my head immersed in that same old silence, punctured by tolling bells.

Day 57 – Kuytun – 5,802 Miles

The descent is an uninterrupted 25 miles, 40mph as you flash by ramps of gravel . . . run-offs constructed for luckless trucks that suffer brake failures on the way down. Although early August, the altitude and the mountain's lakes and rivers kept the temperatures lower than anything I'd experienced since Europe. I appreciated it, fearful the southern reaches of the Gobi Desert would be my home within the week. The dramas of the Uyghur insurrection stayed with me, all communication remained down . . . the conflict itself started to appear at the roadside.

Riding through small towns I heard shouts and a new noise, louder than any I'd ever known – *ka-krack, ka-krack!* – the ringing of gunfire rebounding through the main street as I passed. Around me a building was under siege, a man running in, holding a gun, another running after him holding a wooden bat . . . a horse bolts . . . smoke drifts out from windows as more shots go *ka-kracking*. Men had been laying paving on the street outside, a pile of small bricks pulled up, insurrectionists breaking the things in half, launching them at the compound and at the men making their way inside. Another valuable lesson on my way around the world: insurrection looks better on TV. The ardent tone of the reporter, close-up faces full of rage, bleeding wounds and cordons of armoured police . . . it really makes it, captures all that passion we have waiting inside ourselves never to get out. The reality is somewhat clumsier, lower on drama, sporadic, unkempt . . . only a high-stakes game of hide-and-seek, one that I, student of politics, ardent supporter of any insurrection against the Chinese state, felt pretty sure was none of my business. I pursued my own noble course of action and rode on, faster.

In the city of Kuytun, controversy caught up with me, matters finally came to a head. The police got me . . . took me in for questioning. It was a roadside checkpoint, Uyghur people being ordered from their trucks, cargos searched, guns pointing all too casually about the place. The police did their normal act, behaved as if it were a fun, friendly affair, as if I were as excited by their presence as they were mine. One holds the gun, the other gets to bark at you. 'Passport!' They'd been given English lessons, though not enough of them. I told them where I was going. 'Yes, but . . .' replies the officer, in a good accent too, before he'd stopped attending class and his tongue carried back to Mandarin. I tell them I have no time to waste, not that they understand, and so I slowly pedal off down the road. Someone starts blowing a whistle, an officer runs after me, grabs my shoulder, grips forearm. Gun. Impasse settles. I gesture my intention to eat, fingers picking imaginary food from the bowl of my hand. 'Yes, but . . .' and then Mandarin.

They kept me half an hour at the roadside, bade me wait, blew a whistle and shouted when I made to roll away again. An unmarked car arrives, four doors open to plain-clothes officers and a woman carrying a notepad with the demeanour and dress of a secretary. Last of all emerges an important-looking man, wearing a uniform shirt and spectacles. Built to almost six foot, exceptionally tall for a Chinaman, he introduces himself, finger on chest. 'SUPERINTENDENT!' he shouts triumphantly. 'Passport!' He snatches it, looks at it, has his secretary write down all details once, then twice, in separate books.

She spoke English, just a little, and so I said I was going to Shanghai . . . needed breakfast. Superintendent had also been at those first English lessons, and as he listened to her translation, turned to correct me, incapable of speaking softly. 'LUNCH!' he barked, as if to emphasise how much of my day he planned to take. Secretary explained that I could not go to the city alone, they would drive me in and then drive me back to my bicycle. 'No. Not leaving my bicycle.' She translates for Superintendent. He looks at me, snaps 'YES!' I shake my head, non-confrontational but resolute. 'NO!', 'YES!', 'NO!' . . . a fine bit of dialogue. He shrugs, waves a hand at my bicycle as he mutters something. Secretary turns to me, 'We will drive behind you . . . but you must not try to escape!'

In the centre of town, we pull up at a café. Things don't look promising. A glass cabinet, dressed with hard-boiled eggs, grey peas and balls of fried batter. Superintendent swings into action, bad cop to good cop the moment we are over the threshold, as if all he's ever wanted is to be a waiter. He sits me down at the head of the table, puts a napkin and condiments beside me. The Chief of Police for all Kuytun starts bringing plates my way, his long face nodding eagerly, gesturing thumbs-up or thumbs-down, and me giving a reluctant thumbs-up to the grey peas and hard-boiled eggs. My bicycle is propped up outside, the plain-clothes police officers have become plain-clothes bicycle experts, stroking their chins, tapping their knuckles on the steel frame, holding the handlebars, clicking through gears, squeezing tyres. Beside me sits Secretary, Superintendent ladling peas into a bowl with a happy grin. Two young women appear, also in plain clothes, hair in ponytails, cheerful smiles as they pull up and sit, superb posture, and in unison . . . 'Hello, how are you?'

They are English teachers, plucked from the college next door. I imagined the clamour as the personal address system rang through hallways and classrooms, 'Attention, would any English-speakers please report to reception, where the police and your country await your help.' We all sit down at the table, the plain-clothes officers sitting to my right with Superintendent, Secretary, and English teachers to my left. I'm waiting at the head of the table behind a bowl of peas, an eggshell and some crumbs of dry, grey yolk. Everything settles, Superintendent speaks, the English teachers translate the questions and, from behind peas balanced on chopsticks, I answer truthfully. I was going to Urumçi, then to Shanghai. I was in China for one month, and I came from London, where I was a courier.

'You're not a journalist?'

'No, not a journalist . . . a *courier*.'

'It is very important that you are not a journalist.'

The bastards, they were almost as disappointed as me that I was a courier and not a journalist, really rubbing salt in the wounds. No one had told the Chinese police about the London job market, as if jobs in journalism were two-a-penny and low-hanging fruit. Try as I might, they wouldn't accept it, couldn't see that my writing showed great originality, but the other candidate simply had more experience . . . he was the one the police wanted, dammit! I press the point.

'*No!* I'm a courier.'

'*PASSPORT!*' Superintendent shouts that one himself, his favourite.

'Why do you want my passport again?' I point to Secretary. 'She already wrote everything down . . . *twice*!'

Superintendent is adamant. '*Passport!*' . . . and I hand it back over. He begins leafing through, voice hushed as pensively he licks all down long fingers, unsticking pages as he turns. Superintendent speaks, looking at my passport, his tone slow and serious, deliberative. Pauses. A teacher speaks sharply.

'What do you know about events of 5 July in Urumçi?'

Six sets of sets of eyes narrow into crosshairs levelled my way. Inquiring, accusative, stern, they look down the table at me, where I sit behind the remains of an eggshell, a few bits of grey yolk discarded on the plate beside a bowl of peas, those peas all round and green and unassuming, never meant to have ended up a prop in a caper like this. There's silence, inertia as I lay down my chopsticks with a slow clatter. Superintendent repeats himself, only quicker, impatient, looking right at me, nose twitching with the prospect that he, out in Kuytun, is about to pull off a great investigative coup, earn himself a promotion. He shouts it at me, repeats, his voice springing all over that small café.

'*WERE YOU INVOLVED IN THE EVENTS OF 5 JULY IN URUMÇI!?*'

They're all staring at me, as if I'd instigated the whole thing . . . as if they know every thought and my guilt is already decided. Six sets of Chinese eyes pinned right into me sitting on my stool, a bowl of peas in my lap. I answer them, all in the timing, a weighted, perfect delivery through half a smile.

'It can't have been me . . .' I start – they stir – finish, '*I was in Kazakhstan!*'

And just to prove I'm innocent, I throw my hands up from where I'm sitting at the head of the table, with that bowl of peas and that eggshell . . . but especially those peas, all shiny and green. It was marvellous, supreme. My voice drops into the silence, the teachers give a flickering giggle as they translate. Silence returns and then, finally, a moment later, the comedy hits home. Suddenly laughter is everywhere, rolls from the tiled walls as the crowd melts before me, Superintendent chuckling to himself, nodding agreeably, even going so far as to slap me on the shoulder. With all that over, they start helping me, which was, as it turns out, all they'd wanted to do the whole time. The teachers take over, deliver the state line by heart.

'We know it was not you, but it is dangerous here because . . . *because* . . . some *Wigur*, they might try to hit you!'

'*To hit me?*' It's endearing, the way single-party states make everything into the simplest moral paradigm.

'Yes, *to hit you.*' They lean in, earnest, believe every word.

I gape. 'But where will they hit me . . . in the face, the body, in the back?'

'We don't know . . . but, if you have trouble, you must ask for Han people.'

That was a relief, no shortage of Han in China, but still I needed clarification.

'Are you . . . are you all Han?' Lots of nodding. 'And Han people are good and Uyghur people bad?'

'Yes,' they answer in unison, pleased at such a quick learner as me, 'but *some* Uyghur people are good too, lots of them are peaceful.'

'But still, some of them might try to hit me . . . but not Han people?'

They all nod, and at last I understand what I'd thought was a complicated ethnic situation.

Day 59 – Turfan – 6,013 Miles

After that I wasn't interested in cities. I skirted Urumçi, kept myself to the desert. August was rising as I made my way down to Turfan, a depression 125 metres below sea level, the Dead Sea the only point on the earth's surface that sits lower. The Chinese name for that place translates as 'land hotter than fire' and, with the peak of summer underway, again my nose started bleeding at the rising temperature and drying air. It was sensational, absurd . . . one more madness of the earth. For even there, beat down by heat, I only had to turn my head to see mountains 5,000 metres above that same sea level. As it grew impossible to step barefoot upon scalding earth, so I gazed at snow-capped peaks, squinting upwards from down in a world so hot it was hard to believe snow even existed. I remember the colours . . . and I promise that, if ever you go there, you'll come to understand why the peoples of those lands have always worshipped the sky as their god. Beneath sky the colour of a peacock's neck I rode, the richest blue you'll ever see, staring down upon earth a darker red than even the blood that would sometimes trickle from my nose.

Despite the desert, for millennia civilisations have thrived in that place and, without greed for cash crops or any more than their basic needs, they have irrigated their lands from canals dug beneath the earth. The canals slope down from inside the mountains and water collects beneath fields surrounded by walls of brick and mud. Riding by, it looks like a miracle has taken place for, from that desert earth, so red and barren to appearance, just the other side of a wall there stands the richest clutch of green, leaves of vines bursting full and bright against the sun.

Occasionally I'd stop to check the map, and it was in those moments of unsheltered stillness that I fully appreciated just how the heat had grown. In only a second sweat appeared, droplets seeping from every pore. I'd hurry whatever I was doing, fumble the map back into a pannier, push quickly away and rush to start pedalling again, make passing air breathe life against the water waiting on my skin.

Underneath the road, perhaps two or three to the kilometre, were tunnels, channels cut through the ground to accommodate the melting snow of spring. The walls and floor were set from a concrete the sun never touched, each bridge perhaps only a metre high, but so sacred cool against the desert outside. Whatever wind there was would funnel through those passages and, once the clock struck one, it was the almost perfect place in which to spend three hours cowering from the midday sun. *Almost* perfect. Just as my afternoon's rest required a sheltered spot away from the open road, so too did other acts of human nature, equally essential, though more tainting of the chosen spot.

We must have seen one another from the road . . . I certainly saw them . . . for those were the only hiding places in all Uyghur. Riding that highway, from the corner of my eye I would periodically see the squatting silhouette of a Chinaman, his bare, bony backside pointing downwards, a truck waiting above the tunnel. So it was that I'd pull up at tunnels, peer inside and choose the stretch least littered by the dried-out turds of desperate men, flags of white toilet paper fluttering in surrender. You put yourself upwind of the most and newest droppings and you relax. If you followed those precautions, forgot about the decoration, the arrangement worked fine.

* * *

Across the state line, from Uyghur to Gansu, the Chinese authorities lifted whatever technology had been blocking me from the outside world, just metres across the border my phone working once again. There in Gansu, I began to feel I was entering China . . . the people grew smaller, facial hair thinning and then disappearing, prayer caps gone.

In a roadside service station, past the city of Kumul, one evening I sat talking to a girl as together we ate bowls of noodles. Tired from her bus journey but keen to practise her English, she told me she was from Urumçi . . . only another 700 kilometres before she was home for summer, and these the last five hours of a two-day bus journey from Shenyang, in the far northeast, where she studied engineering.

'That's a long way to go to university, it must be a good place to study.'

'Yes . . . it is a *very* good place to study engineering.'

'Do you like it in Shenyang?'

'No . . . I miss home. I don't like travelling so far . . . I don't like engineering.'

'Then why are you studying engineering in Shenyang?'

'Because my father says I must –' she smiled – 'and so I must . . . for my family.'

Just as I begin to consider this, the fate of children raised without Disney to make them aware of their rights, there comes a terrified and unrestrained shouting, a commotion the volume of life and death. The canteen in which we sit is consumed in chaos, the girl drops her chopsticks, pushes herself back from the table. I look round, expecting an insurrectionist or two, at least a gun, but instead find myself watching a coach, moving slowly but powerfully towards the canteen window. Transfixed I watch, the end too close for me to consider moving, my mind quickly appraising the situation as the coach gathers speed . . . *Coach will hit large glass window, come crashing into canteen. Glass will shatter and spray, surprisingly far, but not so far as me.* As my European head assessed the potential for personal danger, I watch half a dozen gallant Chinamen – eager for martyrdom and disinterested in their own wellbeing – throw themselves into the path of the coach, put their backs into stopping the runaway vehicle on a route to destruction. They brace . . . hopeless against the rolling weight . . . they take the strain, drop the strain, run, retreat and finally jump out of the way. The canteen falls silent, one of those moments when you realise light travels faster than sound. I watch, slow motion as window goes elastic, like a bedsheet thrown backwards, turning to flakes of crystal as the coach hits.

Shards of glass fly into the silent air and then . . . a half second later, a splintering crash falls as glass bursts into the canteen and showers across diners. Crystals fly into noodles, babies lurch into awful song, mothers run and chatter erupts. Men rush to the coach outside, its radiator bent inwards as half of them stroke chins and become experts in coach radiators, and the other half focus on the window and become glazers. I think of that girl . . . her two-day bus journey to satisfy her father's wishes, of those men throwing themselves in front of a runaway coach. And with glass strewn across the floor ... I was in China, where everyone was expendable.

Day 63 – Anxi – 6,535 Miles

The trucks motored behind huge triangular scoops, set across their fronts like snowploughs in case a peasant or scooter should fall into the path of Progress, become trapped under the juggernaut and start slowing things down. In China the individual meant nothing. How can one of anything hold meaning with more than a billion others just the same? That was only half of it . . . that everyone was expendable did not begin to account for the fact that, quite simply, they were insignificant beside the future China had planned for itself. It was religious, fanatical – 'FUTURE WILL BE BETTER' cola was on sale from west to east . . . 'I BELIEVE', the not quite subliminal slogan doing the rounds in English between television adverts.

The masterplan was plausible too, substantiated, for up and down the roads I saw the forward march of China, industrialisation and beyond, the dragon shot full of growth hormone and whipped into a headlong gallop, every bit unstoppable as I watched the future flash by me on trucks. I saw it all . . . saw pylons waiting to be pieced together, the astronomic rollers of a paper mill, nodding donkeys to pump the oil, the rotor blades of wind turbines, four of them in convoy . . . each one the longest articulated lorry you've ever seen, an extending platform sliding out below the trailer and still the rotor hanging 10 metres from the back wheel. I saw the chamber for the catalytic cracking at the refinery, the telegraph poles, a score of tractors piled on top of one another, a gargantuan metal box towed on one articulated lorry and pushed by a second, a man strapped to a platform and suspended between the two vehicles at 70mph. In the wind his cape went flapping, the poor bastard cajoling a box of controls so that the load moved neither too close nor too far from either vehicle. I saw rods and pipes and vessels, coils of wire and steel cable that I could not even begin to guess the purpose of. It was all on the back of trucks, and every fifth truck bore a tanker full of petrol, all set to replenish those stations where the entire frenzy was fuelled.

The petrol stations were themselves testament to China's intent, future-proofed against the day when the Chinese travel about their nation by space shuttle. The automobile is seen as an indicator for Chinese growth and, if the Chinese ever start driving as much as the United States, the whole world's oil will have to be found a second time. Chinese petrol stations dwarfed everything, a score of pumps at any one, they were like amphitheatres or coliseums . . . the roof of the forecourt 50 metres high, ready for the day the blueprint was complete, when everyone was driving and the current youth were telling stories to their grandchildren, stories that ended with . . . 'of course, all that was back when China was just one billion people'. On the car transporters I'd see two-dozen cars, stacked high for an expanding middle class. Some of those transporters went four decks up, others two decks wide, gates and doors across the flanks, like giant farm sheds, so that when the cars arrived in Urumçi they just filled the truck with goats instead . . . sent them bleating back to Lanzhou.

I rode deeper into desert . . . closed in and passed one-third total distance, up on schedule at around 110 miles a day. As I rode I'd smell the trucks coming up behind me. With goods collected by the 1,000 kilo and then driven at 70mph, the scent would leave its impression on the trailing wind. Chickens passed me by, goats, sheep and newly cut timber. A consignment of chilli peppers went past, leaving my eyes to sting and nostrils to tingle ever so slightly. A shipment of fennel overtook me once, brought on memories of childhood stomach upsets. In Uyghur I passed a tomato-processing factory. All afternoon, truck after truck of tomatoes drove by, sweet, acidic nightshade on the air as juice went dribbling down tyres.

Of all I saw, pigs became the most intriguing. Some years back China had resolved meat consumption was to be a marker of development. Eventually they aimed to pull level with the US in quantities of beef consumed, a goal that would require a quadrupling of the world's grazing pasture and animal feed . . . not that trivialities like that were about to trouble China. If I'd thought hard about the forecasted Chinese future that would've been it . . . *Adios!*, so long, record over! I'd have wound up quivering beneath a road in Gansu . . . agoraphobic, tucked up, foetal and waiting for the end of the world to come sooner rather than later. The first marker of meat development had been met when China reached parity with the US in consumption of pork, evidence of which was all down the roads, small trucks with three floors of pigs packed inside heavy railings. They were tightly shut in, rows of bums and pink curly tails that could neither sit nor stand, were kept somewhere between those two positions, buckling under the weight of the sow wedged sidewards across their backs, a line of empty teats and a trotter protruding in some forlorn plea for rescue.

Those wedged in tight were the luckier ones, for the pigs with room to move were simply shaken, banged about, knocked from trotters, smashed upon railings of wall and roof, thrust into a metal floor – covered in shit and sawdust – each time a pothole came out of the tarmac. I looked at them, pink skins shifting red and blue as abrasions and bruises took hold, bled with explanations for the confused trauma in those sad, intelligent eyes. Each of those pigs always had its eyes turn red, whether from heatstroke or general horror, I didn't know . . . but the whites were all shot with blood. Every ventricle behind the ball had torn for good, not that '*for good*' was to be very much longer anyway. They couldn't stop dribbling . . . dribbled out a heavy, white mucus secreted not only from snouts but also the sockets of the eyes so that, if they were tears then they were almost too foul for sympathy. Some of the runts, weakest of the lot, they never made it to the abattoir anyway. I'd find them at the roadside in various states of death, thrown overboard to lighten the fuel economy and give the survivors a little more space. I found one pig, still pink apart from its crimson wounds and the entourage of flies in glass-bottle green. Others had turned black, scorched by the sun into tough leather, only the trotters to tell them apart from a rock, so that at night I was sure Chinese pigs dreamt of being eaten by wolves.

Out in the desert I'd see the future of Chinese energy . . . acres of proof that China was the world's biggest developer of wind power, armies of turbines, spinning incessantly where they stood in the gutter between two mountain ranges. I rode through that gorge with a wind that had blown all across the Kazakh steppe from one direction and the Gobi Desert from the other . . . 8,000 miles of wind pressed into a valley 20 miles wide. The Chinese are not in the business of missed opportunities, and so up went the windmills, orgasms of renewable energy, panting and purring relentlessly, lines of 30 set 10 kilometres deep . . . constant turbine, trucks arriving to deliver still more. There too you saw the development of China, the older turbines with their paintwork eroding, faint but still visible the Nordic names of their manufacturers. Riding on, the turbines grew younger . . . shining in the sun and, there on the shaft, bright-blue paint, the name of the Chinese manufacturer written in hanzi. Why, after all, would you pay someone else to build anything . . . not when you can appropriate the engineering secrets and have a billion working-age citizens to start knocking them out by the thousand. That was another thing: in China there was no such thing as 'working age' . . . if you had an age, you could work. Factories smoked, roads were laid, women with birch brooms swept dust and tumbleweed from a million miles of highway. On walls at roadsides men with rollers painted hanzi, messages of encouragement or advertisement, 20 metres high in bold colours for the passing traffic. The man who has not found formal employment has instead bought a stereo and trolley. Slowly he paces through towns, his stereo pulled along on its trolley, crackling out party music that his fellow citizens can buy from the suitcase of CDs he carries under his arm. If that didn't work out . . . he took to the deserts.

Through those deserts ever I rode, with a half-dozen plastic water bottles strapped over the back wheel. As each one ran empty during those 100-mile stints without habitation . . . I laid them down at the roadside. It was the moral thing to do, for a dogged band of men and women had taken to the sands with wicker baskets strapped to their backs, recovering whatever plastic and metal they could find to sell at the recycling plant. That was the Chinese work ethic . . . and for a communist state it sure had a lot in common with capitalism, right up to the top, where it was said 90 per cent of China's millionaires had direct ties to the state Communist Party.

One morning, just after breakfast, sun shifting warm to hot against the desert rock, I found my defining postcard of the Chinese work ethic. All through China people drove some three-wheeled scooter, a small motorbike with a large crate on the back, a practical but affordable-looking version of a cart. Fifty miles of desert to the next town, I rode over a hill to find one such cart broken down, pulled slowly uphill by a man who'd have been collecting his pension had his mother popped him out a few thousand miles to the west. He was pulling that contraption up the hill, trailer loaded high with scrap metal, his hands on the handlebars and pain on his face. A rubber strap of inner tubes was knotted together, fastened to his vehicle at one end, and then slung high around his chest in a harness. His face was scrunched up like a ball of bright-red paper . . . looked ready for the final pop, an excitable blood vessel in each temple hinting the wish might be granted come the crest of the hill. Veins and sinews trickled thick down his arms, neck and chest, like the wax from a candle long left burning, the flame all but gone, eyes bursting from sockets as if they'd already witnessed his own death and there was no point hanging around much longer.

Together we entered the next stage of Gansu's wasteland . . . and there I was, preparing to ride my 100 miles daily through a desert, making life infinitely more difficult than it ever needed to be. And there he was, that old chap playing chicken with an aneurysm, getting on with labours that had never been any more than daily life. Bewildered, I shook my head. In all the world, let me tell you . . . there's nothing more idiotic than a Westerner.

Day 66 – Gansu – 6,802 Miles

Soon after the lands grew green again, billboards reappeared. Life follows water, billboards follow life . . . the two inviolable features of human habitation, water and selling *stuff*. Cars, colas and clinics rolled by on hoardings as I picked off the cities of Jiayuguan, Zhangye . . . my misgivings about society less important than thirst and shade. The traffic built, coaches coming past me down the highways, travel-sick faces at the windows and bladders of vibrant green liquid thrown periodically overboard, skidding along the tarmac to burst with a stench of warm bile.

Nearing cities and the fashions grew familiar too. The women who passed on scooters had started trying to turn themselves white, kept the sun from their skins with gloves up to the elbows. Those without masks revealed some modern lead oxide all over their faces, Elizabethan-style, a shade of ghost, a yellow line to mark where fake met real skin tone. In countries where skin is dark and the people poor, white skin becomes a point of pride, a badge to show life had never forced those women to work outside like peasants. I thought back to London, where that same August the men and women would be heading for tubes and coffins of ultra-violet light, turning themselves pink and orange to hide the fact that they were ever indoors . . . pale and sun-starved from those inordinate hours behind a desk.

T-shirts with English slogans appeared, me the only person for 500 miles who understood a word of it, and just as the West had taken to decorating its skin with tattoos of Chinese characters, writing words like *'strange'* where really they meant *'unique'*, so had the Chinese, no less in thrall to the romance of a foreign script, meaningless but exotic, dressed themselves in the most bizarre statements. A man with *'Fashion is a Human'* on his sweater handed me my bowl of noodles. There was the waitress with her vest that read, *'Attention: Human Instrumentality Experiment – We need A.T. Field'*. One began ordinarily enough, large font across the front of a truck driver, he grinned above *'Beverly Hills, London, Paris, Tokyo'* before the T-shirt shifted to a smaller text that read . . . *'Explore new world, travel, meet exciting people there . . . and kill them'*. It was either insanity or genius, and sometimes the owner of a slogan, with a basic hold of English, would ask excitedly what the words meant, only to be disappointed when I didn't have a clue.

In truth, that was the least of it, the stuff that passed by as only cultural curiosity. It was when I was thrown into direct contact with the Chinese that things grew difficult, when I was obliged to share a meal table with them, slurping their noodles and wiping the backs of hands across mouths. I wondered whether Chinese couples ever go for meals on dates, both sexes eat with such noise that no romance could ever survive such a racket. The restaurants of China sound like snake pits, a constant hissing, sucking and slopping, morsels of slurry jumping around the centre of tongues, teeth linked by saliva strands, mouths open wide to show their meal to one and all. Or rather to just one . . . to me, the only person who thought any of it even a little out of the ordinary.

The language too, for me Chinese was a nightmare all of its own. Try speaking a tonal language without enthusiasm or conviction. Each monotone, Indo-European attempt, delivered with the knowledge that it will almost certainly be misunderstood, falls tone-deaf in Chinese ears. I don't understand how it's possible to sound fed up or resigned in Chinese, when the tone of a word is itself responsible for the meaning. Come Gansu, the communication was finished, done for, the old certainties had dried up . . . 'centre', 'café', 'restaurant', even 'Coca-Cola' no longer worked. After meals I'd ask a motionless face the way to the next town, repeat a name five times before finally pointing to my map and hearing the correct pronunciation involved a certain strangulated death cry I hadn't quite mastered. Unperturbed, I'd ask for the bill, coming to appreciate just how comfortably I'd been communicating through Kazakhstan and Uyghur. I rub thumb and fingers together. He understands that without bother, holds up a thumb and his first finger . . . two of them, a thumb and a finger, clear as day: two yuan. I reach into my little purse, pull out one yuan, then a second, hand them to him with a small bow of gratitude. He laughs, shakes his head, holds up thumb and finger again:

clearly *two*. I stress the two yuan I've just handed him, and he stresses his thumb and finger my way, one more affirmation of *two* before he takes out a piece of paper . . . and writes '8'. They count differently in that part of the world, once below and once above the knuckle, higher value for thumbs. Eventually I evaded communication entirely, the whole thing too stressful and pointless to endure, the language like a box of wires and coiled springs, rebounding off the walls if ever my foreign face set off a tripwire.

Of all the difficulties, far and away it was the patriotism that was most unbearable. Love of your brothers and sisters, love of your society . . . I can't imagine a healthier thing. But patriotism, the thought that your bit of rock is better than the others, is a different matter, a thing for scoundrels and imbeciles. It was inescapable, and if the idea of the nation state was invented in Western Europe, doubtless it took Asia to really make a goer of it. The nationalism there is not like that found in Russia, nor the one I know from Britain, nor waiting for me in the US, where people all love their nation because deep down, they know it's pathetic, enfeebled . . . a shadow of some prehistoric version of glory they would somehow like to revisit. In Asia it's different . . . there is no sadness, no melancholy, the love for their country is genuine and joyful, the sort of enthusiasm found in children with a new toy. I thought of all those Vietnamese who'd seemed so happy and proud to have been bombed by the US for a decade, just so long as they could say for the rest of history that Vietnam defeated the United States. I thought of 1998, the financial crisis (the other one), with South Korea among the major casualties and every day Koreans rushing to the central bank, not to retrieve their money, but to donate family gold to the national coffers. China was the epitome of all this, indeed, '*China*' was the only word of English anybody knew. Town after town, even 12 months after the event, still they had banners and rockeries and topiary in honour of

'*Olympics – 2008*', when the world's biggest festival of '*everything's OK, nothing to see, here*' had rolled in and out of Beijing, more than 2,000 miles away.

From a TV, mounted on the wall in one restaurant, I sat with row after Chinese row, watching a video of a woman singing her heart out in front of the flag. Transfixed, they watched the screen blend in and out of Chinese soldiers shooting guns and mortars at a faceless enemy the other side of a trench. By the end of the video tears were in the singer's eyes, planes and warships launching rockets from sea and sky, audience engrossed as the proprietor switched on the subtitles for my benefit, whispered one more '*China*' with a thumbs-up my way . . . and in despair, I read lyrics promising a Chinese spirit that would triumph by tender beauty and almighty firepower. After displays like that, I found it hard not to hate everybody I saw. One afternoon, forcing myself to believe some Chinese citizens must have had a balanced, critical view of national politics, a man walked into me. He wore a red and yellow T-shirt, large text across the front . . . simple but to the point: '*I love China*'.

Day 68 – Kunlun Mountains – 6,917 Miles

In all this I had logistical problems developing, a novel dilemma slowly coming to bear. With mid-August upon me, and a flight out of Shanghai on 5 September, China was proving too small and I was fast running out of road. I'd booked my flights to a strict schedule of 100 miles a day, plus an extra day in case of emergency. Even with the lost days at the Kazakh border, and another 1,500 miles to go, still I was well ahead of schedule, ridiculously so . . . all set to arrive in Shanghai a week early. The rules allowed as much, stipulated the clock started and stopped when I reached ports of arrival or departure, yet that wasn't what I wanted. It seemed outside the spirit of things, not to mention the fact that a week in Shanghai sounded as expensive as it did unappealing. The most obvious ways of lengthening my route all involved harder riding than I'd planned but, after days of deliberation, I dived south for Xining, the road climbing into the Kunlun Mountains.

I've done it so many times before . . . and every time is like the first, it never gets any less special. Keeping my legs turning rhythmically, I watch myself move higher, grass and trees growing shorter, hair on the livestock longer. I always set my mood some time before the gradient arrives, and each mountain, anywhere in the world, takes me to the exact same place inside my head. Always the same lesson, or at least a new version of it: the end will not be quick, nor will it come easily. To hurry or to struggle is only to become slower, for time is artificial, it burdens you with impatience, and impatience will only encumber your efforts and soften your wits.

When riding a loaded bicycle, a 4,000-metre pass takes hours. It takes hours going slow . . . it takes hours going fast. You move across something bigger than yourself, it teaches you patience, becomes meditative like nothing I've ever known. Locked in confrontation with the mountain, legs spinning and heart rattling, all sound and sight seems to heighten. Colours sharpen . . . lift off their earthly matter so as to better imprint themselves and their movements as an abstraction of the mind. What would be a mountain or road is untangled from the orderly parcel with which we ordinarily view our world. There, in the Kunlun Mountains, it is as if particles deconstruct, wash over me to leave only colour. Blue, green, white . . . and I become only a subject in a painting, everything perfect at last.

The sounds are even better, for the mountains are a cradle of something mystical, of resting gods, all but silent places in which you hear little more than the winds that pass through, as if inside some corridor with the door to another place left open. I hear the heavy bells hanging from the necks of cows, tolling back and forth in the valley, as tufts of grass are pulled up in their mouths and heads jolt free. When the cows venture closer to the road, continuing to eat, I hear the very tearing of the blades of grass, thud of footfall upon earth. I hear my tyres pulling, peeling on and off the road below, and I listen to the rubber close above the tiny perforation of the asphalt's stones, push out the infinitesimal air, hear that air rush back into the empty space as the tyre lifts back off. Salt water runs from my eyebrows into my line of vision, a stinging warms my eyes, giving way to a place halfway between sadness and elation. My nirvana waits for me there and, though we're told in life that the extreme sorrows we face are only proportionate to our happiness, it is only with a peace such as this, high above the world, that I have ever felt both simultaneously . . . as if you find the meaning of both your life and death in the same place. Up in the mountains everything feels right, it always does . . . I realise I am so very finite, but only that which will perish can ever be truly sacred.

Looking down from 4,000 metres, a road seems so innocent, a human ribbon laced delicately around the slopes where it switches back and around upon itself. I speed down, imagining the air thickening with every metre travelled. Noises begin to murmur, silence abating as life returns. Rock turns to scrub, scrub to grass, bushes grow among the grass and then turn to trees, shooting upwards before forming a forest. You reach alps in middle China. Tumbling streams step through the rocks and then, 30 miles after you began your descent, there comes agriculture, patchwork fields and crops, rooftops, terracotta squares and triangles. Oh, but it's pretty . . . all you could ask for really, under that blue sky and crisp air, the bunting of swept clouds upon the sky. It's peaceful up there, one of those moments of eternity, of effortless speed and sweeping turns with all the world unfurled, floating downwards, back and forth like a falling feather.

Somehow it came to me then . . . waiting in the ecstasy my thoughts turned west to the Midlands, that town I'd always called home. Who knows how that place got out there in middle China. I'm emotionally delicate at heart, all that splendour bust me right down to the tragic. Descending those mountains, free as I was, it left me thinking of all those stuck there without any idea such wonders even existed. If only they'd been aware of it, if only they could see all the world was theirs to enjoy . . . but if that one wasn't the biggest of *ifs*. It's not that I grew up surrounded by folk who wanted to cycle to China and couldn't, their worlds were all so small in the first place. Though the expansion of their horizons and opportunities would not, in many cases, have taken them to China, it might at least have taken them somewhere better than where they wound up.

And so it was that I plunged down, and upon the mountainside I remembered that afternoon with everybody laughing in the living room. He'd turned blue, drunk with alcohol, they said. Wayne had turned blue, his long body, six foot and climbing, was laid out on the living-room floor. Semi-conscious, his balding head rolled to one side, body lank like a beanpole, a blue balloon of a head floating on top with a half-smile. *Drunk?* That was a good one. We all thought it funny at the time. He was a good sort, you see . . . no harm to anybody, a hard time of things but only love in him really, that was why he used drugs in the first place. In such a lifeless world as that, well, it's nice to feel so warm and so big once in a while.

I'll spare you the details, don't expect you to care, but Wayne died that night, turned blue right there in front of his mother. Fresh out of prison, it was the first time in a while, not quite the same tolerance as normal. He died in his sleep, that smiling tower of a man had only love and heroin in him that night and, come morning, all the love was gone. We buried him . . . just as we do most of our problems . . . down there it ended . . . only not for his daughters, nor his mother. It's still ongoing for them, but in lives so hopeless, well . . . they never would have known too great a happiness anyway. I won't go into the detail of it all, not up at 4,000 metres, but the point I'm making is that right there in middle China, coming down the hills into the purity of all life has to offer, I thought of Wayne, and the tears that started from the wind against my eyes turned to tears good and proper, pulled out of my eyes and across my cheeks, peeling over my face and into the wind, back up the handkerchief of that mountainside. Right then it was all just too wrong, too tragically avoidable, tears all down that blue sky above the Kunlun Mountains, half a world and a decade from where Wayne had died on his bed and where his mother found him next morning.

That's where it comes from, that and so many instances too horribly like it is where I got my politics. If ever I sound extreme, if ever I sound deranged, it's only because I grew up so close to the victims of so much unfairness. All of them, to the last, give such sad, damning evidence that our system doesn't work, that some people are born and never stand a chance. I may have cycled quickly around the world and yet, now more than ever, I feel that peculiar alpha-male undertaking shrinks so small when placed beside the challenge of changing our own society. Making it kinder . . . making it fairer.

Day 72 – Shaanxi – 7,333 Miles

If I'd previously calmed my haste using the mantra that there was no destination, only a journey, with Shanghai very much my destination and looming larger on the map, that wouldn't work much longer. Past Xining I started motoring, opened the doors to the engine and began shovelling in coal. It was as I gravitated eastwards too, the density of the population increasing, that situations seemed progressively more fraught. It wasn't that I was fed up with China, but the novelties of size and scale had worn off, while its irritations grew more acute.

They watched me, over my shoulder, peering at the words on my phone, in my books, the computer screen I sat before. It didn't matter that they couldn't understand a word of it, so long as they got the opportunity to peer, breath falling warm on the back of my ears in an unasked-for intimacy. They must all have been hard-of-hearing, it was the only way I could explain how they shouted everything at me, close at hand so that the words could not get lost in that slender space between us, never greater than 15 centimetres. And they stared, most of all they stared.

By putting myself in China I'd become the property of the nation, and thus might the Chinese enjoy me all they wished. They stared right into me, right through me, as if looking at some intriguing new insect. The insect would nod a greeting for them to ignore, the insect repeated it with a smile for them to ignore, the insect started waving his arms as they went right on staring and finally, a good half-minute later, the insect would request, in loud English, that if they must stare at him then could they at least acknowledge his greetings? It was culture shock all right . . . Chinese culture was shocking to me. Those back home who espoused humans were '*the same but different*' had clearly spent very little time in rural China, where the people are, by even the most generous understandings, different but the same.

At the roadsides they got me, entire families of *HELLOOW!* One person would shout, and forgetting that they didn't really mean it, I'd reply with a *hello* of my own, only to watch as they fell about laughing. I was theirs, my privacy theirs to invade, right up until that moment whereupon I actually wanted them, when I asked for their help with directions. It was then that personal space became a valid concern in China, one worthy of consideration. All credit to them, they had mastered the art of rebuff like no other. The insolence of a child executed with the haughtiness of an adult, they turned their heads three-quarters away, drew their lips tight and showed you a palm . . . spread their fingers and waved quietly side to side while shaking their heads. It was like a punch in the face, a gunshot, a statement that I would get nothing from them. They would not even look at me . . . and all I wanted to know, I tell you, was nothing more sinister than if I was on the right road for Lanzhou.

The car horns, ever the car horns wore me down, screaming all day long. They screamed that I move, screamed that they were coming . . . no thing too complicated, no situation too nuanced for explanation by car horn. Each time, for a whole month, it felt as though my eardrum was being spliced open with a blunt dagger. I grunted, grimaced, shouted, grew ever more furious, but it was futile – the car horn is invaluable to Chinese culture, it props up the nation itself. That horn expressed all standard scenarios of the road plus infinite more besides. It was fired once to say '*I'm behind you*', twice for '*300 metres*', again for '*200 metres*', '*parallel*', yet they kept going down the road with still more to come: *I've overtaken you. This is fun. Fast. I like driving in my car. I'm a taxi, you're a pedestrian, let's work something out. Tunnels make echoes. Hello. Hellooow! It's me! I second the horn of the car in front. I'm about to overtake dangerously close to you. Bored. Scooter overtakes bicycle on empty road. Turning. This is going to be close. I'm driving like an idiot, be careful. I've hired this van just for a day . . . I want my horn's worth! This is how my father and brother drive.*

I'm sorry to produce such a list but that was how it felt. I imagined the hidden rage that horn must have buried in the population, grew convinced Chinese society retained its order by use of that horn and the frustrations it nullified. *Listen to this horn!* My culture, history and ethnicity is repressed, *listen to this horn!* They think they've made an emancipated woman out of me but all they did was give me a truck to drive through a desert, *listen to this horn!* I'm a homosexual but don't even know it because of this crushing, sexual conservatism, *listen to this horn!* Ten per cent economic growth? Maybe on the East Coast, *listen to this horn!* China, a great nation, then where are our basic freedoms? *Listen to this horn!* The sky is thick with smog, rivers run black and my child coughs blood . . . *listen to this horn! Listen to this horn!* No use gesticulating either for, if I waved a fist at them in rage, they simply took it for greeting or support and let off another volley my way. No concern could not be raised and answered by a Chinese person blasting off a round on a car or truck horn. Like a psychiatrist's couch, it saved them from themselves, it was their dissent, their protest, their therapy.

Day 74 – Highway G312 – 7,566 Miles

Urban China reared up fast as I made my way to Lanzhou, the city beneath a yellow haze, sheep grazing below the cooling towers of a coal-fired power station, nibbling tufts of grass from the barren earth around the concrete. Beside a line of plant machinery, of trucks and bulldozers, I watched a young boy as he sat swinging on the heavy chain that looped from the hook of a crane. In tiny hands he held the large links of metal, swinging backwards and forwards, a child faced with the hard steel of that contraption, and seeing in it only a swing on which to play. I passed out of the city along the banks of the Yellow River, pensioners performing T'ai Chi to the lapping of the waters, scores of tilted arms and rotating palms turning in unison as night fell. As hours drew on, the elderly relinquished the water's edge to the young romantics, and for two miles, courting couples took up their positions on a line of benches, kissing sounds lifted skywards in secret defiance of conservative families.

I kept east, gained a momentum that took me quickly to Xi'an, the historic terminus of the Silk Road I'd joined back in Qyzylorda, Kazakhstan. Beside me a digger tore through the concrete of a block of flats, revealing terrible wallpaper to the entire street as someone's home was laid bare, soon to disappear forever. Everywhere, old apartment buildings were being flattened, turned to dust between caterpillar tracks, dumper trucks roaring out of the centre to clear the debris for a commercial renewal. On the peripheries I saw new tower blocks rising to replace the old. Shoulder to shoulder they stood, each one identical in height, painted pastel shades of green and pink. I rode out beside computer cafés, building after building crammed wall-to-wall with monitors, watched by vigilant young males unable to turn their heads from the screen. They were interested in neither sport nor adventure games, to the last each one was raising armies, building civilisations and commanding forces on the battlefield, everyone training in the strategies by which they planned for China to rule the world.

Countryside returned, though never again would it be the same. There was little open horizon on my road between Shaanxi province and the city of Shanghai. The road became lined with peasants and smallholdings. Small birds sat on buffalo backs, beaks pecking against the hide. In the hills outside Xi'an I wound through 30 miles of orchard, apples shining ripe and red on trees pruned thin to maximise the yield. Apples covered driveways, piled in drifts as people packed them into crates. Beneath the orchards, I watched farmers bent over double, hunchbacks rising before my eyes. They performed their labour with the musical efficiency of centuries working that same land, conical hats nodding in tune, like a Kurosawa scene, or a toy that moves in perfect accordance with the laws of physics. They harvested maize, miles of corncobs all down the roadside. Kernels were pulled from the cob, before one farmer with a wide shovel would toss them to the air, loose husk pulling away on the breeze, kernels falling back to the asphalt with a patter, a second farmer sweeping them back onto the shovel to be tossed once more into the air. As I made my way south towards Luoyang, the crop turned to watermelons. I watched a farmer with a gallon of pesticide strapped to his back, a hose with a pump mechanism that he squeezed, spraying the chemical as he walked along rows of melon, pesticide dribbling down his hand, dripping onto his legs in their ragged trousers. The harvest landed . . . millions of dark-green cannonballs being piled onto carts, driven through a 10-mile traffic jam of watermelon, to where men and women waited in the hold of larger trucks. Tidily they stacked endless watermelons for the journey to each corner of China, a peasant's offering for the hungry nation that needed to be fed.

Last of all I found coal, the lifeblood of all that growth I'd witnessed. I crested a steep hill, into a new valley, and suddenly coal was everywhere. Long conveyor belts disappeared into the ground, a motor grinding away to lift rock into an austere building made of brick. The building had a second orifice, kept behind spinning cogs and wheels that smashed larger rocks into smaller chunks, spewing them out into piles of coal that reared up in the forecourt. Diggers circulated to keep each pile in check, manoeuvring to refill the line of lorries that pulled up in constant need of coal. If all that sounded orderly enough, believe me it wasn't, for at each stage of the process the people around had been left to tolerate whatever waste product arose.

The scaremongering they put about on the subject of the Chinese environment, well . . . put simply . . . it isn't scaremongering at all. A dusty fog set down and, though the humid air did not look black, after just 10 miles cycling through that valley my body was a source of coal in itself, face and skin covered in a soot that made me scratch and cough as I rode on, dressed as a chimney sweep, coal collecting thicker in the folds of my elbows and across my stomach. The rock pulled from the earth brought with it treacly black water, emptied out to run thick through village streets. People waded in rubber boots, lifted feet from their bicycle pedals as they cycled through the floods, an arc of black slurry spraying from their wheels as they got on with lives inside the crushing footprint of industrialising China.

Day 77 – Yanling – 7,889 Miles

Contorting and coiling, I slept. The mosquitoes had not been there at dusk, when I lay down without setting up my tent, but at night, above mud turning slowly to peat, they swept over me and danced, drinking cocktails of blood and coal dust. I struggled, sighing and groaning through climbing degrees of exasperation that made me even hotter than the humid night. The coal dust irritated my skin, as did too many miles of exhaust fumes. Among it all the plump mosquito bites throbbed red, moistening with trickling sweat. I scratched, scratched until my skin lit up and the blood peered through, my body twisting and mosquitoes dancing a carnival until the sun came up.

Which decided it. The objective for that day, categorically, became less about a hundred miles and more about being clean again. I rode out of the valley of coal, weighing up either a river or the hosepipes at the car washes I sometimes passed. In the final reckoning, fate made the decision for me. After 77 days riding, and approximately 10 washes, finally discomfited by dirt, you wouldn't believe the words that appeared in English on a signpost before my very eyes. It was like an oasis . . . a mirage painted in Latin script and printed on metal in a desert of filth. Some 50 miles into the day it rose in front of me:

500m — Hot Spring Spa

It was a lavish affair, the staff sceptical, my soot-covered face no picture of affluence. I show them my passport, tunes change, they smile . . . turns out I'm a rich man in disguise. They lead me down a long corridor, into the tiled walls of a modern bathroom. The air is thick with steam, lockers are lined along the walls and naked men stand with towels over their shoulders. They have hairless bodies, guts plump to a size seldom seen in China, the physique of men who eat well and work little. My attendant goes to a locker, takes out a pair of short shorts. Long, slender fingers hold them in front of my eyes. Green. Spandex.

Outside was a paradise, waters babbling through tropical fauna and over rocks, slipping through pools with a gentle ripple. Climbing plants crept across a trellis, casting dappled shade over the pathway of smoothed stones crunching underfoot. The spa itself consisted of pools cut into scalding hot boulders of volcanic rock, sides shaped in gentle curves, like kidneys with a ledge on which to sit. I moved my toe in and out, ventured to my knees, waist, scalp. Everything stung . . . the bites, the skin where my nails had drawn blood, sores and grazes I'd slowly been cultivating for months. Breathless, my skin turned red as blood rushed to the surface and then, gradually, the water began to slow-boil me back to clean.

After each spring had bestowed upon me its own particular mineral, I parted leaves and stepped from the main path, moved towards a large pool under a dome of palms. Different from the rest, its waters were alive, frantic, flitting back and forth with silver darts shot beneath a constantly broken, bubbling surface. The entire pool was full of fish, hopping over one another's tails and bellies, mostly small and silver, like sticklebacks in appearance, but among them a score slightly larger, a darker skin and slower motion to their swimming. As I stepped in the fish scuttled away, parting as my feet and ankles arrived in the water, returning a moment later with tiny pinpricks, nibbling, infinitesimally small teeth picking against my skin, the tops of my toes, balls of my ankles, hard and bony faces swimming into me and feeding from me. I stepped deeper, fish parting and returning all the way up to my waist, mouths nibbling and skins fluttering against mine, the whole notion more humorous than unnerving, body rigid, braced against a setting so strange.

I squatted down, smiling, the water cool against my still-hot body. From there I lay down, up to my neck in fish . . . breathed deep, submerged my head, and they began nibbling at the lobes of my ears and the lids of my eyes, bony fingers picking at my nose and pecking at my lips. As I lifted my head back from the water, fish retreated slightly and then returned to the feast, 70 kilos of fish food. The absurdity of the situation grew with all those tickling fingers, those hard, sharp mouths just prodding in my armpits and at my nipples and the soles of my feet.

I started laughing, just a snigger at first, laughter through my nose, before the smile burst and my mouth opened, those heads and mouths picking at my body, every inch of skin nibbled by fish, so that suddenly, and unstoppably, my body split with laughter. Incredible, uncontrollable it came, the purest comedy I've ever known, a laughter at nobody's expense but simply for the hilarity and incredible tickling that comes when hundreds of fish start nibbling between your toes and in all the crevices of the body we normally keep private. I couldn't stop myself, a full five minutes, maybe ten and there I was, bellowing, laughter from the very bottom of my diaphragm, belly rocking, and the heads of passing Chinese gazing into the pool at the Westerner who couldn't stop laughing.

Now and then I tried to get it under control, the whoops and giggles would subside a moment. I'd take a deep breath but no sooner was my mind restored to calm than my attention slipped momentarily back to the fish nibbling my nipple, and I was roaring my way to tears all over again. After almost a quarter of an hour I got a handle on things and watched the activity beneath the water. The scab upon my knee, from where I'd once fallen when my spanner slipped as I tightened a crank, the hangnails from whenever I pushed my fingers deep inside a bag and rummaged, the hardened skin where I gripped my handlebars or where my shoe touched my Achilles.

All that dead skin, tension and calamity . . . those fish simply nibbled it all away.

Day 78 – Anhui – 8,093 Miles

I rolled into the final 600 miles before Shanghai, set a date in my head, gave myself five days to hit Pudong airport beside the Yellow Sea, the far end of that landmass I'd started in Normandy. I thought I was there, home free, and then, on the second of those five days, the northern hemisphere shying from the sun in anticipation of winter, dusk falling ever earlier, my wheel flattened. It wasn't the first time . . . once on the road into Kazakhstan, twice before in China. I've spared you the details of my mechanicals, but on that evening, 70 miles into the day, the puncture became relevant, more than just patching the tube and riding onwards. The air hissed out, turned my tyre to pancake in 30 seconds flat.

It was drizzling, a roadside through farmland and occasional houses, utilitarian boxes of concrete. A muddy driveway led me to a patio with a roof of corrugated metal, a lantern hanging to cast yellow light outside a small shop, only a few lines of boxes, the most basic household goods assembled in the hope of occasionally being sold. A woman knelt, stacking crisps into crates as I put my bicycle on its stand beneath the shelter, removing bags from over wheels. Then he came.

It was an exchange five centuries in the making. Christian missionaries had gone to China in the seventeenth century, trying to unsettle the social order with word of Jesus Christ the saviour, hell-bent on proselytising to heathens. The Chinese upper classes, fearing for their power, taught the peasantry to mistrust Westerners as people who wanted to trick and enslave them. The nineteenth century came, Germany claimed sections of China for itself, enslaved locals to mine coal from their own ground to develop German industries. The British were no better, were worse. Make no mistake, in the annals of history you'll find no scum quite like the British. We mastered it all, mapped out the future. The British perfected the art of doing evil and calling it good. With a Bengali opium harvest to sell, and the Chinese aristocracy junked-up on heroin not far to the north, the British were nonplussed at the Emperor's effort to outlaw opium . . . not with a Bengali opium harvest to consider. They waged war . . . *twice!* . . . argued the Emperor had threatened the principles of free trade. The British went to war to force heroin on the Chinese population and, after five centuries of preaching, exploitation and violence . . . in late August of 2009, weary and exasperated, so did a cyclist lay down his bags beneath a tin roof in Anhui province.

He flew towards me, out of the darkness of his home and into the lamplight, three-quarter-length trousers, a mole on his neck, long, wiry hairs spiralling from it. His hands were leading, outstretched . . . coming at my neck, fingers spread until he downgraded his desire to throttle me, made do with pushing me backwards, shoving the meddling, thieving Westerner away from his wife and home. I stumble back, he keeps coming, shoves at me again . . . his wife, she's terrified, Munch's *The Scream*, fingers pressed on cheeks, eyes and mouth wide in fearful silence as he batters me with Mandarin, lobbing high-pitches all over me, like the firing of howitzers as I raise my palms to him . . . *surrender!* . . . the first Westerner to mean no harm in five centuries in rural China. He keeps at me, right in my face, shouting . . . throws a punch . . . *duck* . . . He picks up one pannier, he throws it down the muddy driveway, it bounces . . . He throws a second at my face, comes and shoves some more as I bend to catch it. I shout – I have to – I shout at him to stop, shout words that mean as little to him as his did to me. He stands over my bicycle, hands on hips, breathing heavily as I take it from its stand, wheel it away.

The drizzle had turned to rain, dusk become darkness, China not exactly a place for which I felt affection right then. Further down the road, under a gathering of trees I put up my tent. After removing the wheel of my bicycle, I took out a new puncture repair kit, purchased in Xi'an to replace the German one I'd set out with. I found a nail, removed it, and patched the puncture before crawling into bed.

The rains had passed on come morning, sun coming up and tyre going down, deflating flat by the time I woke. I'm no bicycle guru, but I've been fixing punctures since before my age was into double figures, and never bought a new tube where I could patch an old one instead. I know how to fix a puncture. I take the tube back out of the tyre, the patch lifting a little at the side, not much but perhaps enough. I pull it off, sandpaper roughens the surface to help the glue stick. Let me tell you . . . I know how to fix a puncture. I take the glue, spread it pearly-white upon the surface of the tube, an area larger than the patch. I wait. The glue sets, starts to go off, turns opaque to translucent, pulling back at my finger as I test it. I set down the patch, orange lip bonding to tube and glue. Pressing it between thumb and fingers, I hold it there. Let me tell you, I know how to fix a puncture. Minutes pass and I check it, see a perfect seal, not a bit of give anywhere in that orange perimeter to the black patch. I replace the tube in the tyre, inflate it. It goes flat. That wasn't in the script. Let me tell you, I know how to fix a puncture, been fixing them since before my age was into double figures and yet . . . Flat. No doubting it. Flat. Once more I took it all apart, the seal nicely in place so that I checked the tyre instead, found nothing, round and round the tyre. No nail, no glass, no nothing. I cut open the bottom of a bottle of water, fill it in a nearby stream, run the tube through the water to look for bubbles of escaping air. Nothing. I take out my pump . . . you're not supposed to pump up a newly patched tube outside of the tyre, the glue stretches and damages the seal. But still, what else to do? I pumped air into the tube, placed it in my container of water. *Pop-pop-pop* . . . pods of air float slowly to the surface.

I pulled off the patch, roughened the surface. *Let me tell you, I know how to fix a puncture!* Patched it, inflated it. Comfortably an hour had passed, some of the locals beginning to take an interest in it all, admiring my misery and tapping knuckles on the steel frame of my bicycle. Tyre goes flat. Pump it up again. A farmer with a straw hat encourages me to follow him. We carry my bicycle and belongings back to a small restaurant. As the tyre flattens, I eat noodles. I fix it again, three hours now gone. I never counted how many times I fixed the puncture in the end that day, perhaps approaching a dozen, palms blistering in the cool damp, my knuckles cramping, arthritic from the effort of heaving the tight tyre back onto the rim each time.

Tyre still flat, I fixed it again . . . well, what else can you do, without a spare tube in rural China? Somebody's child ran onto that patio where I worked, stopped dead in his tracks when he saw my scene. He was timid but not afraid . . . an angel, I tell you . . . incomprehensibly beautiful, a butterfly that will grow to be a caterpillar, evidence humans were conceived in a place of magic and love, then left to exist among this world in which we rot. I promise I'll remember that child the rest of my life, for he engrossed himself in my misfortune. Running round with sandals flapping and skinny arms waving at his sides, pulling his shorts up and dressed in a T-shirt with orange stripes across it. He wanted to help. I remember the way he squatted down beside me on his skinny legs, watched what I was doing, his face barely six inches from my hands, pale skin, thin lips drawn almost to a triangle beneath brown, shining eyes, round, open and full of curiosity.

Every so often I would do something new, and he would turn to me and say a single word, which meant nothing to the stupid adult that I was, no matter how slowly and carefully he pronounced that single word. Each time I would repeat his word, meaningless though it was to me, and at that he would look up and smile. I remember the way he hopped about, how he would hop from squatting down beside me, retrieve the puncture kit from the other side of my pile of bags, jump back to hand it to me, squat down once again, hopping to and fro like a sparrow among the crumbs of my despair. I let him hold the patch between his tiny thumbs and fingers as the glue set, and so seriously, with such determination he made that job his own.

Once again I'd pump up the tyre and he stayed squatting loyally at my side, listening to the air seep from the tube each time. As it did so, as I heard hope hissing out of my tyre and back into the atmosphere . . . he would turn to me, wide eyes full of the earnest desire to make things better, and he'd say a single word, at which I'd nod and slowly try to repeat it with a crackling voice. Come then I was done for, perhaps 10 failed patches, four hours, and, though rationally I knew it was the Chinese puncture kit that was failing me, knew the glue wasn't working, knowing this didn't make my despair any less painful in the moment. I neared the end of my tether, set to cry like a baby as that child beside me hopped back and forth, his thin lips like a beak, that darling sparrow scuttling all around, gathering up the pieces he thought would make things better.

My hands summed it up, so sore and ruined as again I heaved tyre back to rim. The humidity, combined with gripping the handlebars, had meant that for that past month my hands had been slowly festering with some sort of fungal infection, burrowing tiny red holes in my palms and fingers. From heaving the tyre onto the rim, a fit all too tight, I'd formed and then torn open blisters to sting on the base of each thumb. With the air so damp, my fingers having struggled so hard with that tyre, my knuckles began to freeze, clamped shut, seized as stubborn as a corpse. I dropped the wheel, the tyre not yet on but my fingers contorting away from me. Entirely out of my control they tickled stilted goodbyes, twitched without my twitching them. My face gave way to emotion, staring incredulously at hands no longer mine, as that boy looked right into my face, so full of a concern warranted only by the fact that I'm a human being and I'm clearly suffering. That beautiful boy, he takes my hands in his, gazes up at me with those wide brown eyes, windows to a soul that deserves a better world than this. With concern all over his tiny features, muttering tender words of optimism, he takes my hands in his own tiny fingers and one by one, so gently, he lifts my fingers by their tips and, on my behalf, begins to slowly massage them back to life.

He sat me down upon a chair, ran to fetch an adult, those skinny legs bounding disjointedly into the café. Adults appeared, looked at me, a sorry sight I must have cut right then, like Sisyphus with a puncture and certain a new tube was the only possible solution. I knew what I wanted to do, the despair of it all had softened my head, left me giddy, drunk with do-or-die wanderlust.

Hefei was the answer, the provincial capital perhaps 100 miles to the north of where I sat. An engine was what I needed, no less than a motorbike . . . a scooter and the wind in my hair to Hefei. I would tear up and back down the road, buy the tube, then ride 400 miles to Shanghai without rest. The adults looked at my flat, pitiful tyre, waved hands around the immediate vicinity and shook their heads. I go to my bicycle, take out the map and 300 yuan, a man with a straw hat standing over me as I spread the map . . . point to Hefei, point to his scooter, to myself, to Hefei and back . . . then slap down three crisp notes, the equivalent of perhaps £30.

He shakes his head, closes his eyes then shakes his head, points to Xiawuxian on the map, eight miles down the road, points to the motorised cart beside the house and then, the darn capitalist, he takes a pen and writes '100' on the map. His wife watches with a concerned expression, the child hopping from foot to foot and pulling at her arm. I shake my head, he doesn't understand . . . Xiawuxian would never have the right tube, I need to get to Hefei, would take the motorbike and return direct.

I say it again, '*Hefei!*', point to the scooter and turn my hands to grip imaginary steering in front of me, rev imaginary accelerators and, with a face some way past woebegone, I stand there with blubbering lips, going, '*Vroom-vroom . . . vroom-vroom!*' The little boy knew charades . . . *he gets it!* . . . translates, pointing and talking hurriedly, he understands how to help the strange man with the problem that makes him so sad. He starts pointing at the scooter, repeating a word again and again, pulling the woman's arm and, jumping up and down, explaining my masterplan. But he didn't understand, that beautiful child had no idea, didn't comprehend that the adults understood all right, but in the world of grown-ups, where trust is a thing rare rather than implicit, that scooter cost a few thousand yuan and no one was about to entrust it to some odd Westerner never seen before and perhaps never to be seen again.

Confused, the boy furrowed his brow, talked to the adults, talked to me, trying to mediate the whole fiasco. The farmer in the straw hat repeats, '*Xiawuxian*', and points down the road. At which the idiot Westerner shakes his head, repeats, '*Hefei!*', regained his imaginary motorbike and, with a face sadder than ever, stood there with rubbery lips going '*Vroom-vroom, vroom-vroom*'. The Chinese peasantry shook their heads, suggested going by cart to a repair shop eight miles away. The Western graduate shook his head, stood there full of '*vroom-vroom*', revving his fists, advocating a 200-mile round trip on an imaginary scooter.

Eventually I yielded to the Xiawuxian proposal, said goodbye to the child, my little prince, gave him the rear light from my bicycle as a gift of thanks . . . a way of his remembering me for a fraction of the time I will him. He pressed the button, the diodes illuminating red, and, as they did, so his face became a smile. Holding that light in front of him, he pressed the button on and off as I stepped up to the cart, the rain falling once again. Sitting beside the man in the straw hat, waving goodbye to the child, we set off for Xiawuxian, a new tube waiting in the first workshop we entered.

Day 82 – Yangtze – 8,560 Miles

It would not have been possible for me to ride 100 miles each day for three months, some 150s thrown in along the way, without succumbing to the idea of one day riding 200. Starting from Wuwei,

I rode the morning to Wuhu, increasingly excited as I reached towns and cities that I'd looked at on the map for weeks, unable to believe I was finally passing through them, their location henceforth behind rather than ahead. Crossing above the waters of the churning Yangtze River, I gathered momentum as the rains began to pound. Westernised China was in full flow by then, fast-food restaurants and supermarkets in every city, the land resolutely flat as dusk brought up the first 100 of the day, leaving me resolved to sit stubbornly at my saddle until 200 had come and gone the same way.

My shoes soaked in the rain, water coming down at me from the night sky, up from the road where mudguards could not catch the spray from my wheels. That night would have been almost straightforward if not for my feet. I'm not precious about these things, had experienced various discomforts since setting out, but my feet that night were the first time I'd really felt pain. That night I travelled back in time, somehow set about cultivating a case of trench foot. Perhaps nearing 150 miles, come 2am I'd loosened the straps of my shoes, tried in vain to let air at my feet, skin of my toes slipping warm and moist against one another, a burning sensation on my sole.

At a service station I stopped for food, the first rest in hours, the first I'd stepped from that bike since the rain really began. My shoes unclip, I dismount, I fall . . . catch myself with a hand. My knees buckle, shots race through the nerves from my feet, body collapsing, soles unable to take the pressure of my weight. I hobble up a bannister to the restaurant, knees tumbling at each step, walking on the side of one foot and the toes of the other, body falling and rising clumsily with this new sensation. From the restaurant white lights were glowing strong, neatly dressed staff standing to attention, looking at me so that I can say with all certainty they thought I was a cripple . . . maimed, shuffling forwards on the toes and outsides of my feet, lugging my bodyweight behind me like an awkward case of luggage.

Leaning on a rail, I pulled myself up stairs, hobbled towards a chair, feet scraping like knife on stave as I dive at it . . . throw myself down and swing into the seat with an outpouring of breath. They gather round, half concerned and half curious, two waitresses leaning forwards, knees together, nodding at me to confirm I'm fine . . . thumbs-up. I go about my business . . . the one thing in the world I needed right then, moving down towards the ratchet of my shoe, the fastening of that coffin cracking open as I pull it loose. People gather as I heave off my shoe, life flooding back to my foot inside its sock. I drop the shoe, it lands with a clatter on the tiles. Rolling the sock down over the heel, I unpeel it up to my toes, the foot revealed. They gasp. Hands over mouths, sounds of sympathetic pain as the pitted catastrophe goes on public display. My feet are turning yellow, turning grey with the faintest hint of green, great splits emerging between swellings of skin; my feet no longer dirty, but rather, dirt hanging where it seems to have grown from out of the skin itself.

The other ratchet cracks. I pull off the second shoe, the freak show not yet over, more of the same waiting at the end of my left leg. Taking napkins from the table, I press the soft, dry paper against my foot, a waitress shouting at a young man who hurries to the kitchen. I dab napkins at my foot, and though it feels comforting, feels gentle . . . the problem then was less the damp and more the rotten, festering pain. The man returns from the kitchen, hands me a stack of thick kitchen towel. I thank him, place sheets beneath my chair, one for each foot, squarely down upon them.

That I couldn't stop long was the biggest problem of all. With only 150 miles down, I didn't want my legs to seize or my mind to drift off to sleep. I ate, changed into socks of thicker cotton intended for winter. The waitresses looked concerned, half dismayed and half entertained, a nervous laughter as I pointed east and said, 'Shanghai', still 150 miles away. I packed the soles of my shoes with kitchen towel, my feet wailing with fear as I pushed them back down to the darkness, like corpses into rubber bags. My feet protest . . . *there must be some other way!* I pull the ratchet . . . it crackles shut. By 5am I was indifferent to ideas of '*200*' as anything meaningful, nonetheless as resigned as ever to finish my challenge. I pulled over as the computer on my handlebars ticked over to *201* . . . stopped beneath the concrete columns that held a highway overhead. There I unpacked my sleeping bag, unzipped a hole in the bottom through which my feet could stick, everything else bundled snug inside, my feet taking deep, gaping breaths of air.

I never noticed Shanghai appearing on the horizon, not in the way I'd once imagined. On that last day the city crept up slowly, an urban sprawl that grew more intense until I'd found myself on an eight-lane highway, a bullet train flying over my shoulder at a million miles an hour. Twenty million people's worth of tower blocks spread in all directions as the airport appeared, lines of lights illuminated across terminals, rain falling all over again, the runway coming to an end with planes tearing into the sky above the Yellow Sea. Without even realising it, I'd arrived. I laughed. Looked about. But I'd arrived . . . from Rouen to Shanghai, Monday 31 August, some 2,000 hours since setting out. As day 83 creaked shut, with Pudong airport hanging over me, something came to a close. It wasn't that I didn't enjoy the other places in which I rode, certainly the adventure kept going . . . but something changed that day. Perhaps it was experience, perhaps the pressure of money and increasing mileage, one way or another, there was something about Rouen to Shanghai that I fell in love with . . . something I never really found again.

Intermission – Shanghai – 8,761 Miles

It was certainly Shanghai, and, beyond that, I was confused. With five days to kill, I made my way to the French Concession, the one part of town that keeps its colonial heritage. Buildings stand with tiled roofs, shuttered windows, ornate railings, white verandas in the shade of trees leaning across narrow roads and pavements. For all its evil, colonialism sure was pretty. I spent my time in cafés, scribbling away, sipping coffees and watching cosmopolitan China go about its leisure time. It was the women that most caught my attention, glamorous adverts for modern China. The Shanghai women embodied it, dressed in fashions decreed by magazine editors and designers back West, every one of them in a heeled shoe, so that, having spent centuries resisting the practice of having their feet crushed in binds, the women of Shanghai had voluntarily begun strapping their pins into stilettos instead.

Outside the walls of the Concession and it was over. Cultural revolution, cultural revolting, revolting culture . . . Year Zero without the skulls and done on a better budget. It was a building site, the entire city no more than rubble and holes filling slowly with concrete. Most of the former residents, those who had once dried their washing beneath the windows, did their patriotic duty and left when the contractors arrived, leaving the stubborn ones to hold out for a bigger small pay-off. Their mettle had been tested when one construction racket enlisted the mob to murder an obstinate old man who, after decades on the same backstreet, had refused to budge, instead wound up dead in his home one morning. That was when things started getting out of hand, media had piped up. Killing the elderly as part of property speculation, even for China, was a step too far. The murders stopped, but the construction march, which I'd witnessed ever since Uyghur, which in half a century will be known as only Xinjiang, had not so much as faltered.

Above, the sun moved across the sky, cranes rotating through their arcs, like clock hands counting the hours to departure. They had it all, every corporate entity in the world was in Shanghai and planning expansions, yet all the corporate choice could not conceal that the coffee, drinks and food in general were all disappointingly poor, paid for by individuals eager to consume expensive tastes not traditionally their own. Suddenly claustrophobic, I was driven to anxiety by the crowds and pace of it all, walking the city with my neck revolving, disbelieving eyes and head pointed upwards. After three months cycling almost 9,000 miles, and walking perhaps less than one, I was quick to tire, shuffling at the slow pace with which tourists infuriate the natives of cities everywhere.

They had all the names – Gucci, Prada, Louis Vuitton – aisle upon aisle of consumerist choice for Communist workers, handing over banknotes with Mao Tse-tung printed on the face of it all, humbly dressed in his military fatigues and a belief in dignity over luxury. The streets were advertising, or at least the advertising had streets laced through it. Images of picture-perfect Westerners, picture-perfect Westernised Chinese, so long as it looked perfect they'd given it a billboard. There were happy families of one mother, one father and one child. That was telling in the adverts, always, unfailingly . . . *one child* . . . nothing to suggest familial happiness might lie in anything more.

That one child was China's backbone. The resources, the space, the environment . . . China couldn't afford more children. The fine was nigh-on £2,000, a pretty penny in China, for any clumsy pecker who blurted his secrets into a burning earhole. Child number two went without rights to education, health and what little democracy was available to child one; it was a non-citizen. To be fair, the urban Han were getting off worst of all, for ethnic minorities could have – they were *allowed* – two, three or even four bouncing bundles of economically productive joy. In addition, everyone in rural areas could have a second crack of the whip if, first time around, they had the misfortune to land upon a girl. 'But that's sick!' I exclaim. The café owner shrugs. 'Maybe . . . but that law was only to stop them killing baby girls.'

The Chinese state argued the whole thing a triumph without bounds. One child had prompted *economic growth, higher savings rate, resource equity, happier population*. They didn't talk of the forced abortions, the tiny, abandoned bodies . . . that was just cynicism on my part, my own malady, and in the form of Shanghai, so had China and the West embraced at last. There you could buy any one of ten brands of fried chicken, the skyscrapers went straight up, like the hands of only children who knew all the answers. China, make no mistake, was a great success.

Southeast Asia

Day 85 – Bight of Bangkok – 8,782 Miles

I rode out into Thailand, between runways and service roads, planes landing and lifting back to the sky. A heat sat over the land as I laboured pedals, five days since I'd last ridden, my body not grateful for the rest. During my time in Shanghai, the time in the air, Body had forgotten what to do, while Brain had come to enjoy cafés all too much. I pedalled slowly, created headwinds for myself, laboured, shoulders rocking, riding for the coast to the south of the city.

I stopped beside a small house, a bamboo lean-to next to it, tables dressed with jars of chilli, pallets of salt crystals and napkins, crates of glass bottles on the floor. A woman came out to me, an apron and a pair of quick feet, short footsteps in plastic sandals, a big smile, one of those grins that sends everybody back to Britain all fit to burst with 'the people are so happy'. She ate the air from her cupped palm with a pair of fingers, and wide-eyed she nodded her head into a question mark, ushered me to follow her through a doorway. Two refrigerators sit humming along the length of one wall. In the dim light burns a blue flame, a crown of gas floats on the shadows, a slow hiss and the popping of oxygen plucked from the air. From a tabletop, a blade shines with what light is in the room. She takes me to one of the refrigerators, seals of the lid kissing goodbye as it's pulled open. She points to a plate

136

of chicken, a plate of prawns. She nods the question . . . I nod '*yes*' . . . she shoos me outside.

A man watches from across the shelter as I sit down, arms on table. He sits on a small stool, his back against the table, his legs wide open, sandals on the dusty earth. In a short pair of shorts his thighs turn to groin, chest bare of all clothing or hair, his gut round but solid, as if he has swallowed a cannon ball. Tattooed large above his navel is a faded grid of interlocking shapes, rectangles and long-tooth combs set inside a circle. Between his legs he held a pool cue, a pile of them leaning beside him, and with a knife he would flick the dusty tip from each cue, roughen the surface with sandpaper, then take a tube of glue with which he would proceed to affix a new tip.

He spoke to me in English, without looking up from his cues, a gravitas to his manner. In him was none of the uncertainty of a second language, an authority of tone given weight by his surroundings, measured words strengthened by the incongruity, disarming our preconceptions, the idea that high intelligence does not go dressed in only sandals and shorts, with a round, bare belly and a tattoo large upon it . . . the idea that intelligence does loftier things with its time than replacing tips of pool cues. He asked where I was riding to, asked where I was from, my impressions of China, of Thailand. Then he asked why I thought the Chinese might have disliked Westerners, and what people in Britain thought of Thailand. He never looked at me, just continued with his cues as I talked about the British stereotypes of Thailand . . . a place for parties, abandon and hedonism. As we spoke, bowls of curry and rice arrived, prawns in their orange shells, the green of spring onions, of coriander, a red of chilli and the woman smiling at me before stepping quickly away. I ate as he talked, still not looking up at me. He spoke of Thailand and its history, the tone of his voice so steady, without animation, his head rising occasionally, speech punctuated by the sandpaper that roughened the cues.

'There is nothing new . . . not in Europeans coming here without care for Thailand itself. The Thai people, we speak of ourselves as the only nation in Indochina that was never colonised by foreign powers.' He chuckled. 'The truth is there was never any need . . . the Thai aristocracy was always corrupt and lazy, they simply sold the rights to our lands to Britain and to France, instead of making them fight for it. The Europeans extracted our rubber, our timber, took the fur from our animals. The Europeans took everything from us without ever having to fire a gun . . .' He paused. I listened, spellbound. 'That was always the history of Thailand and Europe, and then, in the nineteenth century, it changed. Your countries began their obsession with words and contracts . . .' He sighed, roughened a cue with the sandpaper, eyes flicked momentarily towards me. 'The East India Company made us sign a treaty, a treaty that confirmed all the old terms of trade, left nothing for Thailand but a signed document. The King thought to resist, to demand more, although he soon recognised there was no use doing so, that resistance would only bring about a military campaign, just as the British had waged when the Burmese had refused to sign away their resources.

'As the century wore on, and as the Europeans rivalled one another to take the world captive, the French took the lands of Vietnam, Laos, Cambodia to the east of us . . . and the British took Burma and India to the west. Thailand remained sovereign, but only because the British had already possessed all of our wealth, and only because it provided a convenient barrier, a buffer state between the British and French empires. It suited both nations, just as it now suits the pride of my countrymen to claim they have always been free . . .'

He looked up from a cue, a knowing smile just behind his lips, steady gaze from his dark eyes. 'You would be wrong . . . if you think that Western people coming here, with no respect for Thailand, is a new concern.'

Day 88 – Isthmus of Kra – 8,943 Miles

Thailand was kind to me, the coast drawing me out through canals and estuaries, beneath highways that lifted traffic above the water before sinking into Bangkok. Evenings broke with the smell of incense lit, and I watched people leaving their houses, slipping on a pair of sandals, the heels of which would clap against the ground as they strolled to shrines at the bottom of the garden. They placed gifts, put flames to incense, said prayers and bowed, unscrewing the cap from a bottle of water and setting it down for the dead to drink. I remember the monk, sitting in orange robes upon the rear of a pickup truck driving by. He looked at me with a smile, put out a level palm in front of him, pushed it towards me and picked something from it with the thumb and fingers of his other hand. In his grip he lifted some invisible ball of sorcery, and with a flick of the wrist, he cast it into the air, blew . . . commanded his blessings upon me as his outline pulled into the distance.

The vehicles themselves matched the spirits at the roadside. Trucks were painted silvery-blue, pink and neon, metal studs decorated up and down the rig, waving lines of colour that collected into whirlpools. Where the Chinese truckers had stickers on their doors, stickers of angry robots with machine-gun arms, in Thailand they'd stuck up human forms . . . Bob Marley, Che Guevara. There were illuminations too, blue lights beneath the trailer, so that by night the things floated by on glowing beds. The coaches were no different, similarly ready for a carnival, the roadside fairground all lit in pink, more luminescence, cartoon nymphs with blue hair and green eyes, arms thrown out as they reclined among explosions of begonias. At the rear of the bus they put neon lights behind the grille of the engine, the fan and conch of the carburettor all-aglow, a 1,000-kilogram confusion for the fireflies hovering in the bushes at the roadside. One bus passed me by with more lights than all the rest of them, calling itself the '*Disco Bus*'. I looked up as it moved slowly away, white faces on the inside, foreheads squashed against the glass, the rucksacks, braided hair and beaded necklaces of the young West, looking everywhere for a little adventure, driving south on their five-part installation of Thailand.

The coming days passed no differently. But for the mosquitoes and the sluggishness of my legs everything felt perfect, the air cleaner, drivers more patient and their horns less frequently called upon. Growing in the road verges was basil, leaves of green and purple that rubbed against one another in the breeze so their scent carried into the mist. There were fewer steel rods for the laying of infrastructure, and the earthmovers and pneumatic drills sold at Chinese roadsides were replaced by terracotta pots and houseplants, water features, ceramic models of roaring tigers and elephants raising trunks in salute. The women still swept forecourts, men still chopped trees and hit engines with hammers, turned bolts and cut metal piping, tails of sparks spraying onto the pavement. People still worked in Thailand, but differently to the Chinese, for there was a bonhomie there, as if people had time on their hands again. As I rode by they would wave to me, men leaning against the bare chassis of the truck, oil and grease across their overalls. They called out, I looked, they waved. And that was it, as if I were an individual again . . . no longer just a mere spectacle.

The business changed too, the heavy industry dried up, girders and car transporters replaced by chickens on the roads beside me. Trucks would pass with 60 cubic metres of chicken, a cargo of nothing but fluttering feathers, tumbling over one another and impossible to tell where one bird stopped and the next began. At the roadside were coconut plantations, coconuts in phenomenal numbers. I passed entire mountain ranges of them, palms shooting skywards as a young boy shimmied up the discs of the trunk, tied to the tree by a sling, a machete hanging from his waist. He hacked free the coconuts, threw them down to somebody waiting with a sharpened spear stuck into the earth, the colour of dirty metal with a gleam to its point. The man on the ground would impale that green skull, raising it high in both hands, bringing it back down upon that spear . . . once, twice . . . and the green would fall away to reveal the hairy coconut itself, the star of the show. Moving closer to the sea, salt replaced the palms. Salt beds were dug from the sun-baked earth, between dams separating one bed from the next, some dry and parched, some full of water, others with conical mounds of white salt swept into heaps by men and women with brooms, bandannas around their faces, straw hats on their heads. They walked beneath windmills that pumped the sea onto the land, the turning sails made from a cloth that tore slowly to rags hanging upon a frame.

The 100-mile days ticked by as I passed south and into forest, where monkeys watched me, howling through the foliage and leaping to the undergrowth as I neared. Tiny faces would emerge, turning sideways to assess what my business might be. Sometimes, far in the distance, I would watch a monkey's silhouette pad across the quiet road, tail raised and arms reaching, fingers unfastening the knot on a bag of rubbish. As they heard me approach, the neck would swing to reveal that white face, a half-eaten sandwich tossed away, and the monkey clambering away up a telegraph pole. They sat upon the cables looking down, crouched, baring bright-red assholes, unfurled tails swinging like the pendulum inside a grandfather clock.

Mid-September came and monsoon hit, the air solid with falling water. As evening neared I'd pull into the shelter of restaurants, a gas canister beneath a table, tubes looping up towards two ring burners, a pair of pans bubbling on top of them, one red and one green, steam rising in the cooled air. There was a glass cabinet, a sliding door, steel trays with leaves upon them, bowls with shoots of lemongrass, pieces of chicken, a pair of scissors leaning against a thigh. The rain fell, road became river, motorbikes pulling beneath shelters, cars floating onwards, sailing downstream with wheels disappearing under the waves, sticks and plastic packaging drifting along the road. Corrugated roofs all turned to flumes, each furrow becoming a steady stream of water falling over the side and down towards growing puddles in the mud. A woman stepped towards me, dressed in an apron and laughing at the rain. She pointed towards her bubbling pans, cupping a palm and eating the air from it with her fingertips. Pointing to a pressure cooker beneath the tabletop, she lifted the lid as steam piled upwards through light, burst with the smell of cooked rice.

Day 90 – Sadao – 9,113 Miles

Trouble was brewing, bicycle starting to raise objections. I'll spare you the details, but put simply, the oil had gone from my rear-wheel hub, the contraption in which my gears were kept. The oil was necessary to lubricate the cogs, allow them to move smoothly over one another and keep the whole show on the road, gears shifting and bicycle rolling efficiently. I'd changed the oil once before, when waiting at the Korgas border, but in the following weeks I'd watched as it sweated out into the deserts of China. I'd brushed it off . . . the manufacturers said it was normal in extreme heat, nothing to worry about. For so long I'd observed black puddles beneath my rear wheel, but come that time they'd stopped, dried up . . . there was no oil left to leak.

A rattling began, a grinding of bearings and if not the rattling then an occasional thump, a banging from the rear wheel, two pieces of unidentifiable metal colliding, hammering on the hub and demanding to be heard. From Shanghai I wrote to the factory that produced it, back in Germany, asked what could be done. No reply. Riding south through Thailand, I ignored the noises even as they grew more persistent. I tried to soothe the worries of the machine, winced when the thumping grew louder, spoke to my bicycle . . . *soon it'll be all right, work with me and I'll get you better, I promise.*

Leaving the highway, I made my way to smaller roads, through villages more remote, the forest thicker, alive with strange squawks and chattering where before had been only the hum of traffic. New types of death emerged, squashed on the road the flattened coil of what had been a snake, a silver skin with tyre treads across its middle, curled fang jammed between stones in the road's surface. There was the lizard, a whole metre in length, I must have disturbed the thing for I realised its presence only through my ear. A slithering movement began, a rustling of leather pulled powerfully through gravel. I glimpsed it, a real dinosaur, the hanging skin beneath the neck, broad green back and that gigantic tail, pulled over the ground by long, black claws.

As I moved south, the rear wheel ground on, pounding, a locking sensation followed by release and then the heavy crash of something loosening and pulling free. The rains returned, transforming me from dry to dripping in 20 seconds, buckets of water from above and laughter the only worthwhile response. After the clouds had said their bit, the sky cleared just as swift, as if it had never borne a grey shade in all its days. The world warmed again, and as I headed in and out of Thammarat, so Thailand grew poorer, the landscape changing, pavements turning back to dust and soil, concrete houses replaced by metal sheets and planks of wood, cars turning to cows, motorbikes to bicycles. Life there became quieter, slower, softening as the sound of engines disappeared. Islam emerged, mosques and minarets, the Muslim south the poorest part of Thailand, where the Buddhists, ever viewed so benevolently in the West, become only the oppressive majority. The Thai Muslims protest for rights and, with deaths and brutality, the authorities crush all dissent, the whole thing one more cooperation in that endless, borderless, 'war on terror'.

Out of the hills ran rivers, widening in readiness for the sea. The houses moved from land to water, stilts protruding the weeds and lilies, and tethered canoes pulling slowly back and forth the rope that held them. From a rickety deck, children threw pebbles into a bucket floating in the water, while a mother squatted among tangled fishing nets, fingers working through endless knots. A man floated idly through the scene, gliding home in a boat full of holes, his paddle breaking the still surface with a slow plunge and a splash of water. It doesn't get better than that, truly picturesque . . . poverty that floats. From inside my pannier there came a loud fluttering of lenses, the camera desperate for a peek, whispering promises that if only I let it see what I saw, then never again would I have need of a memory.

From the beachfront I made for forest, for the border beyond Sadao, where opaque, white rubber trickles down plantation trees. The sunset yawns, a heavy blue cast with clouds, final fires of orange light sinking to the mist of dusk . . . a stock-image from a tropical land, the outline of farmers making their way home with shovels over shoulders. Night came down with no light to be had, forest thick and the canopy holding a three-quarter moon at bay. Cicadas struck up, their membranes rubbing a din so consistent that eventually I ceased to hear it at all, the sound making its way inside my brain as only unrealised noise. Slowly, so very gradually, as I move deeper into the jungle a new smell presents itself. No longer the pungent smell of chlorophyll and green leaves, this new odour is something unpleasant, something unnatural, a smell that doesn't belong in the rainforest, but in bedrooms and morning-afters ten thousand miles away. I know it . . . but what is it? I rack my brains, surely the jungle doesn't smell of . . . yes . . . but that's it. Of condoms? I ride on, still unconvinced, occasionally passed by industrial-looking tankers making never-ending deliveries of some unknown liquid. Eventually, on the road up ahead, a large area of white light hums in the darkness, flies and moths move all through this pool of electrified brightness. The smell intensifies, reaches a peak as I keep cycling, pass a chain-link fence, the sign of a multinational corporation. Two simple words, stamped in light on the night of the Thai jungle. Latex factory.

Day 91 – Alor Setar – 9,274 Miles

In Malaysia the road surface improves, widens, lanes separated by well-painted lines. The roads orbit towns, unlike in Thailand, in China, in all the world as far back as Austria, the last country where settlements were anything more than lengths of houses along the road itself.

At a street vendor's stall I stopped for lunch, sitting at a short, wooden stool, knees up and picking the bones from a fish curry, the smell of spices all around. I tear up a traditional flatbread, make parcels of curry to eat with my hands, lick the smudges of sauce collecting on my fingertips. Beside me, hand and flatbread disap-pearing into my mouth, children are arguing over plastic toys, as Malay locals come piling out of McDonald's.

Upon the streets, mosques became commonplace, the Thai

miniskirts grew longer, necklines higher and the fabrics looser, more modest. Calls to prayer came regularly, so too the covering of heads. Periodically a burka appeared, head-to-anonymous-toe beneath that curtain, only a slit for the eyes looking out at me. It's not natural to see such things, by which I do not mean the belief itself so much as to see its presence in Malaysia. In Southeast Asia the burka was never part of Islam, it has arrived as a cultural export from Saudi Arabia and Wahhabism, the most ancient and repressive misuse of Islamic creeds. With no mention of the irony, the West's closest allies in the Middle East open mosques and fund dogmatic preachers in all corners of the world. Between military aid and the bribes of our arms contractors, Western foreign policy has subsidised a proliferation of the most illiberal form of Islam, walking by me on the streets of Malaysia.

It was then that my grubby, tattered vest began to embarrass me for the first time. With the modesty of the female dress and the smart appearance of the men, I couldn't bring myself to walk in and out of shops looking like the vagabond I had been. As I stood making efforts to communicate with those who looked so respectable, I grew self-conscious, and at a market stall I shuffled through a rail of checkers in all different colours, short sleeves and collars to make a man presentable. After choosing an orange number to match my panniers, I paid, pulled the shirt over my shoulders . . . kept it there until a cold Normandy evening in early December.

* * *

Teluk Intan sits on the banks of the great Perak River, the waters of which become shallower each year, soils eroding from the banks, raising the riverbed so that now cargo ships can no longer pass and instead dock at a coastal port 50 miles away. It's quiet. In Teluk Intan they had once shipped petroleum, rubber and tin from the refineries and mines of the interior. The money stopped with the cargo ships, leaving a Malaysian has-been of a place, the universal phenomenon of towns that have had their day . . . where the money dried up, pavements cracked and the roads rutted. Retail properties with whitewashed windows, municipal gardens overgrown.

Among it, however, one building of relevance remained in use, beneath a sign with a picture of a computer. Inside a fan rotated back and forth at the far end of a long room, a man lying back on a low bed, legs crossed above him, a row of computers along the wall between us. He waves me in. I sit in the light of the screen as a computer starts up, rattling and humming between my legs as the screen loads and . . . at last, news on my gear system. A man by the name of Paul Moir introduces himself from Singapore, the one man on the peninsula who can help. Relieved, I read on. A new paragraph, an apology it's taken him so long to reply but in two days he leaves for holiday. As I look at that screen in Teluk Intan, midday on Tuesday, 15 September, I read Paul Moir's words, written in Singapore, 400 miles south.

Happy to help . . . unfortunately . . . Thursday 17th, 5pm . . . fly to Bangkok.
If you can get to me by then . . .

Day 93 – Melaka – 9,567 Miles

That was the start of it, standing in the street of Teluk Intan, looking down at my bicycle with 400 miles and 48 hours running through my head. The numbers broke down fairly well. My 8-hour days at the office would ordinarily yield 100 miles, multiplied by 4 would equal 32 hours, leaving 16 hours spare to accommodate decreasing speed, looking at maps, eating, some sleep and miscellaneous untoward circumstances. I have to confess, it was a nice challenge, sounded difficult and, at the same time, quite attainable, a victory mine to lose. What followed was not quite a steely tale of do-or-die resolve, of mettle in the face of possible failure, that wasn't it at all. My faith that I could overcome was more mathematical than spiritual. Broadly speaking, the numbers were on my side, not out of reach . . . 400 miles waiting to be respectfully dismantled. I'm self-contained, live deep inside my own head, forever deliberating, an endurance athlete of thought, harangued by each decision and possibility, a control-freak and collector in search of certainties. I'm also compulsive, pathological, impossible to satisfy and terminally incomplete. While I'm embarrassed to admit it, riding 400 miles in 48 hours is precisely the sort of challenge in which I can find some meaning for a while. It's a poor route to happiness . . . the same idiocy that led me to that stupid record in the first place. Mark my words, the world will not be improved by someone like me, seeking to win a race for the forces of good; it will be saved by those who laugh at the idea of a race in the first place.

Regaining the bike that afternoon had to be the start of some significant innings. Stepping up to the crease, I needed a first inroad against 400. Small markers struck up at the roadside, white-painted stones at kilometre intervals and 'Klang – 140km'. I crossed the Bernam River, the boundary from Perak into Selangor province, home of Kuala Lumpur and the most prosperous region of Malaysia. The road changed, almost immediately the increased tax revenue was laid down beneath me, the surface shifting from bitumen and cubes of rock to smooth asphalt. My wheels began to turn for Klang, where in 90 miles I would make my first stop.

The country unfurled around me, the shadows of palm plantations moving to cover the land, so harsh and regimented where a rainforest once stood. They chopped down and smoked out a million different plants and animals, replaced them with a million identical evenly spaced palm trees, grown for the oil from which the world makes its shampoo, in which fast-food restaurants fry their chips for that golden hue.

Time blurred, sending me past the roadkill bodies of burst lizards, their blooded guts and spine exploding as one desperate, black-nailed claw tried reaching from the carnage. A metre-long tail pointed from the scene, skin flattened into what would have made such a lovely handbag. Butterflies dropped, perfectly preserved in their collisions, scolding red eyes and little dusts of blue upon the wing. Such delicate death against the hard asphalt, they made the prettiest of corpses, waiting for the tyres that would eventually turn them back to powdered carbon.

Dusk turned to night as shadows gathered into strange, concealed forms. Fan belts, the rubber strips of a windscreen wiper, rope lengths, in the dark it all began to swarm as snakes, coiling and ready to spring. There were serpents too. In the lakes and rivers I saw them floating, the twisted forms of logs, dead and only half-sunken, reels of hose and drainage pipe with necks peering from the waters. Palm trees left the roadside and in their wake came giant needles, voodoo dolls lanced right through, limbs splaying, writhing in the wind, leaves hanging deadweight and falling with a deafening shred of fibres. Fireflies hovered in the undergrowth, on occasion I would see two of them side by side . . . gleaming eyes watching level and steady. The eyes blinked, there came a shuffling of bushes, no longer two fireflies but the eyes of a single chasing dog, claw scratching tarmac as it pelted down the road after me. The horizon began to burn, light filling the sky with the electrical hum of Kuala Lumpur, a white haze eternally lifting and receding like some glowing lung. I made out the tallest of its buildings, spires of light built by secularists as some sign of progress.

Klang came . . . perhaps 9pm and the city rose to bundle me

inside of its neon. I rode through, looking around for somewhere to eat. Signposts appeared, counting down three more kilometres, the tricolour of a French supermarket providing me an arrow to follow. With military efficiency I went in and out, grabbing everything my heart and body might have desired with no concern for cost or ethics. I bought jam made from blackcurrants in France and then flown to Malaysia, bought Brie, a cylinder of soft fat for my body to burn, bought butter made in New Zealand, a chocolate spread produced in the Alps, and a litre of chocolate milk to cleanse my palette. The first 100 miles had taken perhaps nine hours, the likelihood being that the following ones would be progressively harder to churn out. Leaving Klang that night I didn't know what I was planning, to ride as long as possible, I suppose . . . another 100 miles to put me halfway through the total. It was a curious thought, the beginning of the night and without any intention to sleep until the sun was back in the sky. I started to fantasise, more and more I fantasised . . . that was the way I approached so much of it, made stories for the occupation of my head, dreams to alleviate the tedium of what was at hand. Leaving the city, I turned big gears, powered against my pedals, set out against the next century with a vengeance.

Almost immediately it came, a rebellion in the muscles of my legs, electricity howling so that my calves and thighs turned to petrified stone, shooting pinpricks and arguments as cramp began. Suddenly I was on a giant ship, a ship sailing into a storm, the wind crashing and spray throwing itself against the bridge. From behind a cupped hand the captain shouted: *'What's that, cramp, you say? . . . Nothing we can do, old boy!'* And so I pushed at my legs and forced them to continue, for it's when they stop turning that the cramp really bites in, sinks its teeth and locks its jaw. If you keep pushing, driving forwards, then it can't bring you down . . . and slowly, gritting teeth, taking your mind to better places, you continue.

Far more than the weariness in the muscles, it's the sleep deprivation that gets you. The softening of the head is what topples your resolve, convinces you to step from the bicycle. As I followed the coast, reality left my head to be overrun by psychosis and dreams. I remember lightning, high above the clouds I remember lightning storms . . . 16 shells from a thirty-ought-six rattled off high above, flashes of lightning . . . bolts that never broke to the surface of the sea but remained trapped inside that sky. They struck through my peripheral vision, so slight and quick, silently, rarely with the sound of thunder, so that in time I grew paranoid that it was not lightning in the sky at all, only electricity in my own vision, an epileptic haywire in the brain. If at midnight I was admiring the storms high above, come one o'clock I was in fear of seizures. Come two o'clock I was resigned to the fact that I'd always been epileptic but never known it and come three o'clock I was considering how best to adapt my life to live with the condition. By four o'clock, I'd decided to purchase a medical bracelet in Singapore, something to alert paramedics to the fact that I was epileptic, if ever I was involved in an accident. With Sir Hugh Gough charging by, standing high on the stirrups of a horse, his white coat blazing out behind him . . . Slowly, you go crazy.

Sky faded blue as I passed Port Dickson, the second 100 almost over and dawn pulling across beaches. Light fell upon the luxury hotels of the coast, aquamarine swimming pools paced back and forth by jacketed guards yawning into their fists. By then I was tired, painfully so, head lolling heavily from side to side and, though afraid of falling asleep, fearful I would not be able to rise and ride afterwards, as my eyes began to falter and flecks of red and green emerged upon my vision, I knew my body could tolerate little more.

Daylight broke in the villages, landed on a small table upon the pavement. A Chinaman sat there, the Melaka region one-third

Chinese, a demographic owing to the refugees of Britain's nineteenth-century Opium Wars, pushing that Bengali heroin harvest on the Chinese to the north. Once the Chinese refugees arrived in Malaysia, the British forces waiting there had enslaved them, set them to mining tin in the interior. Forgive me, glorious Empire . . . I digress. Back in 2009, I gesture at the Chinese man in Melaka, eat from a cupped palm. He nods, opens a heavy plastic box, full of bags of cooked noodles, white and thin like vermicelli. As I ate, I pointed behind me, over my shoulder, said I'd ridden in China. He was interested, smiling, nodding as I gave him my itinerary, my *Urumçi–Xining–Lanzhou–Xi'an–Shanghai*. It wasn't just idle banter, I had ulterior motives, was preparing to mime a request that I sleep on a stretch of pavement next to his stall. I finish one bowl of noodles, then a second, all full of thanks. Making a pillow of my palms, head on knuckles I close my eyes, before opening them to gaze imploringly at him . . . not an enthusiastic host by any means. I look on, still imploring. He sighs, stands, gestures that I should follow him back behind the house. Heavy bolts scratch, metal surfaces pass over one another as the door falls open to let out a smell of dust and dead wood. Inside are silhouettes of tools, rakes and saws and a scythe leaning against the wall, eerie shapes falling across the floor and then soaking into darkness.

There's a low table, planks of wood set close together upon trestles. He moves towards it, takes an old rag from the rung of a ladder, brushes dust, cobwebs and leaves from the table. From the floor he picks up a newspaper, unpeels it, spreads folds of newssheet across the planks, smooths down the creases. He steps back, walks from the room, closes the door behind him. Climbing up, I swing myself onto that hard surface . . . lying on my back, tools and baskets hanging over me, toes pointing skyward, hard wood at my back like a catafalque, shadows cast against my body as cracks of light slip under the door. The points of my skull, shoulders, coccyx and ankles . . . it all presses hard against the wood, my body lowering into a corridor beneath the ground, stars flooding over me, head journeying through outer space, an intergalactic voyage as I descend into a black hole. And all life is swallowed up.

* * *

After 40 minutes my alarm brought me back, sun up and road waiting, the third 100 miles opening before me. After sleep I was off the front, bearing down the road for Johor Bahru at the tip of the Malay Peninsula. I'm sorry if this gets cursory . . . in those hours in the saddle I saw such wonders, evaluated the world and my life within it so many times over, but there's only so much one book will hold. Don't take my word for it, or anybody else's for that matter, just go out there, and ride.

Day turned night once more, my skin starting to sting, a rash burning, perhaps from the salt in my sweat, from my last swim in the sea, or else just chronic fatigue and a body showing the first signs of deterioration. I never learned which for, after a shower and eight hours' sleep, it disappeared more swiftly than it came. It wasn't just my skin causing problems, my hands were disappearing too, and, after so many hours of constant riding, the pressure on the carpals down my inside arm had stopped all feeling. On each hand my two smallest fingers had faded and lost sensation so that, even as I stretched and played with them, still they grew ever more numb. For the final century I removed all thoughts from my mind, watched the remains of the ride slip by as only numerical fractions in my head. I would roll through the first mile of the day and see one more four-hundredth fraction disappear, a second mile and another two-hundredth. Come the end of 400 miles I'd taken in only three half-hour sleeps . . . caffeine blocking all rest even in a head that craved nothing but.

At Johor I arrived in time for a morning rush hour I'd been warned to avoid at all costs. It floods from Malaysia to Singapore, one of the world's busiest border crossings, a daily event of human geography in the animal kingdom. That border defies all lofty belief that humans are any more than another hungry organism, for on one side, in Singapore, the wages are five times that on the other. Like an army of ants that have found a crumbling biscuit, so do humans swarm across the Johor Strait, into Southeast Asia's most affluent country. That immigration checkpoint was chaos, more scooters through a confined space than would ever seem possible. I don't remember details, it must have been a long causeway over the water, but what stays with me are the tunnels of the immigration facility itself. The road corkscrewed up and down, catacombs through the anthill, scooters racing on with no regard for lanes, headlamps diving towards cubicles at which immigration officers waited with a stamp. A swarm of 20 scooters clustered around each booth, the road behind still filling up with more workers, their engines emitting a pitched drone that echoed through the concrete tunnels. With scooters diving on all sides, rows of auto-pay cameras fluttering at number plates from above, and everyone desperate to reach Singapore first, I pedalled as fast as possible through the anarchy, jumping over speed bumps, squeezing between scooters and bollards, my rash burning and that army of waiters, attendants and bellboys carrying me along on their tide.

Across the border, everything is different . . . that imaginary line a resounding success in keeping two broadly similar places very much distinct. Chinese faces answered my questions in English, signposts regularly in English for the first time since London. Desperate to stop the clock on another leg, again and again I asked the way to the airport, people too flabbergasted to comprehend what I was saying, waving their hands in delirium.

'The bus stop to the airport is 200 metres that way.'

'I don't want the bus stop to the airport, I want to cycle there.'

'But you can't cycle to the airport . . . it's 16 kilometres . . . It's too far!'

Intermission – Singapore – 9,982 Miles

It was nice to be in a home again. Paul Moir was an engineer, his work with bicycles more hobby than job. He showed me the air-tight bags where he kept his wholemeal bread, safe inside the fridge and away from the humidity. From a shelf high above he lifted down the coffee beans and grinder, and then the pot in which the muesli was kept. Placing his hands together, Paul Moir told me very simply to make myself at home. In the garden we washed three months of Eurasian mud and dust from my bicycle, a condition of entry to New Zealand, where immigration controls keep out foreign species of all descriptions. We moved to the workshop, cleaned the interior of the hub, talked cycling as I forced my eyes to stay awake a little longer. Stooped beside me, Paul unwound bolts and replaced paper gaskets, shapes that had either snared into gnarled forms, or else disintegrated altogether.

For a couple of hours we worked on the bicycle, afternoon approaching evening, the Moirs getting ready for their flight, skies darkening outside with the omen of a storm. Paul appeared at the doorway of the workshop, fixing the collar of his polo shirt, a small collection of bags and suitcases waiting in the room behind him.

'I'm sorry we're in such a rush.' He pauses, looks at me. 'You know, if you'd rather not go into the city and pay for a hotel, you're

welcome to make yourself at home here for a few days. Really . . .
it's not a problem.'

* * *

Outside the house and Singapore was a humanitarian disaster, a
model of success in the eyes of the world's economic institutions,
and, as such, lifeless in all other ways. The island was dystopia, perfect and complete because nobody even realised as much, torn as
they were between gratitude to their government, love of money
and a faceless fear of terrorists. It was Smallville, Pleasantville,
Fordism . . . The national pastime was said to be shopping, nature-
walks were pavements beneath skyscrapers, and shoved out of sight
were the squalid tower blocks in which the Malay and Tamil ship-
yard labourers were housed. Closer to the urban centres emerged
regimented suburbs, luxury cars in every driveway and a golf
course at the end of each street.

Out the metro I found Orchard Road, not a fruit tree in sight
as I walked under the sheer, pristine faces of department stores
above, one large boutique grave, dug deep and perfect with a
mechanical shovel. When I ask for an Internet café, a man scratches
his head, grimaces at the prospect. 'I think there is one in a mall
near here, but you should not go there . . .' I ask why not, but he's
unequivocal: 'Because that mall is very old and very boring, it's
been there for almost six years now.'

I walked around, watching Singapore, contempt so loud inside
my head I grew scared someone outside might hear it. There was
no need to worry, nobody paid anyone the barest attention. They
all sat alone, listening to their headphones, using a stylus to entrust
secrets to the screens of their pocket computers, capturing the
world around them with the phone in their camera or the camera
in the phone, whichever was most convenient at the time. The

buildings had banners draped from windows – *Live Better! Feel the Energy!* – though who even knew what that was supposed to mean. A couple sat together on a date, the girl in polka dots, so pretty and entirely left to waste. She prodded woefully at a chocolate cake as I watched her boyfriend ignoring her, devoted to a game of shooting rocks in Outer Space. Children sat down with their mother, teeth braced so that as adults they could have perfect smiles, skateboards under their arms so they could remain credible on the street meanwhile. They sat at a table, the mother staring vacantly as the kids produced hand-held video games, one with a motorbike and the other a gun. And nobody said another word.

New Zealand

Day 94 – South Island – 10,091 Miles

Somebody broke my bicycle. A baggage handler, heavy turbulence, a conveyor belt, a holidaymaker's suitcase . . . something was to blame. Something clobbered it good and proper. The front wheel had fallen out when I reached the airport at Dunedin, a bolt had been fully dislodged, at the time was missing, presumed gone forever. I told an attendant, dressed in a fluorescent jacket and shorts, a pair of boots with the laces trailing. He disappeared back into the hold, looking for one bolt in the hold of a jumbo jet. It was a valiant effort. Five minutes later he came back, no luck. I tied my wheel into the forks, a piece of string bound around the skewer.

For a while I'd been excited about a return to the English-speaking world, had forgotten how rarely anyone says anything worthwhile. After three repetitions of 'but it's cold' and one of 'you can't cycle to Dunedin . . . it's 25 kilometres', I set off hesitantly, the front wheel falling out and back into the forks with every bump. My rear light had broken too, the cold at 30,000 feet stealing the last life from its battery. Night came, headlamps on the highway behind me, long shadows and car horns, always the car horns. Those motorists thought I wanted to be on their highway without a rear light, thought I must be having a whale of a time, a real thrill-seeker. It's not so dangerous that they would think to slow down . . . I'm not so invisible that they can't see me from 500 metres away and start firing on the horn. Eventually the headlights behind me get heavier, white light, and then white light with blue in it, swirling blue on the road before me. A discotheque, a siren, the police had arrived at last . . . just in time. Who knew what might have happened?

He was a young officer, not accepting excuses or taking no for an answer, insistent. After bundling my bicycle into the back of his car, together we drove the remaining road to Dunedin. Like police everywhere, really he was a decent sort, but with an air of restraint about him, the air of a man who feels he is behaving convivially, although he has the right not to, as if his decency is a favour. He listens to himself speak, a lot of respect for what he has to tell me, his eyes set on me instead of the road. 'They say Dunedin is a nice place, that New Zealand is safe, but in ten years there have been five homicides . . .' He always calls them 'homicides', can't use the word enough, no plain old murders for this one. He rounds it up. 'I was first on the scene of two of those five homicides . . . nowhere is safe.' That's the crux of it where police are concerned, convinced of danger everywhere.

I ask if Dunedin had a park, an open space where I could pitch a tent. He strokes his chin, feeling it for options as if it is a map of the city, lots of stroking, finally an answer. 'You'd be a target for certain, they'd target you.' The guy's unstoppable, what does he mean . . . 'They?' He straightens up. 'Gang crime . . . Monster Mob, Black Power . . . the main threat here. I'll drop you at a hostel.'

* * *

Next morning I visited a bicycle shop, pumped up my tyres and fixed my wheel with a new skewer. After three days in the Moir household, and a day in airports and aeroplanes, I craved open roads and turning pedals in fresh air. Things could've been easier.

It was cold, that was the main problem, humidity and monkeys far behind, my body was still waiting in the tropics, not the least bit acclimatised as I left Dunedin for the hills above the city. I wanted to obliterate it, eight days to Auckland was the plan, only it never works like that . . . the faster you want to go, the slower you progress.

At the roadside were yellow-flowering gorse thickets, stacks of chopped wood, axes lodged in tree stumps and the smells of bonfires and horse manure lingering in the valleys. It was Britain again, familiar, a northern European countryside on the other side of the world. Small drifts of snow melted slowly in the verges, red berries dotted among white crystals. The wind was from the south, almost directly out of Antarctica and as cold as you'd expect. It blew me north, towards Auckland, but left me uncomfortable, sweating uphill before freezing on the flats, always eager to find excuses that would allow me take a break.

Behind a hot counter, aglow with chips and batter, Jen Lockerbie stood in front of me. '*Lockerbie* . . . just like the bombing,' was how she introduced herself, returning me to a world of meetings, a change from my fleeting impressions of foreign cultures. She had time for people, that was the thing with Jen Lockerbie, standing there in her green apron. Even as I jumped back into English with a hundred infernally stupid questions about fish, potatoes and batter, still she had the time of day to give. Of her five children, four of them went running around us, in and out of the kitchen. One of them was hitting another with a spoon, the two of them laughing, laughing, one more hit with the spoon . . . a hit too far . . . and the tears began. Her son runs to Jen, buries himself in her green apron to dry the tears, sobbing for all he's worth.

'I have one son who's not here,' she puts in. 'He's sixteen . . . down in Dunedin with his grandmother. He wants to go out drinking, live by his own rules . . .' She shakes her head as she tells me, 'That's fine, but not under my roof, not with four young children growing up and looking for role models. That's the problem, the children these days have no role models, and no respect either.'

New Zealanders have their golden age like the rest of us, but still the place was so traditional, it was hard not to smile. A 16-year-old, sent to live with his grandmother for disobeying house rules. Gangs and all . . . New Zealand is the most wholesome dysfunctional society I've ever known.

* * *

Three hours more riding left me few miles to show for it, the day at an end. In front of me were large windows to the living room of a house . . . big armchairs, the kind with a foot rest that folds out as the chair reclines. A television was on, four sets of slippers propped up in front of it and visible beneath the curtain. Before setting out, people had told me New Zealanders would be happy to let me camp in their gardens. My shoes crunched down the driveway as I chose my words, prepared to test the advice.

He opened the door wide, looked at the stranger standing there before him, the door wide open to the night, not a trepidation in sight at an unexpected knocking after dark. Standing there was Ray. He opens right up, letting all of the warm air out too. A quizzical hello and then, 'Yes, you can camp in the garden tonight. Not a problem.'

Taking my tent and sleeping bag, I walk off down the lawn, happy with the soft, flat earth on which I'm about to sleep. A few seconds later and he's following me back onto the grass. He's calling out, 'Say . . . if you'd like, my wife could just fix you up a bed in the spare room?'

In the house we talk, sip tea with Ray's wife, Carole. Carole works the telephones in a dairy, selling milk to the South Island.

'Nothing but foreigners now,' she tuts. 'I'm the only Kiwi left on the phones, dialling or answering. A Chinaman, Filipino, Vietnamese. The cities are worse. You won't find a Kiwi left in Auckland.'

Ray interjects, a man not one for giving opinions on matters beyond his own eyes. Ray chides gently. 'I'm not sure that's quite true now, Carole.' He turns my way. 'You must be tired, get on to bed if you like . . . it's all made up for you.'

There's a bathroom attached to my room. I sit in the tub, a shower held to my chest, hot water breathing over me in spurts as I squat down, knees up. In the bedroom, beneath the covers I'm watched by photos of cows, children and grandchildren, sets of unfamiliar eyes all peering from their frames in the walls.

* * *

'You've hit it just at the worst moment. A week ago it was like summer, folk on the beaches at Christchurch. This wind's from the south, Antarctica . . . perishing it is!'

Ray had made breakfast, inch-thick slices of bacon, fried tomatoes, eggs, toast ready and waiting. He forked rashers onto plates, asked of my trip and why I was doing it, why a record? I had ready-made responses to those questions, it all depended who asked.

'Some guy did it a couple of years back. I always loved travelling by bicycle, and he went and gave it to big businesses, rode around the world and endorsed banks and investment funds with it . . .'

At that Ray looked up, lifted his head from a line of pink rashers on the grill, looked me in the eye as he asked, incredulously, 'He didn't?'

Quietly surprised, I smiled. 'Yeah . . . he did.'

That response summed up Ray. Possessed of such spirit he does not believe what has happened to the rest of society. In London, selling the soul for whatever price can be fetched was good marketing, but to Ray, down on South Island, it was still shocking. For an hour he told me about his farm, the animals he sold to an abattoir, keeping back enough meat for himself. Ray told me his stories . . . I collected so many stories that never made it to this book. He told me all about the *riggerjoist*, with which he hoisted the calf out of the lame heifer who couldn't push. I interrupted, and together we deciphered our same languages, learned that a rig-gerjoist was a winch. He finished the story, sad and slow, recounting how he had to fetch his rifle in the night, put the mother out of her pain after the birth.

Before leaving, I asked Ray to sign my little book, the logbook I kept for the bureaucrats, full of signatures from people I met, proof that I really was cycling around the world. Ray sounded out the letters as he spelt 'Hilderthorpe' . . . musing whether it was an 'A' or an 'E' in the middle of the word. 'Carole always says my spelling's awful . . .' He chuckled, clutched pen in fist, not the least self-conscious that he couldn't spell the name of the town he'd lived in for a decade.

I could have spent hours in his company, just listening to him and asking my stupid questions about cows, undoing all the harm of my education, that stupid brain that won't hold still with its dis-section, analysis and pointless critique. I think Ray would probably be bemused to hear I hold him so highly, wouldn't understand what all the fuss was about. I can still see him standing there with his breech calf as I left that morning, a large milk bottle in his hand, his white hair and dark eyebrows. A black leather hat was tipped forwards on his head, a braided bead sloping around its well-worn brim, leaving a shadow on his face. Ray's face was like a furnace, nothing but warmth, the mouth always a little open and ready to start smiling. Just listening to him was calming, in living life as he does he teaches you what matters in the world. I'd have loved to see him in London, walking through the City in his hat and white Wellingtons, a milk bottle for his calf under one arm. He'd have put the place right, brought in some humanity, or at least I'd like to think as much.

Day 98 – Marlborough Sounds – 10,468 Miles

Nights were drawing in. The clocks had gone forwards and, though down in the southern hemisphere the days were lengthening, a week later I would be back north of the equator with winter on its way. The Antarctic winds blew me through the Bight of Canterbury, the flats surrounding Christchurch. It began to rain, cut to the quick with cold. I made hard work of it, low on finesse, slugging it out as the wind turned on me, and I started riding deeper into the night to amass shorter distances than ever before.

I rode on to the Kaikoura Peninsula, making my way to Picton and the boat that would take me to North Island. That stretch of coast is supposed to be beautiful, stunning even, but for 200 miles I could see no further than 10 metres down the road. I was beside the Pacific then, my first time and the world's largest ocean a mean disappointment. Ill-tempered, it impaled itself upon beaches, cliffs and rocks, so that under grey sky the grey waves went wrecking themselves against all they found. It didn't get any easier. Sometime after dark, with a flooded ford across the road and cars queuing to pass where the current was calmest, a man wound down his window, leaned out . . . 'It's already cold and wet, it's getting pretty dark too. I don't mind offering you a ride to Picton.'

'No, no, thank you . . .' I respond as I shivered, cursing at my idiotic record.

He starts, confused. 'Really? . . . Why not?' He won't make it easy for me.

I shrug, out comes a barefaced lie, 'I want to ride.'

Day 99 – North Island – 10,557 Miles

Wellington was a monumental moment in my circumnavigation. The record-keeping bureaucrats on Drummond Street decree a circumnavigation must include a set of antipodal points. Wellington is an approximate antipode of Madrid, which is to say that the two of them, to within 100 kilometres, would line up through the centre of the earth. After half-sleeping a three-hour ferry crossing, I woke expecting to ride a useful number of miles. I managed 10. I stopped. Put concisely, I was a wreck. It was no fun, fun had sunk without a trace.

Matters didn't improve with the morning. This doesn't get any better . . . there'll be no happy ending. New Zealand did not go well. My willpower disappeared as soon as I mounted the saddle, legs trudging against the pedals towards a region known as the Parapara. It rained . . . it rained and the wind blew, the land before me rearing up with what was to come. I'd no stomach for a fight that morning, yet the roads on my map, on reaching the Parapara, those lines went haywire, turned spaghetti, fraying all over the place to seek out something like a flat route through the hills. There is no flat route in the Parapara, there the land folds and falls like a heap of dirty laundry. I would plunge down a hillside, into the wind, pedalling hard only to descend the hill. At the bottom the road would rear back up . . . a concertina, a wall . . . and so slowly I climbed.

After two hours, with Body screaming that this was impossibly hard work, I stopped at a house to refill my water bottles in central nowhere, among the valleys, waterfalls and mudslides of the Parapara. I knock at a door, pane rattles frame . . . a shadow appears. His name is Tom Irirangi – Tom Irirangi of the Parapara – once a forest ranger, a Maori man. From across cups of tea at his kitchen table, he looks down a billed nose at me. 'It's all the same, mate. *Maori* or *settler,* it's all about *sharing.*' He emphasises key words, speaks slow. '*Sharing*'s what this is about.'

As we talk, his two daughters go running around us, one of them under a duvet, the other chasing, taking the duvet herself, and then running around under the duvet until being caught and the duvet changes hands again. He tells me history, how the Maori warriors had met a better fate than the Aborigines of Australia.

'We fought 'em see! The settlers . . . the Maori Wars! Before the Europeans, the Maori had a parliament, and folk were represented in that parliament according to how many of them got off the boat when they landed. Because the Europeans could relate to that . . . and because the Maori could relate to representation for folk on the island, it worked out better than in Australia.'

Tom spent an hour over that information. Repeating it all, he spoke slowly, forgot, lost his way mid-sentence, beginning sentence, end of sentence . . . Tom Irirangi was *high* . . . was high as a kite. The house smells of dope, resin seeping from the walls. A woollen hat sits on top of plumes of thick, black hair. Looking across at me steadily, the man leans a wide chin on a large hand, he talks slow. Don't get the wrong impression here, I'm not painting some layabout, Tom is a good guy. He's worked his time as a woodsman, provides for his children, lives modestly as no harm to anyone and with nothing to reproach . . . but that doesn't stop him being high-as-a-kite stoned. He is hospitable, moving slowly over to the tap, filling my bottles with a shout. 'Purest water on the island, straight out the mountain!' I nod, yet something on the table grabs me.

Beside our cups of tea, steam rising, sits a baking tray of roast potatoes, parsnips too, staring at me, me staring right back at it. 'From the garden . . .' Tom tells me, pushing it my way, and then, continuing his train of thought, he stands, moves to open the oven and there, on the centre shelf, shines a leg of pork hacked half away. He points. 'Want some?' Do I want some pork to go with my roast vegetables? He pulls out a pan of mashed swede, pale orange. A jug of gravy follows, the plate grows higher. I ate my roast dinner, listening to Tom as he talked, lost his thread, scratched his head and carried on unperturbed. Body loved Tom Irirangi dearly right then, gnawing a bone and mopping at the gravy. By the time I left he'd smoked even more, offering me the joint after I ate, his head floating higher before walking me to my bike. Tom told me I was over the worst of it, said the Parapara would flatten. He looked at my bike, gripped the frame with a large, woodsman's hand.

'I travelled all over these islands . . . with a motorbike, though.' He paused, thoughtful. 'You can't hear the birds though, not with your head in a helmet and through an engine.' He tapped his knuckle on the bicycle frame . . . 'I think you've got the right idea with this one.'

The rains stopped as the afternoon grew old. Tom Irirangi had been right, the worst of the Parapara was over and, under a pink sky, I pulled up at a house. A light was on in a garage, a man busying himself with tools. He was short, stocky, looks up as my shoes disturb the pebbled driveway. We exchange hellos, and then 'Of course you can stay in the garden . . . but you can sleep inside, if you like?'

Day 100 – Manawatu-Wanganui – 10,655 Miles

Soon after, it started happening. They'd been telling me about it all through South Island, said the North was richer, had more money, bigger cities, that it wasn't so nice. Perhaps I needed it . . .

perhaps you can't leave South Island and go straight into the United States of America. Maybe you need North Island to ease you back to the world we actually inhabit. It came at the roadside. I saw it there, signs nailed to stakes and then buried in the earth, like half-anonymous markers on a mass grave. There were signs for *'Psychic readings, holistic therapies, all major credit cards accepted'.* Or else there was an estate agent: *'Prime development opportunity, one hundred acres of unspoilt coastline'* . . . yours to spoil . . . *'Auction October 1st'.* Then there was the shop window, the sign there: *'No more than two children in the shop at the same time'* . . . they can't be trusted, not the children. I went indoors, had tea and cake in a café, and there it was on the counter, *'Toilets – Strictly for customers' use only'.* That's our world, everyone convinced that everyone else is having an easy time of it at their singular expense . . . shit in your pants for all I care, let your bladder sever, get your own toilet!

The Western world, right on schedule and absolutely terrifying. A novelty when you first arrive, when you step off the plane into aisles of chocolate and fudge, it's not so bad at first. The cheese, pastries and slabs of meat are welcome, but soon it gets to you, when you're unwrapping the second sheaf of plastic from the sausage roll . . . saturated fat, gristle and rusk without a vitamin in sight. That's when depression sets in, aisle number two, surrounded by bread in plastic, potatoes in plastic, meat in plastic. Whatever you want to eat, endless dietary variety so long as you don't mind it wrapped in plastic. The need for sustenance had brought others off the streets too. Motorised wheelchairs were parked up, humungous creatures busying themselves beside me in the supermarket aisles. They looked partly human, but with a great bubbling bulge that first led and then followed them around. To move forwards they shuffled from side to side, a loud hissing of breath in their wake and an exhausted sigh, a groan, whenever they reversed.

Facial features obscured by mounds of fat, they were genderless. All had breasts, none of them a groin, some under-evolved sea creature that swaggered from the depths, cursed by gland problems, a gland problem that inhibits exercise. In those shops more than just obesity was waiting for me, for mealtimes had also washed up a wrinkly or two, those pre-dead who would be better off staying indoors but, damn them . . . they just have to venture out for their eats. There she was, ahead in the queue, drool running off her hanging lip, down a crinkled, stubbly chin and no one around with enough courage even to speak to her, let alone wipe the slobber away. Iris opaque with cataracts, she stares out, stares flat into the developed world that has no space for her.

* * *

Upon a house I came, long after dark on the last day before Auckland, the town of Te Kuiti. The door opens to me, a man in short hair, goatee on his chin . . . 'Of course you can sleep in the garden.' Fingers count silently as I move back to my bike . . . one, two, three, four and here it comes, regular as clockwork: 'Or we could just make you up a bed in the garage? I can fetch some swabs.' I turn, guilty for anticipating the hospitality.

'That sounds amazing . . . but what are swabs?'

'Swabs are mattresses . . .' He laughs. 'Don't worry, we'll see you right.'

His wife looked after me next morning, sat me beside the baby in his high chair, just as welcome as I'd been made all over New Zealand. Four other children sat in front of the television or bowls of cereal. Poached eggs, perfectly round, were put before me atop two perfectly square slices of toast. Rain beat the windowpanes and, from out of the corner, the television speaks of worse to come, of a tsunami in Fiji.

There had been an earthquake beneath the Pacific, only small, nobody hurt, but enough for the television to take up the lead . . . do their duty. Heads on the screen were talking catastrophe, talking chaos and carnage, emergency shelters and evacuation, the threat to Auckland and *make for higher ground!* They harangue the coastguard, the Navy, the emergency committee and the mayor. The interviewing is all done by an agitated man, short, dark and not at all handsome. He doesn't let go of anything his interviewees say, doesn't let them say a thing, would rather interview himself, and then, when they utter just one word, he growls like a dog with a stick.

He's dressed in an open collar, with that perennial suntan, testosteroned . . . no tie but always that jacket. They go for the disarming look: effortless smart, bleached highlights in thinning hair, a subtle assurance that here is a man who knows the world, yet still knows style. He can dispense cheap puns and wisecracks for hours at a time, given the opportunity and he'll belittle a pharaoh. There is no one that this man with his self-titled breakfast show is not afraid to depict as stupid. In every developed nation, he runs the world . . . the modern orator, paid to sound irate about the trivial, to be incensed. A professional enrager, he represents the common man, unafraid to demand answers to the most trifling, short-term of questions. He gets the hackles of his viewers up, puts Nuremberg in your own front room, on your breakfast table. He won't rest until his airtime is over, his allotted slot at an end, whereupon he goes happily home, and there never was a tsunami.

It was still raining when I left the house. The man's wife agonised on my behalf, wringing her hands and wanting to drive me to Auckland. Once a woman has raised five children, she's happy to look after the whole world,

'The airport is almost 120 miles . . . can you do that in a day?'

All I knew was that two weeks ago I could have. 'It should be easy . . .' I sigh. 'But it probably won't be.'

* * *

The trucks grew as I neared Auckland, 18-wheelers, illuminated down each side. Rain turned rainbow, evaporated into dusk before the road turned motorway and I had attention only for traffic. As day ended, the road delivered me to the airport. I stopped the clock, took a photo . . . airport and me. Ray called from Hilderthorpe to congratulate me, to see if there was anything he could help with, his voice coming down the phone like a pat on the shoulder.

Pacific Coast

Day 104 – Pacific Northwest – 10,905 Miles

From a backstreet in Vancouver, a lank-haired woman in a leather jacket moved towards me. 'Say mister . . . you got any swabs?'

'Sorry . . . *a swab?*'

Condescending, irritated, she snaps at me. 'You got a cigarette?!'

America took time coming, my fantasy jet-lagged and slow getting up to speed. My preparations for that place had been meticulous, plans the best part of a decade in the making. From de Tocqueville to Dylan, with Kerouac in between, not since *The Mayflower* has anybody hungered so much for a landfall. My road moved south, past Seattle's coffee houses, the city on a perfect autumn morning, the air crisp, rowing crews skating across the bay, oars cutting in and out of the water. Under the monorail my shadow pedalled, beneath the Space Center upon its Needle . . . Out the other side, riding my bicycle through the addresses of Boeing and NASA, factories larger than towns, where they make contraptions to fly above the earth and into space beyond. Castle Rock and Longview came and went, places small and large, urban sprawl surrounded by the wood yards and forest that sustain the economy with lumber to be shipped to the outside world. Steady and unspectacular I rode the days, the Pacific Coast all that I wanted.

After three days I passed into Oregon, the town of Astoria and a sky turning pink to blue for evening. From the moment you reach Astoria, which appears on the map as only a small dot like all the rest of them, you sense something different about the place. It must have been the old, wooden buildings, or the newer ones made of stone and brick rather than concrete. It was the cafés with awnings, restaurants rather than diners, a theatre . . . Astoria felt like it had age to it, like a place more confident than the other small towns, a place that knew something of the world beyond. In front of the Colombian Bar I pull to a halt, the sign written in a mosaic of broken tiles, a movie theatre in the upstairs of the building, a small box-office with a silhouette reading a book in the lamplight. Outside of the Colombian, a girl sits alone at a table . . . petite, blonde hair, button-nose . . . a striped jumper, dungarees over the top of it, a cardigan with a hood . . . *a scarf* . . . my God, but if she wasn't wearing a scarf! It aches, I'd have married her there and then, so long since last I'd seen a girl in a scarf. Three months alone with just a bicycle and I'm an even bigger sucker for bohemia than usual. She sat alone with a rolled cigarette, watched the sky . . . she the final evidence for Astoria's metropolitan credentials, you don't find girls looking like that in the real backwaters, they get bored, suspect there must be somewhere with a little more life, move to Astoria. With me a stranger in Astoria, pulling to a halt outside the Colombian Bar, there really was very little for it other than to interrupt Maria from her cosmos . . . all polite and British, aristocracy shows up in Oregon.

'Sorry to bother you, you wouldn't happen to know anywhere serving food?'

She looked round, already smiling. 'Right here, they do great pizza.'

Oh really? The hammer hits, the puck slides up, the bell rings.

'My friend is the chef . . . they have a prosciutto, a margarita . . .'

She finds the pizzas on the ends of her fingers, counts them off. 'There's a vegan option too.'

'You have vegans? In a small town in Oregon?'

Maria smiles, cocks her head to one side, lets me in on the secret . . . 'Astoria is not like most small towns.'

She asks what I'm doing in Astoria with my bicycle. I give a version not quite so abridged as normal, enough to suggest I'm maybe worth talking to a little longer. I name-drop 'world-record', 'cycling in China' . . . ask what makes Astoria so different. Maria talks of the fur trade in the nineteenth century, Astoria the first settlement on the West Coast. In days gone by, Astoria, Oregon, had been mentioned in the same sentences as Los Angeles and, though the town eventually made the decision to remain small, the place still had a certain atmosphere. It attracted young people, still enticed the 'sort of Americans who want to drink espressos', that's how she put it.

Maria rolled a cigarette as I ate pizza, one watching the other. I sipped at my beer, gasped, smiled. The beer tasted so good that night, strong flavour, dark but lots of hops, like drinking down a meadow. Her eyes watched me . . . big, brown eyes, hazelnut brown . . . American eyes, perhaps a little undereducated but just bursting with hope, with vitality, eyes that wake up to see a world that makes sense to them. An American goes through all the same pains as the rest of us, but despite that it still makes sense, their eyes don't bear witness to it . . . they're at peace, hold no grudge against the world or confusion at their place in it, some sort of spiritual ease. It's religious, be it a faith in Jesus Christ or a faith in America . . . it's as if they believe that they, as humans, are magical creations and as such everything else is fine. She starts talking, an avalanche in whichever direction her mind takes her, no pause for reflection, only a stream of consciousness, biography that could not have occurred in any other country.

'Well you see I've got a southern accent because I grew up down in Florida my parents are still down there but they're divorced now. You know Florida is a strange place because down in the south it's all like Miami Beach and palm trees but up north it's all hillbilly and my father – he's a dentist – he had an affair with his secretary and so my mom divorced him. He likes it down in Florida because he loves shooting turkeys. Turkey shooting is a strange sport because you're not permitted to shoot roosting turkeys . . . there is actually a federal law against shooting a sleeping turkey. *CAN YOU BELIEVE IT?* So what a turkey hunter does, what my dad will do is go into the woods at night to find where the turkey is sleeping and then he gets up at three in the morning . . . *at 3am!* . . . he will go and wait for the turkey to wake up and when the turkey wakes up then he'll be waiting and the turkey gets shot straight away.

'My mom she's happier too. After the divorce she kinda realised she'd never been able to live her own life and my mom she's obsessed like totally obsessed with fairies. Now she's doing what she always wanted to do and she's a queen of the fairies at Disneyland which I figure is kinda cool because now she's following her dreams . . .' Maria pauses, a half-second American pause '. . . and that's what you have to do in life . . . you just follow your dreams.'

I'd stopped my jaw falling until then, but . . . '*Queen of the fairies?*'

'Yeah, queen of the fairies! You don't know the queen of the fairies? She dresses up with a big pink dress and a wand and she has her hair up, and she'll just walk through Disneyland and talk to the children about being a fairy.'

My world spins, stumbles. Mouth open . . . 'That's amazing.' I'm not lying either. 'And what are your dreams?'

No need for a pause, dreams on tip-of-tongue . . . 'Well, I really always wanted to be a folk singer so I'm just working a job in a coffee shop and having guitar lessons here in Astoria and I've joined a choir on the other side of the bridge connecting Astoria to Washington. I go to there twice a week on my bicycle and I sing. I'm not the best singer there is but I think it's important that I'm just following my dreams. I love just riding my rusty bicycle over the bridge and singing into the wind as I go.'

It was touching stuff, truly spellbinding. In response, I told Maria as much as I needed to about myself . . . the record, cycling as a really beautiful way to live, Kazakhstan the most amazing place, completely deserted. I added a little flourish with that one, something emotive, calm and slow and European . . .

'All that space, you find yourself alone in the middle of the most desolate surroundings and I suppose . . .' I searched for the words, allowed the intimacy of the moment to roll over me, a gentle wafting of the hand. 'I suppose with nothing else around, you sort of make a peace with yourself . . .' I pause, smile, look up softly, a scoundrel . . . 'It's really special.'

* * *

She'd been apologising in advance that it was humble and yet, as key turned through the lock and the door opened, the room shone with all the warmth of a home. A shopping list upon a chalkboard, postcards on the refrigerator, walls with the same black-white photography of Paris that finds its way into houses everywhere. We stood in the entrance of a large room, a living room and kitchen in one. In one corner was an armchair and a small settee, a wood burner with a flue disappearing into the upper wall, a wicker basket with blocks of wood, a newspaper and box of matches inside, pine needles and bark piling into drifts upon the floor beside it.

'Maria . . . do you think I could perhaps have a shower?'

I'm as polite as polite can be. She smiles my way, such a smile that girl had, not quite enough to have me abandon records and start a new life in Oregon, but there was real purity in that smile of hers, a good soul. She opens drawers, hands me a towel, doesn't say a word . . . just points to a door in the corner.

* * *

In clean clothes I walk from the steam of the bathroom, step out into 24-carat cliché. Maria has slipped into something more comfortable. She's let down her hair, removed her cardigan and dungarees, only a pair of loose trousers now, a thin vest over her breasts. The lights are off, only a lamp in the corner and the fire burning keen. There's one last touch, the *pièce de resistance*. A guitar. Her bare feet are raised up on the settee, guitar about her middle, Maria plucks randomly from a small range of gentle notes.

From my armchair, I watch Maria watching the fire. She speaks softly, tells me she's written a song, '*a song about life and how sad it can be*'. She plucks the guitar, a few aimless strings, starts to sing. Such a tender smile, a lovely little house, hospitality to match and a really gentle spirit. Don't mistake me, I don't mean to criticise, but Maria needed those singing lessons, the guitar practice too, possessed of the ability that comes third at the talent contest in a small village. Maria rolls from one sound to the next, words of love, life and sorrow enunciated periodically at the fireside. It was bad all right, unbearable even. I can accept our emotional differences . . . the American candid to the British reserve but, even allowing for as much, it was painful to sit there with Maria and her guitar making such a quiet racket in the name of tenderness. I watch the fire, nothing else for it. I try to look transfixed, contented, mesmerised by the moment until . . . mercifully . . . Maria puts down her weapon and we watch the fire in peace. I listen to more life stories, the moments that define her . . . hitchhiking in Oklahoma, ignoring the American-Indian chief who warned of rain. You have to let people talk, get themselves lathered up with their own voice, their personal poetry. Given the time, they talk enough that they start falling in love with themselves and mistaking it for you. Captured by their own eloquence.

With the fire abating, Maria uncurls from the settee . . . moves towards the open door of the wood burner. She stoops down . . . back to me, begins taking wood from the wicker basket to fuel the fire, turns embers, regales flames . . . her back to me, the thin fabric of the vest and the crowns of bare shoulders above it. There was the moment, if there was to be a moment that night then there it was in front of me . . . the catalyst at which a wholesome and friendly evening becomes more than just an end in itself. As she works the fire, I lean forwards in the chair . . . I reach in her direction, fingers spread into the vast air between us. I move forwards through the air, pushing through all those rejections as a stinking-poor courier in London, my hand almost sleepwalking as time ticks so slow and until my fingertips finally dock, make contact with the warm skin of Maria's back. Fingers spread outwards, palm arrives, suddenly my whole hand placed upon her, pressed there soft. Maria takes my touch as she finishes . . . she stands, turns. She's looking down at me, down into the chair that holds me. She's smiling, eyes aglow, face flush from the warmth of the flames, smiling that smile as she goes on looking warmly down my way. She puts one knee one side of my legs . . . her other knee to the other, lowers down into the chair.

The blaze inside the burner whipped up, dead leaves upon the twigs threw out scatterings of sparks, recoiled within themselves, shrivelled and then disappeared to strip the branches bare and burning. The fire glares as matter turns ether, flies up to the opening of the flue with a panting of hot air. Flames contort, licking at the open door, glowing against the night and bursting into life as knotted wood gathers, gathers heat, gathers heat and then explodes. Resin seeps from out of the blocks of conifer, oozing molten from the wood to bubble and spit. In the moving flames, time burned away, hours rising in the shadows until the fire lets out failing gasps, passes to dying embers.

Next morning I bounded down through the garden, past the tree stump with the axe lodged in it and the splinters of wood all around. I waved goodbyes to Maria, laughing at the kitchen window as I rolled out to Astoria, a smile wide across my face, the corners of my mouth reaching all the way back up the road to Vancouver and down the road before me to Tijuana. It was then . . . that was where it happened . . . that was where America began for me, the first days like a suspended animation before that moment beside the Columbia River.

For the Columbia River comes down from the Rocky Mountains on high . . . and there, right there at Astoria it sees the Pacific for the first time and its mouth, its mouth falls open, agape, dumbstruck . . . its mouth falls open and the Columbia River pours out into the Pacific Ocean. And, in the morning light, everything was glistening, glistening white, rays of the sun split open on the oils in my eyelashes, refracting until my entire vision was aglow, as if all of the world were inside a chandelier set in crystal. The Columbia River and the vast Pacific Ocean, with fishing boats at anchor, birds pulling worms from the wet sand, the studs of an old boardwalk dotted into the waters as I headed on to the Oregon coast, the world as I'd known it disappearing down inside that chandelier.

Day 108 – Highway 101 – 11,356 Miles

Everything I'd seen since arriving galvanised then, came upon me in a wave of disbelief, as if I could've started speaking in tongues. The whole of America was crawling, teeming with life . . . life gone wrong, convictions of right and wrong, everybody with their own personal struggles and myths. Riding out of Europe and into China might well have been something, but growing up in Europe and then finding yourself taking in America is a concept far harder to get your head around.

There was religion, religion everywhere. I remember riding past the churches, each one with a small billboard out front, a different slogan for different days, sermons and moods . . . '*God gave his only son to save us – isn't that awesome?*' Or else it went stricter: '*The Bible is not a menu – You do not choose only the things you like – Pornography and Homosexuality are sins.*' They were not just empty words either, people believed, they believed with fervour. The locals spent Saturday mornings waving Christian placards, working for money during the week and for God on the weekend. They were distributing leaflets outside anonymous buildings with parking spaces on the road marked 'doctor'. The placards were consistent . . . '*Abortion is murder*', '*Every child is a child of God*' . . . always easier to love a foetus than an actual human. If not religion it was politics, death penalty . . . that toilet door in Washington, a rubber flyswatter and a picture of a squashed fly upon it. In the centre ran the question, '*What do we do with flies?*', to the right the words, '*We squash 'em and we kill 'em*', and to the left, '*We don't catch 'em and release 'em*'.

Down the main street of a town I would walk, past the bar, diner, library full of books, grocer with crate of apples, pet shop with flea-collars and warmers for artificial pooches suspended in the window, past the post office, past the gun store. The gun store . . . a window with row upon row of firearms lined up, guns the size of children, handguns stacked on shelves like boxes of eggs, rifles to kill from half a mile away, guns that fire 200 bullets a minute. The posters on the walls too . . . *'There is no such thing as a bad gun, only a bad person'* . . . or else the banner above the doorway, *'The Second Amendment protects all the other amendments'*. And this was the Pacific northwest, liberal heartland of the United States. I thought of maps I'd seen, maps showing election results, the blue of Democrats down each seaboard . . . where they said trade and travel had forced internationalism, a more liberal mindset that sandwiched the Republican red of all the states between. That's what I'd heard, but it's only inside America that you discover all liberals might well be Democrats, but not all Democrats are liberals.

The one about the grocery store, that's a good one: a small hamlet in the USA, European walks into a grocery store. There's a gathering of houses and one store among the forest – *nonincorporated* – a settlement where the woman who owns the store says becoming a formal village or town just brings taxes and bureaucracy, of which the people want neither and already have too much. She owns the store, a Democrat-voting woman in the liberal heartland of the United States. She tells me that a month ago there was a break-in, in the middle of the night a local boy named Cody had got in through the front door. She'd fired a shot in the air, sprang downstairs with her handgun when she heard the glass shatter.

'He's just a child . . . ran when he heard me coming. Sad story, really. Father cleared out, left Cody and his sister. The mother kept his sister, put Cody up for adoption. Must feel awful . . .' Head shakes. 'Rejected by your own mother. Cody's gone from foster home to foster home, never had a family, always in trouble.

Now he's going to jail.' She pauses, thoughtful. 'Best place for him, really . . . a short, sharp shock in the penitentiary with some real criminals is just what he needs.'

That's when you know how European you are, when you realise all that feathery, social-democratic stuff was hardwired deep into your heritage . . . listening to a grey-haired woman who owns a grocery store telling you her views on the penal system and the importance of handguns. She sneezes mid-sentence . . . *atishoo!* 'God bless me,' she murmurs, taking out a handkerchief with daisies on it, then blows her nose in exactly the same way as a woman who did not own a lethal weapon would be expected to.

A tinkling of bells . . . Tracey walks in with a sigh, curls of peroxide hair, shorts and a pair of sandals. Her leg, that's what catches my attention. Upon her pale fleshy calf swells a blister, positively medieval, weeping and throbbing away. The thing's the size of a small melon, glows like a siren, you can't help staring at it. Tracey says her hellos, gets milk and beers from the refrigerator, walks back to the counter with that crimson mess dribbling from her leg. Cigarettes are handed over, storeowner notes the spending . . . Tracey's gonna pay when she's got some money. Tracey says goodnight, takes her blister back out the door . . . a tinkling of bells.

'*Too much government spending! Too much social security!*' That's what I'm hearing the moment Tracey's safely out of the door and earshot. European pipes up, 'But I didn't think America had social security?' Storekeeper is aghast, pantomime, as shocked as if I were little Cody breaking in through her door all over again. '*No social security? . . . Food cards!*' first line of attack. 'Oregon state issues food cards once a month, on the first of the month. In the old days you could only spend them on food, but now you can get whatever the hell you like. They get almost $100 on a card that's topped up at the start of each month, and if they spent it on good food, on bread, potatoes, vegetables, then it'd go a long way. But you see it every month, when the credit gets added to the card. They're in here buying beer and ice cream and cigarettes. By the end of the second week they're putting it on the tab and waiting for the next instalment . . .' She isn't finished yet, another lungful . . .

'Tracey, she's a good sort . . . but she's typical. See that blister on her leg? Well, she got that riding on the back of a Harley. She was riding on the back, the exhaust gets really hot, her leg touches the exhaust and now she's got that enormous blister. *A week* . . . it's been there a week, and I tell her she needs to go see a doctor because otherwise it'll get infected and she just says, *"I've got no insurance."* '

European rolls his eyes, shakes his head in dismay. A tragedy of the so-called free market, when sick people can't afford a doctor . . . a blight on the conscience of any society. But there it is again, Mars and Venus. I'm European and she's American, a Democrat even, but firing a salvo, blazing back across the counter.

'She *could* afford health insurance! You can get a basic health insurance policy for $50 a month, and that covers going to a doctor with something like that blister. They say they don't have $50 a month, but I see 'em spending it in here on cigarettes and alcohol every month . . . and in the end it's me who's got to give her $40 to get herself to a doctor.'

She made a convincing point, I'll give her that much, and so I pried, pressed that I'd heard something about the new president and a reform of the healthcare system. She rolls her eyes, shouts something about a bastard . . . *'Yes, he's reforming it!* I'll tell you what, he's doing things even the Nazis didn't do . . .'

Day 110 – Highway 101 – 11,592 Miles

I saw it all down that coast . . . As far as first impressions go, America punches you in the face. Signpost at a crossroads, small track intersects highway, two arrows pointing in different directions. *'Nursery School'*, that's on the topmost arrow . . . beneath it on the second, *'Shooting Range'*. It was a lot of things before it was subtle. Money was everywhere, on every street *'Bail Bonds – 24 hours – a fast and friendly service'*. Then there were signs promising quick money for those who had to earn it all too slowly: *'$700 cash-advance on your wages'*, *'We cash cheques – almost no commission'*. The automobile traders, signs on the forecourt . . . *'We welcome bankruptcies'*, just drive in with the pickup you can no longer afford and they'll give you a morsel of cash in return for the asset that left you eyeballed in debt. Pawnbrokers roared from every corner, *'Trucks, gold, heirlooms . . . anything of value!'* They said that, barefaced, 'anything of value' and they'd take it from you in exchange for the pittance that would keep you afloat for one more week. The entire country was painted green, billboards educating the population, offering counsel on how to spend the stack you hoped to acquire: *'Big Lifestyle? Skiing, hiking, mountain biking, friends, parties, kids, computers, jeeps . . . What you need is a BIG house!'*

That was another thing . . . *the size of it*. With a nation the scale of a continent there's no reason not to make everything proportionately huge. People twice the size they ought to be, ice creams so tall you don't need to lift the cone, you should see the cups for all that carbonated sugar they're swigging all day long . . . a standard aluminium drinks can resembles a thimble in an American hand, the receptacles they drink from are the size of gardening buckets. Then there were the pharmacies, pharmacies the size of supermarkets . . . *drug stores* . . . warehouses full of chemicals for body and mind. The actual supermarkets were the size of industrial estates, outside were shopping trolleys the size of a practicable European car, the automobiles themselves bigger than a generous European van. Down the Pacific Coast I shared that highway with a steady procession of recreational vehicles . . . RVs, American for a camper van, some of them the size of trucks, satellite dishes on the roof, press a button and a whole bedroom starts sliding out the side as simply as a drawer of clothes. That wasn't all though, that alone was not enough . . . because towed behind the RV would be a pickup truck, and in the back of the pickup truck a pair of scooters. Why, after all, would anyone travel with one combustion engine when they could take four instead?

At every moment in each coming day I found some new thing in which to become mesmerised. Ice cream in the late afternoon, Oregon's Tillamook ice cream . . . famous nationwide. That's another thing to learn, everything in the US is *famous nationwide* . . . needs an epithet by which to become worthwhile. I rode south, past the 'world's narrowest bridge', past the 'world's smallest harbour', a half-dozen *world famous* attractions. Americans stand accused of lacking internationalism, and yet the truth is they're obsessed with the outside world, always falling over themselves to locate their own curiosities in the global or intergalactic context without which a thing is substantially less worthwhile. 'World's smallest harbour' . . . without the rest of the world that harbour would've been puny, inadequate. Through the use of the outside world it became something else altogether, a champion of the small scale, nobody builds small harbours quite like the Americans.

But stop me. I know how people take this sort of thing . . . they think I'm criticising, insulting. Those Americans are so accustomed to being slandered and done down they get all defensive at the first sight of an outside observation, judgemental or not. The truth is you can learn a lot more about a nation and its characteristics as a stranger looking around, than as a citizen with everything right under your nose and entirely out of sight. Besides, I had no judgement, at least not then. On the Pacific Coast I was smitten, the United States had me besotted, out-and-out fairytaled. It was as if I'd set foot upon the centre of the universe, like I was living a dream, *the* dream.

At last and my God, so help me but it was America: twentieth-century mythologies everywhere I turned. That waitress in the diner, apron gathered like a circus big top around her breasts and a gut full of comfort eating. She flashes her nicotine smile, the powder of her made-up face and the tattoo that reads '*nobody's fool*' on an arm handing turkey sandwiches over the counter. Pretty quick I fell in love with the trains there, with all those boxcars passing full of beatniks, songs and vagabonds . . . double-decker boxcars-boxcars-boxcars went rattling by, and even as I rode one way and the train chugged the other, still it took two, three, four minutes for the thing to pass, trains a whole three miles long. On the back of those trains I saw the American economy, the budget deficit locked in freight containers that read *Hyundai, Hanjin, Yang Ming, China Shipping* . . . all moving from East to West, to countries that now sell services instead of goods. I remember it all, remember the mornings when I'd pull up outside a diner, walk on in, removing my jacket and placing it over the back of my chair as if sitting down to an office desk. Pancakes . . . I'd order pancakes with hot syrup, they dish them out, three at a time . . . scoop butter from a tub as if it were ice cream. Three scoops . . . one, two, three scoops of butter melt into each pancake as you pour on your very own jug of hot syrup, watch as it all turns golden and shines, the butter melting into tiny discs of fat. I'd eat it down, cleansing my pallet with bottomless coffee, cups the waitress keeps refilling from the jug that's spent two hours stewing in front of me. The bill settled, I'd pull my jacket back over my shoulders, tanked-up to ride 1,000 miles if calories were all that mattered, gut fit-to-burst and sugar coursing through me. Juddering . . . trembling, I stutter towards my bicycle and get on. Puffing and panting, feet turn slowly at the pedals, fingers and chin shaking, trembling, all trembling like the last leaves of summer that go on trembling from the branches. The leaves . . . *Wow! Those leaves* . . . I arrived at the beginning of autumn and the leaves gave meaning to words that had only ever sounded like pretentious artistry before: magenta, vermillion . . . suddenly magenta and vermillion had a meaning for me, because the leaves . . . they were magenta, they were vermillion, painted in tempera and just tipped with green, brushed at the top. My God, but they were beautiful, and sometimes: sometimes there was one green leaf left among the red, and it hung there, making that red all the more red, just waiting in defiance of all that aged around it.

I made my way south, unwound the seasons, the weather warming and hours of daylight lengthening even as summer slipped further from me. I moved towards the equator faster than the northern hemisphere tilted away from the sun for one more year. And yet in spite of that, my progress was so wonderfully slow. Those first two weeks in America I was on holiday, rode the most generous Pacific tailwind and still turned out the slowest fortnight of the whole six months . . . all of it lost in discussion of capital punishment and gun laws, watching the Pacific, singing aloud, full of Dylan as every state in the union went down into my soul.

Oregon. It was Oregon that really did it; it was Oregon that sank me. I rode through Oregon, through Oregon, through Oregon . . . I want to ride through Oregon every day for the rest of my life. All down that coast you climb up into the forests. Climb up. Climb up. The road tilts, hugs cliffs, hugs hillsides, runs under cover of the trees until you reach the top and begin to pick up speed . . . lots of it . . . more still, and then you're sweeping back down, and up ahead the dark of the forest gives way to the light of the sun, and you sweep out the forest so that the sun hits everything at once. And the trees, they are emeralds . . . and the Pacific, it's sapphire, and it all glows white in the sun, and the Pacific . . .

my god, but the Pacific it's such a good name for an ocean. Rocking and fluttering and sparkling, with the turning pages of books and stories and gossamer yarns, the ocean moved against white sands with their dusty trunks of driftwood, washed up and tossed to the beach, like dinosaur remains and whale skeletons, a cemetery of rib cages and tusks from creatures of another world.

I would ride down those hillsides, my head would fall to one side, my nose and the corner of my mouth would lift in enquiry, eyes glazing in search of clarification. *Really . . . are you sure?* Excuse me, but there must be some sort of mistake . . . *for this cannot be.* I died about five times a day down that Oregon coast, don't hesitate in saying it ruined the rest of my life. The air from the Pacific made me sad to think one day I'd have to breathe the air of the deserts, the air of a city, the air of any place other than that Oregon coast where I rode my bicycle. I saw infinity there, that was the problem. Right there in Oregon I glimpsed infinity. The history of the world came down to meet me, revealed all of the serene chaos that wound up beautiful. I saw it all in the palm of my hand, and with it my mind blew open, so that afterwards, once I'd pieced myself together again, so it was that I saw how small I was against it all, my blink of an eye that passes for a life. I know I probably don't seem so very old to most of you, down here and still shy of thirty . . . and yet, once you've seen infinity . . . you come to realise how soon your time is up, how quickly it all goes by. Live life like you're dying, that's what I'm getting at, my advice in all this.

Day 112 – Big Sur – 11,771 Miles

Oregon turned California . . . I headed for San Francisco, moving into redwoods, forests 100 metres high, two millennia in age and still another five centuries to go. Now and then a tree had been felled, cut half to its heart and torn apart by the toppling of its own weight. I would look at the remains of the trunk, where rings of age were too numerous to discern one from the next and had blended into solid blocks of red, orange and brown. It felt strange to me then, looking in at history, at a tree that had grown from the Roman Empire to the Berlin Wall. Round about then my six-month race against time came to feel more peculiar than ever, my haste to cycle 18,000 miles genuinely embarrassing, the redwoods offering a benevolent ridicule that went laughing softly through the needles of their leaves.

* * *

My little tyrant was starting up ... above me Brain was far from happy with the situation on the ground. Unable to hold still, immune to all pleasure, he began cultivating a profound funk at the slow progress, nagging away at Body and Soul to stop relaxing and begin picking up pace. In fairness, he had a point. Record aside, I'd been bankrupt for some time, and come California I was feeling the pinch. Already the black of my account had turned red, the bottom coming quickly into sight. Diners had to be swapped for general stores, bread and peanut butter became all too much a staple, and my dwindling finances replaced the record as my fiercest opponent.

The romance of America waned along with the excitement of a race. Around then I met with another signpost, a second that distinguished Europe so completely from the US. A trail made its way from the road, an unfortunate coincidence of two arrows on the same post: *'Juvenile Correction Facility'* and then beneath it: *'Animal Shelter'*. Fair's fair, maybe the juvenile correction facility had to be located at the end of the same trail as the animal shelter, but somehow it was just too impossibly cruel. Before setting foot in America, I was accustomed to slurs more subtle. We Europeans disparage more politely, and the world of America seemed so very black and white. That woman in her store north of Eureka . . . you know what she asked me, at 9am on a Saturday as I bought apples to see me through to breakfast? The first question: *Where are you from?* The second: *What are you doing here?* The third: *Are you optimistic about the future of mankind?* Word for word, that's what she asked . . . the sort of question that takes a European years of friendship, a life-changing event, a large meal, bottle of wine and starry firmament. In America they pop it out over the counter with your change before breakfast on a Saturday. I guffawed, came over all European, defining *optimism*, defining *mankind*, defining *future* . . . she wasn't interested in that nitpicking . . . and so I mumbled something about environmental destruction, the first thing that came to mind. She sang back, 'But prevailing winds blow soil from the Amazon to the Sahara. In seventy years the desert will be a rainforest!' Scuffling my feet, I said I wasn't sure. 'Well I saw it on the television . . . and they don't lie about things like that!'

It wasn't the naivety that got to me, it was the pretence, the lip-service and platitudes I was starting to see straight through. Where they'd first seemed so stirring, those big hearts blazed across those big sleeves, come then it had worn thin. The backs of the RVs . . . '*America the brave*' . . . land of the brave, of valour, of courage . . . all bullshit, I'd never been surrounded by so many cowards. They were chickens, pussies, with livers the colour of lilies and bellies like buttercups. The road into each town bore the sign '*In emergency – dial 911*', as if the presence of danger haunted each and every street. Three hundred million Americans, all taught to believe they were worth killing, that their life was so significant someone they'd never met wished to end it. Try telling an American they'll be killed by a falling shelf, loose electrical wiring . . .

that most accidents happen at home and each night they were shut inside with the only people who wanted them dead. Everywhere was the threat of disaster, calamity, malfeasance. They all had guns, concocted lethal injections to stop the hearts of their most evil, yet still the living went on searching for new things by which to be petrified.

'*Get your flu shots!*' . . . $25 for two . . . '*Get ready for winter*' with a course of antibiotics, '*wash your hands!*' . . . wash them again! . . . '*undercooked meat or eggs increases risk of food-borne illness*'. Those Americans were genuinely spooked by germs, invisible assassins, merciless and two million on each pinhead. Once the masses are in such a funk about bacteria, there's little hope for a calm analysis of whatever else might be going on. If people weren't afraid of the contamination, it was disease in general, the lawsuits that would take them to the cleaners. '*Disinfectant products and some ingredients used in this restaurant can increase the risk of cancer*', try that as an aperitif. It was an epidemic, everyone scared stiff, scared of strangers, of shadows . . . a state of terror at what the neighbours were capable of doing to them, what the neighbours were *going* to do to them . . . for money, for property, for pure hatred. Nobody trusted anybody. If people weren't afraid, they should've been or soon would be. Only one good man remained, or at least so said the dollar bills and the motif upon the RVs. That man was God . . . '*In God we trust*'. They sure didn't trust anybody else and, if God *had* shown up, I'm sure they'd have begun questioning his credentials for honesty, too. 'Wait outside while I fill your water bottle, you might steal something' or else 'Yes, I hold a licence for a concealed firearm . . . because otherwise you just don't know!' Or their awe at my supposed courage, 'I'd love to go travelling like you . . . but it's just not safe.'

Unfortunately none of that scepticism was enough to knock off their sentiment, a real stamina for emotive mumbo-jumbo. '*United we stand*' was one strap-line, '*One nation under God*' . . . both doing the rounds on the back of the RVs. *One nation* . . . America was one nation with '*even the blacks*' involved, Hispanics too. Then there were the criminals . . . *Criminals!* . . . People spoke of criminals as if an entirely independent breed. I saw criminals with my own eyes, periodically obliged by terms of parole to work the highways. They put road signs out, one in front, one behind, flashing lights . . . '*inmate work-gang*'. 'Inmate' was stamped on their jeans too, in case of confusion at which subsection of '*one nation*' you were looking at. Nationwide, it was no different, the Pacific northwest 'a whole other culture', Texas the *Lone Star State*, wanting as little as possible to do with the rest of the Union. '*California Republic*' were the words on the flag and Alaska a different matter entirely. I heard of billboards in the Deep South emblazoned with a Confederate flag and the words '*Never Forget*'. One nation, one fiction . . . you can't trust any national mantra, especially one so short and catchy it fits with aplomb on the rear end of a campervan.

I don't profess to understand America, but I saw what I saw, and a great muddle of inconsistency it was too. Intrigued, I interviewed everyone I met so as to get to the bottom of America. I sat down to dinner with Danty and Nita Busbee, from South Carolina – you'll meet them later – the sort of folk who help you make sense of America. I walked into the restaurant, bearded and with long hair by that point. Nita said I was their son, only 10 years younger, and invited me to their table. I picked brains, cross-examined the nation, asked how it could be that so many good and stirring sentiments could come to mean so little in the way people thought. Danty raised a hand either side of his grey hair and glasses, made fingers chatter against his thumbs, like chirping birds. He sang it in his Southern rhythm and with a knowing smile, 'Why it's just people talkin' out of both sides of their mouth.'

They paid for my meal, the first of so many generosities, and Danty gave me the number of a friend in Encinitas, near San Diego, a bicycle enthusiast. 'Erik Christensen, he'll be happy to have you stay. I'm gonna call him and say you're coming. When you get to the Atlantic coast, if you want to stay with us in South Carolina, then you'll be most welcome.'

At the end of an hour talking, Danty's parting words confirmed the sort of people I'd met. It was one sentence, a single quip that elucidated his entire personality. He wished me luck with my travels, whether or not we'd meet again. I laughed, replied with idle chatter and said, *'I'll probably need it!'* Not that I believed that myself. Among all the scaremongering, all the dread and Hollywood fear of America, Danty replied instantly and with a smile, that same sing-song way of his: *'Oh, I don't know . . . you probably won't!'*

Day 113 – Emerald Triangle – 11,843 Miles

It was in low spirits that I moved towards San Francisco, emotions fluctuating, the fire in my belly extinguishing. By then I'd no interest in beating the record, doing so was all too easy. The challenge was no longer challenging and the real reason for my ride, the protest about a better world . . . Well, the less said about that the better. Back in the UK the anticipated media frenzy was proving shy to say the least, and it seemed safe to say that my protest had fallen squarely on deaf ears. Out on the road, my record became a near-hypnotic endeavour, a kind of sleepwalking . . . half-voluntary movements on behalf of some confused urge of the subconscious. Apathy lingered, wrestling with the coming time when I would have to wake and raise my game in the name of a record I didn't care for, but was bound by my own stupidity to complete.

It was with precisely this despondence that I rode into Garberville, one of those moments when a higher power is at play, when your thoughts are read and some presence of fate acts accordingly, as if to tell you to keep on with your beliefs despite the evidences ranged against them. When you think about it, there comes a point where the act of resisting a belief in God requires an effort of faith hardly greater than religion itself.

A single street is all that Garberville is, high among the redwoods, a small turning from Highway 101 that I hope people continue to ignore and drive on by. Leave it be. Dusk was falling, the light softening before it disappeared for good, the evening warm and the lamps, one by one, fluttering on and casting spots upon that single street. I saw a café, an old coffee house, a sandwich bar, a young guy with a saxophone looping out of his mouth, hitting bum notes but playing nonetheless, one foot on the pavement and his back pushed against the wall, his other foot against the brickwork. A thin scarf was tied around his head, a suitcase beside him and over his bare chest a denim shirt with the sleeves cut off.

Marijuana floats on the air next to a theatre, a white light for its sign, 'Garberville', along the top, black letters stuck against the white light to spell the name of that evening's band. At another café, two men sit outside at a table, both leaning against the wall, one of them with his leg folded and a guitar held upright against his body, plucking chords, finding the right notes before eventually beginning to play . . . the two of them looking out onto the road and singing, sweet and gravelly:

You are my darling, the one true darling
Who makes me happy, when clouds come in
I'll never leave you, I'll always love you
No matter what hard times begin.

194

A young guy and a girl sit at a table with crumbs on their plates, open faces smiling up at me. He calls over, 'Where you going with so many bags?' I tell them what I'm doing, what I've done, sit down to join Ian and Jess, under a sign in the window that reads 'no shirt, no shoes, no service'. They laugh to hear I've cycled through China, welcome me to Garberville.

'It's a nice place, but not always so warm to outsiders. It's got a reputation, marijuana heartland. This area here is the Emerald Triangle, between the counties of Trinity, Mendocino and Humboldt. Some young kids . . . they come here and go nuts, lose all discretion . . . don't respect the way of life.'

We ate together, joined by others they'd met on the road, all of us gathered around that table. They explained Garberville, that the whole town was high, the place full of dope, fields of it among the redwood forest. The climate was perfect, local law enforcement was in on the trade, a kickback here and there and the sheriff friends with farmers who'd been growing cannabis for generations, decent citizens selling high-quality stuff to regular and refined buyers, no cheap crap to sell to kids. In the dope capital of America there were millions of bucks to be made, an honest, household business until recently. Changes were afoot, the Mexican cartels had begun to register interest in the trade, move in, had started making folk uncomfortable. If cartels were the illegal threat, the pharmaceutical corporations were their legal counterpart, with no scruples concerning how to grow and distribute quality cannabis in an ethical manner. Fertilisers and hydroponics all set to go, corporate cannabis was gearing up to profit from the legalisation of medical marijuana.

We were an interesting crowd, each with our different lives upon the road. Two were saving money to buy a car for the drive home to Washington, another had spent his airfare back to British Columbia at the summer festivals in the Nevada Desert, needed to earn it back. One more was on his way to grow medical marijuana in Colorado, had skipped town when a faulty propane burner in his growing operation blew the roof off his flat in Portland, leaving the city night to smell of smouldering marijuana. In Garberville they'd all been looking for work together, said the town would give you a chance if you showed up respectful and level-headed, if you weren't taken for some young hothead who couldn't keep his mouth shut in a bar in the evenings, and who couldn't get out of bed to work in the mornings.

It was harvest time as I rode through, buds needed trimming from the plant. Everybody spoke of rain. For days, all along that coast I'd heard a storm was coming. They said the farmers in Garberville wouldn't want the crop damaged by a storm so close to harvest. Ian smiled, spoke with certainty. 'They'll start hiring . . . The storm'll be a flop, it won't live up to the talk, but the farmers won't take the risk . . . they'll start hiring.'

* * *

That town stays with me . . . it's a special place. Though I didn't fit in with the whole Garberville thing, I was happy there for a night, happy to find it existed. The way those guys called buildings '*joints*', called people '*cats*' and southern California '*Babylon*' . . . they were all following a script, all living Kerouac, Woodstock and the sixties. Up there in Garberville they had created an artificial reality for themselves, were following a cliché, and yet, because nobody burst the bubble, because they were all in on that same constructed adventure, it had become as resilient and rational as property ladders, marriages and careers. We're conformists at heart, no one wants to make too much of a stir, and so in Garberville I gave voice to the elements of my personality that resonated with that town, kept silent the parts of my head that come from university, still live in the city of London. There's a little of Garber-ville in everybody, and up among the redwoods, in that town it's drawn from you . . . you seek to fit in, and so it fortifies itself again.

We sat swapping stories as buskers played and laughter rolled on Main Street. A guy came wandering towards us, a young girl on his arm, cocoa skin, a pair of jeans diving south of his pubis, a leash leading across his bare chest to the neck of a Siamese cat. Short white fur, pale-blue eyes . . . it peered down from where it sat upon his shoulder. The owner speaks slowly, floating, half-asleep, 'Say, you guys, what you doin'?' Ian canvasses the table for an answer, responds on our behalf, 'We're just chillin', friend . . .' The guy with the cat looks down at us . . .

'Good . . . *good* . . . because sometimes, when you got nothin' better to do, there ain't nothin' better than just chillin' . . . and sometimes, sometimes when you have got other things to be doin' . . . well . . . still there ain't nothin' better than chillin'!'

Day 114 – Mendocino – 11,916 Miles

The hills grew sharper, steeper. Forest shifting from redwood, thinner trees leaning over a narrowing road cut directly from the rockface. Rocks scuttled down sheer walls, the road winding tight through forest. It was quiet, without cars, mist burning from the sky and giving way to hot sun. Slowly he came into sight, a white beard, dirty yellow raincoat draped over the back of his bicycle, a sign on the back of his trailer: 'We need a ride'. He stood beside his bicycle, scuffing his feet into the dirt, gazing listlessly into the world, as if not quite sure of where he was.

For a cyclist who'd pulled in at the roadside with a sign say-ing, 'We need a ride', he might have been less surprised to have someone stop and ask if all was well. He mumbles, 'Yeah, it's fine . . . Everything's fine . . .' There's a dog with him, a black dog, nose buried in a box of meat held between his paws, lying down beside the bicycle. His bicycle tows a trailer, a second trailer connected to the first by a length of cable. Offering his hand, he tells me his name is Super Dave, headed for Santa Barbara. Super Dave lived in Seattle, each year rode down to Santa Barbara to see out the winter and sleep two months on the beach. As he talks, he pulls his beard. 'The journey takes about four months. First time was 2002, right after my second divorce . . . happy just living on the road now . . .' He sucks in his lips, moustache into mouth as he finishes speaking. I'd seen a few like him already, tearing down hills on buckled wheels, the homeless that travel America by bicycle, men who live only to cycle around the country. Back in Europe, touring by bicycle is a bourgeois pursuit, while in the US it's the homeless who pedal the nation with lives over their back wheel. Something of the spirit at work in America, I suppose . . . a tenacity of faith, the idea that magic awaits you on the road, that the world holds wonders just waiting to be witnessed, if only you dare go out and open yourself to them. You have to search hard for such a spirit in Europe; in America it's ubiquitous, even in the all but destitute, still they are convinced life is beautiful.

Super Dave fussed in one of the bags beneath his yellow raincoat. The coat was a mural, drawn upon in marker pen. There's a ban-the-bomb symbol, then written in big letters, 'Smile! Be Happy' . . . 'Keep the faith, Super Dave, you've got it figured out' . . . 'All who wander are not lost.' Super Dave pulls a small pipe and a lighter from the bag, crumbles resin, sparks a flame, breathes deep . . . right back, a crackling from the pipe as he closes his eyes, offers the pipe my way.

'It's legal, medical . . . I had an accident, a car crash . . . almost paralysed, still a lot of pain. I've got prescription for the cannabis.

Shouldn't need one, it's natural . . . God made it, the deer in the woods eat it.'

We exchange talk. I ask what he does for work. 'I've got money,' he responds, a point of pride. 'I've got a few thousand saved . . . it'll be enough to see me through. Sometimes I accept some coins, but only for food for the dog.'

Super Dave had humble down to an art. His face was the real draw, looking at me so steady as the story shuffled from out that slowly moving beard. What gravitas the name 'Super Dave' may have lacked was compensated for in that face, fit for a coin or a bust, the proud nose, ears drooping with age, lines of thought ploughed across his forehead and two pouches wherein those eyes were set, grey and still, blinking slowly as they watched me. There must be academics, politicians and poets who would kill to have looked like that man, captivating, etched with life and noble struggle, quiet wisdom. I've met travellers in a few corners of the world, all of them seeking to cultivate that timeless mien of knowing . . . little did they know the whole genre had been mastered and perfected by a West Coast space cadet who'd taken to calling himself 'Super Dave'.

He was a continuation of Garberville, a dropout still living in an age of stories, in a time when stories were the currency that made a person and if you didn't know how to tell your story, you were nothing. We've been liberated from all that now . . . swapped it for the freedom of 5,000 digital photos of fun, profundity and the poignant for all to see. Super Dave is from before that time. He tells you how he almost drowned, falling through an ice hole in Montana, of the friend who died beside him in the car crash in Nebraska, how Jesus saved Super Dave's life and each time, as he did, the word *testimony* was whispered in his ears. When the road turns quiet, high up in the forest of Mendocino, and that face starts telling you its story, it fills a void in this world of mine. I'll take another man's insanity over the tyranny of the normal they've got in store for us. I'd love to tell you more of Super Dave's life as I heard it then . . . really I would . . . but there simply isn't time.

Day 115 – The Russian River – 12,011 Miles

Weather shifted. A copy of the *San Francisco Chronicle* announced it: 'California prepares for biggest storm since 1973'. The landscape grew cold. Aside from the wind that seared against me, the cliffs became ever more cragged, slate-grey beneath cheerless clouds, the Pacific dashing itself against the rocks, the road plunging deep down to the bays and then climbing high back above the furore that raged along the shoreline. The shelter of the forest had disappeared, and out of the ocean there sprung a relentless noise, a wind that howled like a hungry stray, the only silence marked by rolls of thunder and pitches of lightning through the struggling light of day.

Where the forest had been, there emerged only a dusty, yellow heathland, grasses tall and thin, bowing beneath the wind and spread across the coast, swarming around the rocks and boulders . . . the dark-green thickets, grey stakes of dead trees left shooting bare from out the earth. Those trees that still lived did so in small clusters, never more than four or five and almost keeling over. Half-petrified, they grew back inland at angles of 45 degrees, cowering under the winds of the sea. The knots of their roots had been exposed, bubbling from the dry ground as the trunks above threw up their arms, endeavoured to flee from where they had been rooted.

The Russian River, that was the name of the place, signposts for Sebastopol a little inland, for Fort Ross, the southernmost settlement of the nineteenth-century Russian expeditions that went through Alaska. The Russians only stopped because the Spaniards had already taken everything to the south, back in a century when America was no more than easy pickings for established powers. There is an opening in the line of a small picket fence, oak encrusted with lichen. All around, the wood has been bleached grey by sea and age, the knots and grain turning black. A gate is missing, a gap stands in the fence, with grass trodden down to reveal footprints making their way in and out. It's a peculiar site . . . there in California. That cross with a diagonal rung below it, a long way from the Ukraine, from Russia, Moldova, out of place but unmistakably the Orthodox Church. I'd recognise it anywhere, that emblem the priests carry down streets at funerals back in Slavic lands.

Trampled earth and bent blades of grass took me into the gathering crosses, tufts of dusty grass about their bases, rocks to stop the crosses being ripped from earth by wind. Among that grey oak, rock, sky is the purple of small thistles. I stepped silently among the crosses, guiltily, a voyeur stealing the sentiment of a faith not mine, only curious to have found it in California. The crosses held no names, no dates, no inscriptions. Behind that rickety fence the graves waited, simply waited, as all time went blowing over them and out to sea. A car comes into view, pulls up beside my bicycle . . . a man steps out. He is wearing thin spectacles, white hair smartly cut, a white beard, trimmed goatee-moustache, a white collar on the neck of a black shirt. An Orthodox priest walks towards me in that cemetery on the Pacific Coast. Tentative greetings, he's suspicious, eyes me like an intruder. He slides spectacles down his nose, looks at me with blue eyes, the authority of a priest and the hard melody of Russian demands to know where I'm going.

I try to sound assured, but polite. 'To Mexico. I rode through Russia three months ago, through Kursk, Voronezh, Saratov . . .'

He nods approval. 'Saratov's a beautiful city, my wife is from Saratov . . .' He pauses. 'I had to stop, to check on you. These crosses . . .' He looks around us at the cemetery. 'There aren't many left, the Americans steal them.'

'Why would anyone do that?'

He shrugs. 'For fun . . . a joke . . . to tell their friends, hang on a wall. They love to be fools, don't think about what it means to somebody else.' A soft smile. 'I would like very much . . . to be back in Saratov.' The priest looks out on California, goes on, 'I came here during Communism, the 1960s, state atheism. As priests we had to flee, had to escape, Beria, the KGB.' He sighs painfully. 'It's a long story. I wish I could go back . . . so sick of the culture here, the consumerism, the fear . . .' he pauses.

'There is nothing here.'

Day 116 – San Francisco Bay – 12,099 Miles

Reluctantly I left, first my sleeping bag, and then my tent, started riding the same headwind of that storm I'd left the night before. For all I was worth, I rode, determined and without regard for the future. After three miles I'd decided to wait . . . to see if the future would perhaps be kind to me.

Breakfast and a diner pulled me off the road. A man and his wife, a Mexican couple, welcome me in. He takes my order as I take a table. I scribble away, writing America and how it feels . . . I try to concentrate and yet it's always there, preaching from the corner above the till, serialising images, screen reflected on white tiles, a version of the world flowing from that god in the corner. I tune in to *'Lady, step outside of the car, don't touch the ignition. We have reason to believe there is a bomb in your vehicle. It's OK, we're FBI . . .'* The Mexican couple watch, devout, the diner empty.

A couple wobble in . . . large, fat. They sit, pulling the fabric of their jeans above their knees as they lower themselves onto stools, lifting a leg over the circle of red leather, gaining enough altitude that they can let themselves drop onto the cushion beneath, the person and the cushion both collapsing with a sigh. The Mexicans continue watching the TV. A man in a helmet and padded suit hugs a little lady in a dress. The fat couple lift their heads silently, eyes straight to the god, as if right from where they'd left off. Mexicans and Americans, united under one faith, watching that visionary, watching a robot with a mechanical arm roll underneath the vehicle with the suspected bomb inside it. *Bang!* A plume of fire. Darkness. Light. '*We need power all through the day* . . . Coal covers our energy needs when we need them and not with the cost and uncertainty of nature. Modern coal power is cleaner than old, making coal a resource that is environmentally friendly, cheap and readily available. Darkness. Light. '*Do you suffer from depression? Find it hard to motivate yourself, get up in the morning, shake off the bad days?* Ask your doctor about Pristine, formulated to stimulate two chemicals that control mood within the brain.' A second voice comes in, quickly, technical, boring: '*Pristine is not guaranteed to cure depression, may induce feelings of nausea, vomiting, migraine. Stop taking Pristine in the event of suicidal feelings* . . .' The audience snap out of it, shake off the trance to talk weather, talk storm, apparently the remains of a Japanese typhoon.

'Just imagine how hard it must have hit there,' the fat lady pipes up. 'I heard from my friends in Japan this morning . . . said it was really blustery but it passed on OK. I'm just happy they're safe . . . they live in Singapore, I don't know about the rest of Japan.'

* * *

It was after dark by the time I reached it, rearing up in front of me, a shade of pale red under the night . . . lights of the city across the Bay, the wind surging over the water. I step from my bike, soles tapping with the metal of the cleat on the gangway, the hollow echo of the void beneath. I peer over the edge: rocks, churning waters. Slowly I walk down the bridge, down that landmark, one of those icons that seem to stand for more than just the matter from which it's constructed.

Walking on the Golden Gate Bridge feels for some reason more significant than walking on most other places. Cars flashed by the road, diamonds of red wire separating me from them. On the other side are the red girders of the bridge itself, huge bolts, a low balustrade . . . truly terrifyingly low. I'm not afraid of heights, but I'm petrified of possibility, my abstract fear that always envisages doing the worst and most irreparable of things. I sense the fear that no physical obstacle prevents me from jumping from the Golden Gate Bridge and into the San Francisco Bay, where they say you're travelling at 70mph by the time you hit the water, more suicides than anywhere else in the whole world, one a fortnight. The clear-headed and chemically altered, believing they can fly or hoping to do nothing but fall.

That bridge is notorious, people flock there in such gentle, cutting indictment of our society, the embarrassing problem whereby we can't build high structures without people wanting to jump off them, out of life and into death. It's a funny thing, to take a human icon as the theatre for your death, your final moments . . . as if to place value and meaning on a creation of this world, to adhere to human culture, even in the very act of declaring the world meaningless, departing from that culture. I walk the bridge, echoes of my metal cleats as I pass telephones, the telephones, always the telephones, one every 100 metres, toll-free . . . *'Need to talk to somebody?'* . . . *'The consequences of jumping from this bridge are fatal and tragic'.*

Americans don't deal well with suicide . . . it bursts their bubble, as if life wasn't magic after all.

* * *

204

I breezed through San Francisco in just six slices of pizza. Hometown of all of those poets and writers, the parties of Sal Paradise and Dean Moriarty. My San Francisco passed with just six slices of pizza, 80 minutes.

Day 119 – Salinas – 12,387 Miles

Weather cleared, the last of the typhoon blowing over, the sun warming a dusty earth that bore the twisted vines of wine country. Long lines of Mexicans queued outside agricultural warehouses, waiting to pick their weight in grapes as I rode south, out of towns and into Steinbeck country, the Salinas River a little inland, the parched earth so quiet and still, with a misty heat hanging over the road.

Away from the city the people grew patient again, less convinced the world was out to make their life difficult. It was a cook grilling a burger who summed it up, a couple of drawled mouthfuls slapped down from where he stood at 6ft-something. A woman at the counter had directed me to the kitchen to refill my water bottle. Through I went, arm outstretched in my shirt and shorts as that cook reared up above me, looking quizzically down from under bushy eyebrows and a moustache. I pre-empted his complaint, explained myself, looking up at that cliff-face of a man, explaining that I'm a customer, just filling water bottles without wanting to trouble anyone. He paused, smiled, not quite taken aback, moving his eyebrows up and down, looking at me like I'm a ladybird, something small but friendly. I can still hear his words, the rhythm in which he said them . . . 'Does there seem to be a problem here? There ain't no problem here . . . you're in the country now, boy!'

* * *

It must have been around that time I confirmed the return date for Rouen . . . 4 December, a little under two months away. I suppose I said goodbye to something then . . . it represented the end, the end of the holiday, of quality of life taking precedence over mileage. I had to start thinking about 150 miles a day rather than just 100, to start suffering more than I'd previously been prepared to. In short, it was the start of my stupidity. The bank balance was what made it possible. My eventual acceleration was not about heroism and grit so much as that I couldn't afford to take any longer about it than I did. Events conspired against me, my wallet aching as the Californian countryside became unspoilt in no time at all, grew picturesque, peaceful, the sort of place where people with money live the good life and drive up the cost of living for everybody else. You have mansions with ocean views, electric gates with signs to warn intruders, 24-hour armed response security teams. You can see the helipads from through the trees, the swimming pools being cleaned by minimum wage Mexicans.

It was lucrative there . . . houses for sale, houses for sale by *Sotheby's* and, aside from the Mexicans, not a common man in sight. They swept leaves from the driveways with broomsticks and a waiting-to-die expression, scratching that broom against the concrete for a handful of dollars an hour. Those Mexicans will be the ruin of that nation . . . the US will not be taken to the dogs by bankers, government or pharmaceutical companies, it will not be ruined by greedy corporations and environmental disasters . . . *No, siree!* It's the Mexicans who pose the real threat to the future of America. That man with his overalls, sweeping leaves from the driveway of a Californian millionaire, standing there all innocent with his broomstick, as if he hadn't done a thing.

I rode on, the fleshy leaves of ice plants covering the earth, swarms of spiders, flickering flames, the land ablaze as those leaves turned green to red for the late-summer months. The plants

scurried down to the sands of the sea, up to the rockface above . . .
tiny flames, the coast erupting into colour and at about that same
time . . . *Bang!* So a spoke exploded in my rear wheel. That was the
other thing, additional to the high cost of living, my rear wheel in
the process of failing. I haven't troubled you with the particulars,
it only became relevant around that time, but I'd already replaced
six or seven spokes in my rear wheel. The thing was badly buckled,
flapping side to side with gusto. I'd had it repaired once in Auckland, again in Oregon. Come California the spokes no longer
broke . . . they simply pulled themselves clear from the rim instead.
Nothing could be done to realign the thing, and it became a case
of how long I could postpone the need to buy a new one.

It ground me down. Mechanics and financial worriment left me
irritable, eager to find fault. '*Private Property*' became my first griev-
ance with America, '*Prohibited*' the second . . . everything forbidden
and every stretch of coast laid claim to by some millionaire convinced they owned the very earth beneath them. The signs were up
around every dwelling: '*No trespassing*', '*Prohibited*', '*Hitchhiking
prohibited*', '*Fishing prohibited*', '*Hunting prohibited*', '*Parking prohibited*', '*Sleeping in vehicles prohibited*', '*Camping prohibited*',
'*Photography prohibited*'. All that respect for private property and
litigation made you wish some poor Iraqi over in Mesopotamia had
thought to put up a sign on his house saying '*Bombing prohibited*'.
Each day I rode over the 'historic bridges' of the Pacific Coast, a
commemorative plaque set on every one. The Americans loved their
history all right . . . they loved *their* history. Cuneiform tablets over
in Mesopotamia, 5,000 years and the oldest forms of written communication . . . *Kaboom!*, they blew them up . . . or if not that then
they blew open the museum doors for the looters to take them
instead. Five thousand years wasn't history, it was irrelevant. But
that was the Middle East, another world, another matter entirely.
Over on the Pacific Coast the Americans had put markers on each

and every bridge for 1,000 miles, a concrete bridge with a concrete balustrade and a little sign embedded in it: '*Historic Bridge Forty-Seven – 1933*'. Any older and history got boring. It wasn't just me who thought that way, one day I met a road cyclist . . . thin wheels, Lycra, tinted lenses over his eyes. Together we rode, talking for 10 miles, the man far more exasperated with America than I was. I ask how he started cycling, he puffs out his cheeks. 'Well, we've got no culture out here, not a lot of history either . . . gotta do something with your time I suppose.'

There was another thing that really got my goat, left me ill-tempered at the nation I pedalled through. Come California, Mexico had become a regular topic of conversation. Everyone wanted to know if I was going there, though they didn't put it quite like that. '*You're not going to Mexico, are you?*' . . . that was the correct form in which to pose the question. I *was* going to Mexico, not in any blasé fashion, not to court trouble . . . I didn't go to Mexico looking for a story. I went to Mexico because I wanted to go there and was convinced it would be just like anywhere else. That didn't go down well, not in the US, where every ten news items concerning Mexico comprises eight killings, one kidnapping and one corrupt chief of police. Even truths can be used for dishonest ends and, after all they're shown, your average American is not inclined to believe Mexico is a place like any other. It's a parallel universe . . . lawless, the streets are on fire, dark horsemen patrol the horizon, nowhere is safe, you can't trust a soul. I can tell you the lines too, save you the trouble of ever trying to have a sensible conversation about Mexico with an American, at least not before the Ministry for Propaganda decides it's bored with the drug-war. There were four sound bites: '*Third World shithole*', '*Narco drug-state*', '*Kidnap Capital of the World*' and '*They decapitate people for fun there*'.

One man collared me outside a petrol station on the Big Sur.

He leans in. 'You're not going to Mexico, are you?' I'm chipper, 'Planning to . . .' He sucks cheeks. 'You know . . . there's a route east of San Diego, up into the Rockies, high above the desert. It's beautiful up there, a really wonderful route. You can see for miles!' And I'd be in the same mountains, high above the same desert, about 50 miles south of the road he spoke of. The man was devastated . . . those 50 miles were the crucial part. I could either be on American soil or in a Third World shithole the wrong side of an imaginary line.

* * *

I began homing in on Los Angeles, reckoned it to be three days away, three big days. After Los Angeles I would need one more big day, 125 miles to Encinitas and the friend of the Busbees . . . Erik Christensen, the bicycle enthusiast. I thought perhaps he could help me with my rear wheel, called ahead, a Southern voice on the end of the line. 'Sure, Danty told us about you. You just keep steady, we'll have a bed waiting when you get here.'

* * *

Sun at my back, my skin turned golden two days after San Francisco, as if the stamp on a passport that crosses into Southern California. I swam in the Pacific, surfers paddling out to those waves that come rolling so perfectly and consistently back to shore. Relaxed, I forgot Rouen, ignored the cost of living. Maybe that was what happened, at about that time, perhaps it was then that the US became a reality instead of a dream . . . a place in which I had good days and bad days.

There's another thing I should tell you about, the first instance of something I never expected, never looked for. I'd pulled up at a shop, an opening in the forest where a couple stood beside their car dressed in holiday clothes, sandals, sunglasses on heads. They remark on my baggage, ask where I'm going, have been. So far and this is nothing out of the ordinary, but they seem interested, ask particulars: where I slept, ate, my mileage. They smile, crack jokes, say kind things and then ask why I'm doing it. I tell them of the record, my history in a nutshell, and they wish me luck as we part. I am choosing food inside the shop when the woman comes walking back towards me. She takes my hand, lifts it to hers . . . places 20 dollars in my palm. 'God bless you,' is all she says. 'Buy yourself dinner on us.' I said I couldn't, stammered, but she pressed my hand and smiled, nodded her head.

That was the first time it happened. I never asked for it, made to refuse, yet again and again it happened. America humbled me with generosity. I don't know if it was because I was poor that it humbled me so, because I actually needed that money and their help was invaluable to me. I don't know what I did to deserve all those kindnesses, but they outweigh every criticism I voice of America. The Americans who survive the fear, the consumerism and mass-produced ignorance, those who see through the bread and circus, who keep souls and wits about them. In those people you find a humanity purer, more warm, than you could ever imagine.

Day 120 – Gold Coast – 12,422 Miles

Through San Luis Obispo, the occasional spoke bursting, I rode on to Santa Maria, only a day from Los Angeles. By then I was in supermarkets . . . no more diners, no cafés, no grocery stores even, only a supermarket was cheap enough. I bought my meals according to price and calories, as many for as little as possible. Cookie dough became an important component in my diet . . . sugar, flour, eggs and broken pieces of chocolate. I'd squeeze the tube into my mouth and feel the granules crunch between my teeth as the paste stuck to my gums. It was the start of something unpleasant, a fixation with calories. Having heard I couldn't get enough of them, I rose to the challenge and ate. And ate, and ate.

It was under floodlights outside a supermarket in Santa Maria that I met John Baum. Standing with my bicycle, his hand was outstretched and waiting to be shaken. He told me he rode a bicycle, that it was unusual to see a bike with bags in Santa Maria. There was something agitated about him, heavy sighs that punctuated his talk, frequently he would pull his fingers back through curls of fair hair as we sat beside one another on the kerb. He was of a soft nature, hesitant in his conversation, not wishing to intrude. He wore shorts made from a pair of cut jeans, trainers without socks. A calm face, pale-skinned, his forebears from northern Europe.

He was rare, a man not well at ease, a man who had slipped through the net, woken up from the American Dream to find that it caused him anguish rather than peace. You can't say that of many Americans . . . even the liberals who disagree politically with the US still find themselves culturally at ease, still find a bookshop or a pancake to buy into. Not John Baum . . . in him was no shred of patriotism, no faith whatsoever in the US and what it meant. We talked about banks and politicians, talked Goldman Sachs and the Treasury officials who had all of them worked there, the government bailout of AIG that had gone straight to the repayment of debts to Goldman Sachs. He laughed, said Americans didn't know these things. I talked about the size, the size of the shopping trolleys, of the cars; that it was all so big to a European. Baum had a loneliness inside, as if he were alone with 300 million strangers. He told me he was a carpenter, that his great-grandfather was German.

———

'Americans don't even know how to say my name, don't care . . . they always call me John *Boom*.' He snarled with laughter. 'They've no idea of the outside world.' The tone of his voice peaked. 'They're almost *proud* of it . . . *proud* to be stupid, proud of this dislike of anything that isn't America.'

I thought to soothe his train of thought, asked if he knew any German, if he'd like to live in Europe. He almost shouted it.

'*Like to?* . . . I'd *love* to be in Germany! I *hate* this country, this country ruined my life. I had an accident, a car hit me when I was cycling. I had to have two operations on my leg, didn't have insurance. I can't ever work a real job now . . . I can't ever be a fully legal citizen because I've got tens of thousands in hospital bills against my name. What kind of country does that to a person?'

He fell silent, I fell silent, unsure how to resurrect conversations with strangers who tell me their life has been ruined. People were still going in and out of the supermarket, trolleys rattling as John Baum confessed his life. He repeated it at a whisper, slowly to himself, a resigned laughter. 'This country ruined my life.'

I took him on board. We parted company shortly after that, perhaps an hour after first shaking hands we were doing so again, the two of us going separate ways but my head all full of John Baum's life. I'd comforted him, or counselled him, or listened supportively to him . . . some combination of all three. I remained upbeat, focused on the positive even as he fumed at all that was negative. I think he appreciated it, I think John Baum enjoyed talking to me, a lighter touch to his tone as we said goodbye and he told me he was happy to have met.

He stuck in my head as I rode south for Santa Barbara, the first time that I planned to ride long into the night. I gathered momentum, eyes pinned and heart rattling with the life of John Baum, a world so cruel, that demands to be hated and yet must simply be accepted as some strand of the inevitable. What does it say of us, to accept such high costs in our business-as-usual? Or perhaps that was it, perhaps they were not high costs at all, for John Baum was expendable, and all those like him too. His greatest problem was not physical, not material . . . it was a lack of faith. A perception of the world as it truly stands had put paid to the happiness of John Baum. The world could be worse, the world could be better, it would still be only the world, the only virtue of making it a better place would be that its inhabitants might have the luxury of getting similarly upset by lesser grievances. It's all relative . . . only I wish that it wasn't . . . wish there was an absolute, some meaning to cling to.

* * *

Santa Barbara is prim, turns out quaint in all the worst ways. The cyclists outside cafés do not wave back, the proprietor eyes you suspiciously, the bicycle shop will not lend their spanner. Shop windows are full of calico, bonsai trees and threads of beads, floral maternity gowns, ceramic casseroles imported all the way from France, face creams from Germany, olive oil soaps, pumice and organic detergents. Having spent so much time assembling the finer things in life, having purchased their conscience, the people of Santa Barbara are not about to waste time with niceties towards some touring cyclist looking as bedraggled as I was.

I headed for the farmers market, my American ritual each weekend. Up in Bellingham, in Arcata, Santa Barbara was the last one I troubled with. Different from the others, it had more money, less patience. I bought an apple pie, sat down with my fork and watched flowing dresses glide over wicker baskets, the best-dressed farmers I'd ever seen. River hats, leather belts around pleated, knee-length shorts, jute sandals and sling bags bulging with a hundred dollars of organic wine and sourdough bread.

Among it was one scene less full of life, conspicuous in its sober tone: a wooden bowl upon the floor, dollars and dimes, a didgeridoo upon the wrinkled mouth of an old lady producing an unresounding sound. Her thin, white hair fell down the shoulders of a long-sleeved linen shirt, her nose squashed against the ridge of the didgeridoo, eyes closed in concentration. She was sitting, one hand rested on her instrument, the other on the arm of her wheelchair, a wooden sign leaning against her knee . . . 'Help me fight Cancer'. The free market had come right down to the farmers market, the free market had sold her the wheelchair, sold her the didgeridoo . . . *my word* . . . she really wasn't so hot on that thing. Don't get me wrong, she played didgeridoo better than any other old, terminally ill woman I've ever seen, but she just couldn't cut it. A tough crowd too . . . cancer plays didgeridoo or the wild rocket quiche, your choice. But all was not lost, for you never lose hope, not in America. With the help of the free market, that old woman had the world at her disabled feet. She could buy didgeridoo lessons to improve her playing, improve takings at the farmers market, increase revenue from her donations, eventually stump up the cash to give to a giant insurance company in return for her treatment. A dozen corporate bosses would take a fair share of the profits for themselves, use them to pay Mexicans two bucks an hour to cut back the rose bushes with their teeth, scrub the pool with fingernails and, soon enough, everyone would be better off, thanks to trickle-down economics. One day they'll rename it dripdown, avoid people getting their hopes up.

Day 121 – The Armpit – 12,501 Miles

It was only going to get worse after that, Los Angeles my goal for the day's end, that city so famous for its soulless wealth. I moved out of Santa Barbara into Ventura, to Oxnard, through harbours of yachts, a naval base, fields of agriculture, pipes spraying plumes of water in wide arcs, a metal board rising up and down to collide with the shoot of water and disperse it in droplets carried on the wind. I hauled my bicycle onwards, rear wheel slapping away, steadily worsening and *Bang!* . . . another spoke.

Los Angeles came at dusk, the traffic soared. Saturday night along Malibu Beach with children fishing on the sand, sun going down over the sea, cars stopped all along the roadside. Drivers parked up, long bonnets buffed to a shine, the sunset splayed and reflected in the metalwork of American sports cars, their proud owners holding them under one arm, a girl under the other . . . happy families. That's where John Baum had gone wrong in life, he should never have got on that bicycle, should have bought himself a sports car and leather jacket instead.

* * *

The sun was already warming when I rose next day, pulled my head from my sleeping bag to reveal Hermosa Beach, about half-way through the hundred-mile sprawl of Los Angeles. Around me, lifeguards were performing stretches in red swimwear, standing at their huts as people put up nets on volleyball courts, paddled in the shallows, the dorsal fins of dolphins cutting among the waves, oil rigs large along the shoreline.

I climbed up onto roads above the beach, around the perimeter of cliffs, into a stretch of suburbia. At a petrol station I bought food for myself, came out to find a man looking at my bicycle. He was tall, substantial, broad shoulders and a stone face, pale with tinted lenses over his eyes, a tiny baseball cap keeping the sun from his head. He was squeezed into a Lycra jersey and a pair of shorts, a small road bicycle beside him . . . the sort of guy who owns just one bike but loves it dearly. Down-to-earth, a pure spirit without any great cycling ambition beyond the happiness it brings. Doug Schultz was a teacher in Los Angeles, had moved from Minnesota for the sunshine. Tired of cold and snow his whole life long, he'd been in Los Angeles for 10 years past, lived there with his wife and child, riding home to them for breakfast.

'I always wanted to ride across the country, probably won't find time now . . . I'm at that point where you stop living for yourself, start living for other people.'

We rode together. Doug pointed off ahead . . . 'You should head towards the port, towards the Armpit, follow your nose.'

'Why's it called the Armpit?'

'Because it stinks, the armpit of LA . . . The other side of the Beverly Hills story, really industrial, oil refineries, fumes in the sky.' He wafted, pulled a face. 'Smells awful.'

Doug rode on my rear wheel, remarked how big the buckle was, that the thing looked ready to break. He said it then, the first time he said it, 10 minutes after our meeting. '*Think I got something at my place that could fix that wheel, wouldn't mind a photo with you too . . .*' Gratefully I declined, said I simply didn't have the time. That much was true, but with the metal of my wheel splitting, the rim fracturing, I knew he was wrong, that nothing he had could fix the thing.

We rounded cliff tops crumbling steadily into the sea, the coast eroding and the land strapped back together with wire nets. Doug pointed to water pipes running above the surface of the soil so as not to be torn away in the landslides, talked about the contaminated water that he would never let his family drink. Golf courses came thick and fast, full green among the orange earth, just one or two players out walking them. Doug said he didn't care for golf, and I remember the way in which he presented his thoughts as neither right nor wrong, but only his thoughts, and irrefutable as such. Riding past another course, he said simply that it seemed a waste, that they would use so much water for so few people to actually go out and play golf anyway. He was so gentle in his sense of justice, the sort of arguments that can never be defeated because they are so humbly expressed. For a while we rode silently, and then he said it again . . .

'Pretty sure I've got something at my house that could fix that wheel . . . and I'd sure like a photo with you for the memory, my house isn't so far.'

* * *

A modest block of tenements, the smell of the Armpit and the cranes of the port just down the hill. We stop beneath a row of identical-looking houses, a stretch of concrete for a shared garden, doors painted sallow green, white paint flaking from boards below a kitchen window. Doug disappears inside, returns with a plastic bag, explains its contents. He towers over me with a softly booming voice, like he's nervous, self-conscious. Large hands going in and out of the plastic bag as we hold a handle each. 'Here's a banana, and an apple . . . Couple of cereal bars, like I have for breakfast . . .' He fades.

Taking the bag, I thank him. Doug lifts his camera from around his neck. There we are: me, me and my bicycle, bicycle and me, bicycle on its own, and then me and Doug, Doug with a little smile on his thin lips. He lowers the camera . . . 'got something here that should see to that wheel, too' . . . he's standing beside me, moves to his pocket, me clueless as to what tool in all the world could even plausibly fix my wheel. His hand withdraws from the pocket and I see it . . . a flash of green presidents, a wrap, coming towards my pocket. My eyes open, open wide. I move away, land a hand on his as he pushes it into my pocket. My eyes horrified, shaking my head, moving my hand into the pocket after the wrap. 'Don't look at it, *don't look at it!*' . . . Doug almost raises his voice, asserts himself, grabs my wrist to hold hand inside pocket. My fingers feel the paper, the girth of the bundle. 'Don't look at it,' he says a final time, more softly, shaking his head with a smile. I choke, I swallow . . . I don't know what to do. 'Thank you' comes out, those two words never so inadequate. Doug changes the subject, back to the port of LA, the directions to take. In a daze I listen, humbled to the point of sadness and nothing I can say. I pack the food into a pannier, we shake hands. I roll away down the hill, waving goodbye over my shoulder. Doug's standing there, large beside his small bike, just as I'd first found him.

I felt it there, could feel it as I rode into the Armpit, that enormous Armpit that stretches for some 20 miles of sparse service road with the occasional truck booming along them. I didn't look at it, did as Doug had said . . . I didn't want to look at it, didn't want that kindness to change from its essence into only banknotes. After an hour I stopped at a kerbside, the stench of oil on the air, flaring gas, smoke stacks, telegraph poles and towers for catalytic cracking all poking into the sky behind corrugated iron and chain-link fences. In the shadow of freight containers, cranes and cargo ships I sat on the kerbside, a deserted road, silent. Surrounded by engineering and industry I pulled the wrap from my pocket, unravelled it . . . and Doug Schultz had given me 100 dollars. I thought of how early he had said it, that within 10 minutes of our meeting he had told me he had something that could fix my wheel, so quickly he had decided to give me 100 dollars to help pay for a new one. Doug Schultz, a teacher who said he'd reached the time where life becomes about living for other people . . . a wife and a daughter and him, living in that modest tenement beside the port of LA with the stench of oil. It's him more than anybody else, more than anybody else I ever encountered, it's the thought of Doug Schultz that makes me believe life has to be about making the world a better place, however unnatural that ideal might be. He didn't ask anything in return for those hundred bucks, but I feel that to become passive, to accept all that is wrong without resistance, however futile that effort might prove, would be a betrayal of his kindness, of all those kindnesses.

Day 122 – Encinitas – 12,649 Miles

Together we sat in the back garden, Erik Christensen and I talking bikes, Catherine resting hands on his shoulders. 'Beautiful night,' she says with a sigh, a sigh that becomes a pause before Erik replies simply . . . 'Isn't it?'

He loved cycling – really loved cycling – in the European sense, said he still shaved his legs as a badge of loyalty to the sport. He listened as I explained the peace I found in cycling, the nobility of patience, of suffering, those duels with your mind. Erik nodded knowingly as Catherine smiled. A short woman, pink cardigan tight around her, disconcerted, she laughed. 'That's how Erik talks . . . I'm not sure I understand suffering as a positive idea.'

They put a plate of food in front of me . . . rice, spare ribs. Politely I set about cutting the meat from the rib using a knife and fork. Erik watched for a minute, then two, as I struggled between the bone and the meat. He smiled, threw a napkin at me, 'I can't watch this any longer, *please* use your hands . . . ribs are finger food!'

From that moment, I felt comfortable in the company of Erik Christensen. He'd owned a bike shop in San Diego, 10 years before going bust. He told me of the club rides setting out on a Sunday morning, spoke of baking brownies that the young riders would come and devour once they'd finished their rides after school. 'That's what it was about, really . . . the community, the spirit of it all.' We discussed my wheel, looking across at it, destroyed through and through. As I ate my food, Erik disappeared to his attic, returned with a rim held like a halo above his head, grinning.

'Well, would you look at that! A *Mavic Open Pro*, brand new from 1992 . . . the year the shop folded. How about you take the day off and rest here tomorrow? We'll build the wheel when I'm home from work.'

* * *

Next day I looked at maps, planned my route to the East Coast and how to find as many miles as possible in doing so, move closer to my 18,000. That day I resolved to ride hell-for-leather across America, to scream to the Atlantic, ruin myself on the way but recover with a rest day in Edisto, another in New York, then an easy return through Europe. It all seemed so easy that day . . . looking at those maps.

Encinitas was another of those episodes, a short story in its own right, still more people and still more generosities that, come my return to Rouen, had grown too numous to recount them all with the detail they deserve. Erik and I rebuilt my rear wheel, discussing government and gun laws as we laced each spoke into its eyelet, myself a self-confessed liberal, Erik an arch conservative with the purest of hearts.

We were still talking as we rode south the following morning, discovering we had common sense in common, that thing so easily lost once thoughts are manhandled into wings of left and right. Preparing to part, we cleared a hill some 10 miles from home and *Bang!* Not another? A spoke in my front wheel bursts right in front of me. Erik sent me home, and that evening we rebuilt the front wheel as we had the rear.

On our final evening together, I sit with Erik and Catherine at their garden table. Darkness had already fallen for the day, small lanterns lit, casting soft shadows around us. Erik straightens a moment, looks up from a book, as if realising a profound thought that has only just occurred to him. He pauses, elbows on table . . . a concerned expression on his face. 'You're not going to Mexico, are you?' Looking back at him, I nod. Erik puts down the book, lets it hit the table. He shakes his head. 'They roll heads across the dancefloor there . . . just to let you know who's boss.'

Along the Bottom

Day 125 – Tijuana – 12,703 Miles

The border came at midday, queuing traffic and soldiers with guns three-quarters their own height. 'Where you going? Why you here? Proceed!' I walked through the domed tunnel, out into Mexico, into the *'Third World shithole'* and *'Kidnap Capital of the World'*. I won't deny what it was I saw across that border. Right after the armed soldiers, in an underpass beneath the road, was a parked-up motorcade of police motorbikes, 20 of them down to the left. Down to the right were pickup trucks, a dozen police trucks parked orderly . . . I can't dispute that the Mexicans were doing their bit in making a to-do about the whole 'war on drugs' business, putting up a show of force to stop the line of cocaine on its way north to the nostrils of Los Angeles and San Francisco. We criminalise the poor society supplying cocaine, then indulge the rich who buy it. That inviolable American faith in the free market: demand will create supply, the market finds ways to provide if only there is profit to be made. Somehow the Americans had excluded the drugs trade from that logic, no one had told them loud enough that you cannot wage a successful war on people making money, whether it's to get rich or simply get by . . . you'll always be out-numbered, there will be too many martyrs.

Even though I had ventured into Mexico, I still wasn't inter-ested in an evening in Tijuana. Tijuana is a destination for reputable

US citizens under the drinking age of 21. They cross the border to inebriate themselves with alcohol, temporary population exchanges with disreputable Mexicans of all ages, crossing the border to find honest work. I headed for the desert, the mountains, a wind from the ocean blowing me inland and up the hills. I bought water again, some supplies of food, the first time since Gansu that I strapped a gallon to the back of my bike before riding into the desert. Everything becomes rudimentary again, life returns, little choice but only a simple thought for carbohydrates, fat and a little taste. Once the gluttony and excess of our standard lives recedes from habit and into memory, come that time you realise it offered very little worth missing anyway.

I slept in a small clearing, the mountains outside La Rumorosa framing the skyline with crenellations, white lights from the town far below . . . chimneys smoke, the occasional shout of excitement, a complete soundtrack to an ordinary life. All that scaremongering, those fearsmiths and doom harbingers back the other side of the border, they'd got to me. That night I took pains to scramble from the road unseen. I climbed behind boulders, a small patch of soil among the stone. Dusk had come and gone, the sky orange and dark blue, with cirrus rising from the bowl of the mountains up into the turning vapours of a slowly simmering cauldron. I watched the final silhouettes of the desert grasses, barbs that wound above me . . . dusty flowers with their seedpods burst open and leaning over me like stars. The night gathered, a silence came, the most complete silence I'd felt for some time . . . a place without sound, with no one around to make any.

* * *

Early morning. I need 150 miles and to outrun the day's heat. Through orange rock on blue sky, walls of mountain shutter me in . . . both sides . . . I can't see out. Boulders, rounded rocks bubble downwards, like stampeding cattle, hides and haunches bucking through car wrecks towards the bottom. As I climb up, a sign in English and Spanish: 'Check your brakes'. I finish reading. The road slopes down, a wall of rock looms, road sweeps in front of it, points left. I lean a little into the turn, veer out from under rock, under shadow . . . and there it is.

You can't read it down here on the ground. I can barely bring myself to write it . . . but up there it makes sense. I tore down, speed falling over me, the road stitching through the rock, leaning this way and that as it swept around and around, sinking down the banks of that heart-shaped mountain above the desert, rocks and sands the colour of bliss. I was so high above it all, and without a cloud in the sky I could see the entire surface of the earth, every hill, rockface and contour as if only a small wrinkle on an old face. I'd no idea I'd climbed so high, no idea the desert under me was so vast. I'd never known a horizon so distant, a landscape so empty.

There was nothing out there, nothing but the morning sun rising up and letting down its heat against the face of the earth. A set of curtains falls open, and some strange creature goes screaming with delight as he cascades down a mountainside somewhere to the east of the San Andreas fault. The mountain undressed me, tore the clothes from me, pulled my shirt over my shoulders and tugged at its buttons. My legs turned jelly, eyes gaped and then streamed, pelvic floor twitches and then the mountain returns to me wits enough to brake as late and as light as I dared. Into the next turning I flash, calm chaos as heart tries to breathe and lungs beat, the bicycle diving between turns too sharp and the rockface opposite calling loud to me. My heart . . . jumps out of my mouth . . . cushions impact, a violent lurch of life affirmed, a surge of fear that reminds you so simply that you're alive, so magnificently alive and terrifyingly in love.

I rode 30 miles without need to turn a pedal. Imagine it, not just the number . . . imagine 30 miles and think of doing nothing throughout it, nothing but shredding through the clear, empty air of a mountainside, the Sonora Desert and all the rest of the planet beneath, as if you were possessed of a power and a spirit greater than that of just a clumsy human with his upright gait and regimented marching between the places in which we waste our lives. I'm at peace, at play, flying for almost 60 minutes of that thing called time, scaring myself into faster and faster for the next plunge of mountainside. I can't give you these things as they happened, sitting sedentary as I write . . . it's not compatible with what comes from 30 miles back to sea level, back into the desert itself, where a man waits with a hand-drawn sign and a box of burritos. He welcomes you back to the world of humans, back to the desert. Above you waits the mountain, innocence streaming down it and there once again . . . right there on the road, is all you ever wanted.

He stood beside a deckchair, a tabletop of burritos and a keg with a carpet over it for shade. His hat was back-to-front, his skin dark, the shade of a man working in a desert. He had his shirt tucked tight into his jeans, a shined buckle on his belt, a calm face, the same sort of nonchalant, slowly changing expressions that exist with less pigment in the rural parts of the US. I bought the last of his burritos, began to eat as he handed me a plastic cup of some cold, red drink, hibiscus floating in the bottom.

'Put sugar in it.' He points into the cup. *'Aguas frescas* . . . Mexican cola.'

I sip at it, ask about life in Mexico. He pushes his hands deep into the pockets of his jeans, palms facing outwards, shoulders shrugging.

'The temperature is good today, it is cool at this time of year. Three months earlier and it was almost 50 degrees in this desert.'

He doesn't get it . . . doesn't understand that I'm a greedy foreigner on a quest for political gossip and talk of hardship, I can chat about weather back home.

I dangle a line. 'Mexico seems calm . . . compared to what they say in the US.'

He laughs a little, like I'm predictable.

'Ciudad Juarez,' I dig, asking him about that city some 500 miles east, at the El Paso border. Back in the US they called Juarez a warzone, the worst place in all Mexico. I press . . . 'Does the country get worse near to Juarez? Does it get dangerous?'

He smiles, shrugs, squats down with forearms resting on knees. He turns his palms outwards, framing the picture between his hands. 'Americans talk a lot about war . . . do you see any war here?'

Day 126 – Sonoyta – 12,849 Miles

Soon after it came, reared up on my left. I'd heard about it, one of those projects that has to be seen to be believed. The Fence. Standing tall all through the desert, five metres high, it forms a 2,000-mile monument to human stupidity . . . an installation, man's finest work of concept art and satire. Across Sonora it spreads . . . rust-red sheets of metal, grey folds of corrugated iron, evenly spaced pillars of concrete, a metal grille, whatever the Americans could find in quantities large enough to make a fence through 2,000 miles of border. It's stark, an affront to the landscape, the road dead-straight and narrow, raised a little from the desert floor, the paint of its markings fading, asphalt at its edges sinking back to the sands.

About 10 metres to the north of the road is a small picket, white stakes rooted to the ground, barbed wire running parallel to the big one, standing so surreal, so absurd and incongruous with the

vast indifference of a desert. Berlin, Palestine, privet hedges in suburbia . . . nothing captures human idiocy quite so perfectly as a
good fence. In the summer months, the border patrol hang pouches
of water on bushes and thickets for those attempting to cross.
Some people thought the parched corpses showing up in the desert
a sort of burden on the national conscience. Others disagreed,
thought it a fair warning. Still more go further, take to the hills
with their rifles . . . shoot the immigrants using known crossing
points. They don't report them to the border patrol, they want
them dead, rather than deported and primed for a second attempt.
Patrol jeeps drive the far side of the fence, tyres towed behind,
attached to the tow-bar by lengths of chain. The tyres scuff and
bump through the sands, a plume of dust following the jeep,
sweeping away old tracks to leave a smooth surface on which to
spot new footprints.

Eventually I reached the point at which that American fence
was patched against the beginnings of a mountain range, sheets of
iron meeting with grey rock, crags of cold stone that shut out the
horizon and all that lay beyond. In all of the world, no sight looked
so ridiculous as that tiny human fence patched against a rockface . . . that poor fence must have felt inadequate, sitting beneath
a mountain like that.

Night came, sunset the same bargain of blood orange and navy
blue, a crescent of moon sliding upwards. I rode late for my 150
miles. The road stretched perfectly straight into the distance, so
that I could see headlights from far away, small lamps that grew
bigger and then gushed past me on that narrow road raised up
through the sands. In the *Kidnap Capital of the World*, a Westerner
with a red flashing light on his bicycle rode safely into the night,
through a desert without anyone around to hear him scream, and
without any sign of the law. After not too long . . . you find that
Mexico is only a place like all the rest of them.

Day 127 – Organ Pipe – 13,016 Miles

Arizona, Lukeville ... I cross back across the border, the line through a desert. The guards made me unpack all my bags, put the dog's nose in my sleeping bag, made the poor mutt sniff socks. Mexicans were waiting, a dejected line outside with their cars, or sitting on chairs in a waiting room. Lots of waiting ... waiting for X-rays, for searches, for lawyers. The guard stood in military uniform, po-faced, another of those men and women told they would be protecting the nation's frontiers and who never quite got over it. A slug of a moustache crawled along his lip, hairy hands planted on round hips, his feet parted, planted firm with all the weight of his authority. Short on humour, he was short on anything humane about him, no interest in people that extends beyond the need for another person to talk down to and feel power over.

'Where are you going?'

'Boston.' Straight and honest answers, not a peep out of me.

'Where have you been in Mexico?'

'Nowhere, just Tijuana and the desert.'

'Got any drugs?'

'No, I have no drugs.'

'Why not? Why don't you have any drugs?' he said with a laugh, adding, 'You don't have any marijuana with you?'

'No.'

'*Why not?*'

'Because I don't like marijuana.'

'You don't like marijuana ... you like cocaine?'

I suppose I lost my maturity ... scoffed at him, 'Not on Tuesdays.'

He smiled, did the one thing he wanted to do ... made things difficult, pressed a button on his radio. He liked that radio all right, cradled it lovingly beneath his chin as if it were a violin. He grinned a slow, contented smile as he spoke into it, 'Can I have someone for a full bag search . . . he's been to Tijuana, says he likes cocaine.'

* * *

The town of Why is the first across the border, nothing more than a junction with a petrol station, a store with a bench outside. There, I went into the store to buy bread, some cheese and tomatoes. The bread is white, bleached white and with a rubbery crust, the cheese primary colour yellow, as if painted in acrylic before being wrapped in plastic sheets. I can't see any tomatoes, find an assistant . . . 'Excuse me, do you have any tomatoes?' Her response stays with me . . . stark, joyless. She drops the words, 'We don't do fresh stuff.'

I ride back out, into the land of the free.

Day 128 – I-10 – 13,137 Miles

Interstate 10, the fourth longest in the US at 2,500 miles, stretches out across the width of America, from Santa Monica, Los Angeles to Jacksonville, Florida. American law allows a cyclist to ride the Interstates if there is no alternative road available. In the deserts there are rarely such alternatives . . . why would anyone build roads when there's nothing in a place apart from the need to travel through it? I was with Interstate 10 intermittently on my way to the Atlantic. That road became an emblem of my ride between the coasts, and I would leave and return to it with the same sort of fidelity the Danube River demands back in Europe.

I rode in and out of Tucson, stopped at a supermarket six months before someone failed in his attempt to shoot-dead Senator

Gabrielle Giffords in the same spot. Out to the boneyard the road led, five square miles of fighter jets and bombers, dumped in the desert to slow the rusting in trillions of dollars of military hardware. I turned out one-fifty, one-fifty . . . 150-mile days, three in succession, enacted a dull efficiency of regimented stops and robotic riding.

The nights reminded me again of those in Asia . . . and once more I played old games, watching the sky for a shooting star before trying to sleep. For a while I lay there peacefully, the Interstate quietening, sky motionless apart from a slight trembling of the stars. Peace would find me out beneath my thicket, or I found peace already waiting there, one of those resting places where I ceased to exist within the world, entirely unbeknownst to any who came passing. The sky remains still. For five minutes or more it is resolutely motionless, refusing to entertain me . . . and then it comes. Somewhere over to the right, the corner of my eye, closer to the horizon, screaming above a rockface. An enormous ball of rock flies through the air, burning into a thousand tiny pieces on its way to destruction in our atmosphere. To think such a thing could ever have looked so calming.

Day 129 – Sierras – 13,280 Miles

Dawn . . . half-asleep, that time when it gets to be so quiet, before the sun rises and all those faraway cities begin to wake with the decibels that winds carry across the earth. Moments like that and it's as if you can hear everything. I lie, listening, listening as the grains of sand scratch over the hard rockface, as rodents and scorpions clamber and scuttle after the sand, over the same rockface, tiny claws scraping and tapping as they go. Above, the birds croak and caw their grievances with the world, and some desolate town puts out a heavy bell, ringing from a church constructed by Spaniards a century before anything else had been built in the United States.

The night, it lines up, the day lines up . . . just as they have done since time began, the morning ritual to which both know the outcome. Every day they face one another, steady, and then turn on their heels, backs meeting. Forever opposed, they begin to step, take paces, the sun reverential and solemn in anticipated glory, night exhausted by repetition and knowing. They step, footfalls echo in the silence, and all goes steady . . . waits . . . until 10 paces are taken and stillness settles. For just a moment it hangs in the air, suspended, and then there comes a piercing crack, a howl . . . and then it arrives, all grand and glowing. Night slumps down, its final laces of blue fall from the topmost shelves of the sky, and the poor loser bleeds downwards. Throughout the dawn he bleeds such crimson red, melting over the black wisps of cloud, rockface crags, melting in such stark reds that all turns black against it. And there it is . . . the world cast in red and black, brimming from the desert. For a few moments the drama persists, and if you happen to be awake, you are immediately transfixed, mesmerised until . . . slowly, it emerges that the night has merely passed just one more time. The light moves from red to pink, the rocks from black to blue. Once those church bells have sounded just one more quarter-hour then it is over . . . the night is dead, the sun risen.

* * *

Desert towns moved by, rumbling roads cracked from heat, telegraph poles the highest things on every street, and rings of rocks around the foot of each one to stop the wind blowing away the earth in which they stood. I crossed over the railroad tracks, came upon houses spaced far and wide, as if the neighbours couldn't stand one another, or simply wished to make use of as much desert as they could lay their hands on. Small boxes of prefabricated house, a chain-link fence covering an area of short, yellow scrub 10 times the area of the house. In the garden, a rope length is tied around the neck of a muscular dog, head resting on the cusp of a water bowl. Net curtains hung forlornly in every dusty window, concealing the darkness where they had not been devoured by moths. A diner beckons me inside.

Full-pelt air-conditioning, a walk-in refrigerator among the desert. Breakfast brings with it the standard scenery . . . the same, heavy menu options of fat and sugar for a comfort-eating nation. All around me the usual confectionery is available and waiting for purchase. That day, however, leaning at the rail of the counter was one sight more peculiar than most. It came to me at once, a sight too stupefying to be conceived of. His back and elbows leaned upon the bar, legs crossed over one another in a pair of jeans, boots up to his shins, spurs on the back of the boots. On his head were a cowboy hat and a bowl of grey hair, a face that looked not to have smiled since the success of the Civil Rights movement, and there on his hip the leather holster of his gun. That gun was the crowning glory. Growing up all feather-wristed and European, a cannon on the hip at breakfast time can strike you as a bit excessive. I gaped at the butt of it, so long and wide, white ivory with some brass star emblazoned on it, a golden hammer and the golden curl of a trigger appearing from the shadow of the holster. The butt of that gun must have sat at the foot of his ribs, disappearing down into his holster, with the barrel, long and thin, protruding out the other side and covering half the distance to his knee. End to end, that gun must have been more than a foot in length . . . and he just stands there, leaning on the bar with a mug of coffee, not yet 10am on a Sunday, nonchalant as you like, a weapon of murder on his hip as I order pancakes and syrup. Finishing his coffee, he walks back out into the dust. I watch him go . . . thinking of Arizona, all desert and rock, a man who eats breakfast with a cannon on his hip, more than 2,000 miles from the seat of his government in Washington, DC.

The state line comes with '*New Mexico. The Land of Enchantment*', my wheel running flat for the second time that morning. But for all the cactus-spine punctures I could well have fallen in love with the space of New Mexico. Interstate 10 cutting through Big Country with the goods trucks, 18-wheelers rushing two-abreast down the road, stickers on their rear end, advertising job vacancies . . . '*Drive for us: 1-cent per mile*'. I never understood whether that was a homage to the size of the US or the poor pay of its truckers. Alongside the Interstate ran the train tracks, every so often with one of those three-mile, double-decker goods trains ploughing forwards. Freight containers stacked double-decker, coal trucks, oil tankers, all under the cirrus strafed high above. The horizon was hemmed in on each side by the sierras, walls of rock, road signs warning against sudden dust storms as the wind whipped through.

My rear wheel was thumping on the floor by the time I made it to town, one thump per rotation, wheel protesting the state of affairs into which it was being led. I pulled from the Interstate, stopped at the first truck stop. Bowie, San Simon, Lordsburg . . . those towns are non-entities, built in opposition to the desert. One day the desert will get its way, push out what little life has made its way there. During the Second World War, they used Lordsburg to lock up 3,000 Japanese-Americans . . . unsure where their loyalties might lie when the fighting began. That's the sort of thing a town like Lordsburg is good for, where it really comes into its own. Food and water is brought there from faraway places where humans were intended to live. Humans were not supposed to be in Lordsburg . . . the town exists because drivers have flat tyres on the

Interstate, a couple of shops and motels feed and house them while they await repairs. A church and a library nurture 10 mechanics and their families, one-third of them below the poverty line and receiving monthly food parcels to augment their wages. Food parcels in twenty-first century USA, the richest country on earth.

The truck stop is a small cabin in the centre of huge slabs of concrete, like an airport runway with rigs parked up or pulling out. I walk into the cabin, empty chairs around a desk, a calculator with a reel spewing from it. Behind the desk waits a face, still and silent, not yet old but ageing rapidly. His hair fades grey before me, a matt face waits, two-dimensional, eyes that didn't wish to open each morning and found slim cause to do so before closing again each night. 'Excuse me, could I pump up my tyres, please?' He's put out at even my voice. 'What? Air up your tyres?' He points past me . . . 'Ask those guys . . .' I spare him my linguistic observations, how interesting I found the American habit of using nouns as verbs.

They were scuttling around the deck, a pair of ponytails and baseball caps, broad forearms with tattoos in faded ink, passing hoses underneath a truck, the driver wiping food from his gums with a finger, leaning against a wheel while the men worked around him. The hissing of the airline came on and off, a heavy hammering as a switch was flicked and the pump restarted. The truck stop sat beside train tracks, a junction of rails blending together and switching directions, lines of grey tankers waiting for an engine and stretching out of sight, dormant boxcars, doors rolled open and the pink graffiti of a faraway city tagged along their flanks. A truck pulls in beside me, the driver climbing down, wiping his brow with his sleeve. He disappears under the trailer's chassis, crouches . . . unfastens chains, chains, chains clinking and then thrashing over one another rapidly as he moves away. It crashes, slumps down, black and tattered . . . run ragged, frays of rubber and wire shooting from its limp body like some beast shot dead. The driver heaves it out, half the size of a man, wire twisting into knots, one of those planks of tyre I sometimes hit when riding at night.

I ride back to the desert, sense my tyre getting softer. Out in the quiet, in the middle of nowhere, the voice of the Lordsburg mechanic keeps haunting me. 'You be careful . . . the state motto is "Land of Enchantment" but we call it "Land of Entrapment".' He chuckled through missing teeth. ''Cos once you're here, you never get out.' The tyre splays, the valve hits asphalt, hits asphalt, hits asphalt.

The Kazakh pump is drawn from its bag, called to give service. As I pump, the barrel gets hot, hotter . . . thin wisps of smoke go lifting into big sky, resistance slips, the seals break. I look down at the cylinder of metal, resting sorry in my hand. The pump's done for, desert's still going strong. After half an hour of vain efforts, a white van pulls up. Out leans a Filipino by the name of Oscar . . . brown, smiling face, glasses shine. 'You need help?! I know bicycles!' Relief. Oscar gets out with a roll of electrical tape, a screwdriver and a pair of pliers, all clutched triumphantly in his hand, Oscar smiling like a lunatic. Relief turns dismay. Gently, I explain that pliers don't help with flat tyres. Oscar goes back to his van. Is gone.

I start walking, wheeling my bicycle along Interstate 10 . . . 50 miles to Deming. The rear wheel creaks along the floor, the weight of the bags pushing the metal rim against the asphalt, rubber flapping helplessly. Forget it. I turn on the road, light starting to fade, right arm rising perpendicular to my body, a flexing in my thumb, lifting up until my arm is outstretched with a thumb sticking in the air. Giving my finest look of dignified despair for the oncoming traffic . . . I was hitchhiking.

Only for cars to stream right past. I laid my bicycle on its side, so as to give the impression there might have been an accident, tug a heartstring . . . make them stop. I needn't have bothered, not after all that television, not after the good Lord had sermonised so memorably and consistently on the dangers of picking up hitchhikers.

Stranded in the middle of the desert with 40 kilograms of bicycle and luggage waiting at the roadside, what could have been more perfect? A killer just waiting to bludgeon them to death with his bicycle, the dull thud of a bicycle to the temple . . . *thwack!* . . . right before I set about rifling their clothes and tearing off their wallets. Cars sailed past, faces in the windscreen looking at me as they drove on by.

An hour passed, the light failing as headlamps sailed by, tail-lights receding into the distance, and then disappearing. The dusk makes it easier for them, justifies their fears, no need to look you in the eye either. Sun set, the ridges of the sierras, breadknives along the horizon, sharpening their black against the orange firmament. Silhouettes of cat-claw bushes stand proud, the grasses leaning, flattening themselves in the wind. Crowns of cloud lift in coronation upon the orange horizon. Glorious, stunning . . . the end of an awful day turning to an awful evening.

I don't know how far I'd gone when lights appeared up ahead, a motorway rest area. Cars loaded with families, children peering from seats, parents shooing me from the window. Nobody has anything but irritated rejections for a stranger in the night, asking hopelessly for a pump. To be honest, I don't know why I was asking for a pump, knew it wouldn't help, not with my tubes in the state that they were, and me unable to find the thing responsible for making each one of them flat. I suppose it was a proxy, the only appropriate thing I could have asked for . . . I couldn't have asked for what I really needed, for a lift to the next town.

Amid the rejections I saw one man, pinned a last hope upon him. With a quiet confidence he walked on his own, headed back towards his truck. Not elderly but senior, that brief period where a man stands with the confidence of a life lived, and just before that time when the burden of age wilts his shoulders. A toothpick hung from the corner of his mouth, steady surety to his step . . . the one man in that rest area I'd wager was not going to be afraid of strangers approaching him after dark.

Ken from Tennessee shook hands with an unassuming authority. Jeans a perfect cut, shirt buttoned to one below the collar, plumes of white hair billowing out of his neck as if a cravat. A goatee, trimmed short with jet-white whiskers, icicles falling from the curl of his hair to the corner of his jaw. He'd kept just about abreast of changes with the fashions of his time, but aside from that Ken walked as if he were calmly leaving the field at Gettysburg, unconcerned by the madness of the world around him. He had the manners of a scalpel . . . direct, perfect, to the point and without abrasion. 'You need a bike shop? . . . We'll strap it on the back of the cab. Course it's no trouble to me, I'm going to Deming anyway.'

I climb up to the passenger door, over the bathtub-sized petrol tank, beside the tower of the exhaust stack, my shoes clicking on the metal of the step. Sinking into the seat, I bounce back up on a bed of springs, leather upholstery, padded rests for arms and elbows, the land a long way down. Ken climbs into the driver's seat, his own armchair bouncing beneath him. He makes adjustments, turns on lights. The cockpit illuminates with dials and navigation systems, an orbit of light around the truck, spotlights beneath the rig. The cabin disappears a little behind us, a red curtain drawn across, fluttering with movement from behind . . . more movement as a withered hand emerges from between the parting. The curtains open, and a tiny woman sits on a bunk behind us, wrapped in a cardigan and peering up from out of a pair of glasses, her bob of fair hair turning grey, a shrivelled face with a warm smile. Ken clears his throat, 'Julian, this is Josie . . . my wife.' The ignition fires, the cab shakes, settles down and silently pulls away. Ken rests a hand upon the wheel, silver rings with gemstones set inside, he taps his fingers to a silent tune and begins storytelling.

'My great-grandfather came from England. Our family did pretty well, owned plantations outside Atlanta, Georgia . . . round the time the Civil War started up. My grandfather, he worked as a sniper, shot generals for the Confederacy . . . suppose that's why we lost the plantation.' Ken laughs. 'No idea what became of it, but doubt I'll see any money or land from it ever again. Just trucking now . . . nine years . . . me and Josie, we share the driving.' Josie smiles, nodded by way of confirmation, peering up from the bunk behind us. 'I sleep while she drives, then we swap. We're on the road all year, living in the truck apart from two weeks at Christmas when we go to my daughter's in Oklahoma, visit the grandchildren. Every week we drive from the West Coast with produce . . . every mile of Interstate 10 to Florida, then Florida back to the West Coast with orange juice, the whole trip almost 6,000 miles.'

We floated through the night, the Interstate so far below, drifting by on that carpet of lights, cars passing underneath. Right then I wanted to stay there, to continue to Las Cruces, Fort Worth, all the way to Jacksonville . . . just sitting there in that armchair with my legs still and the world rolling past, asking questions about America and never turning another pedal-stroke, abandoning my quest at last.

Ken looked at me as he spoke, ignoring the Interstate, fixing those keen eyes my way, speaking in calm, deliberate tones, pausing to place his words just so. He started giving his thoughts about America, the miles to Deming ticking slowly down, cars rolling beneath us in the light. He didn't like the last guy in office, didn't like the new guy either . . .

'America used to be a good place to live but not now, not anymore. This new guy . . . *well*, he's doing things even the Nazis didn't do!'

There's that line again, the same words from three weeks ago, the shopkeeper on the Pacific Coast.

'Something needs to change. I mean . . . this country was founded on freedom, the right of every man to make his way in the world.' He looks across to me at regular intervals, checks I'm following before jumping to his point. 'Thing is . . . I'd be willing to fight for your right to come to this country and get rich.'

I laugh. Ken's hurt, protests, 'No, *really*, *I would*. I mean that!'

'But I don't want you to. I don't want to get rich. Don't you think a country needs to be more than that, more than getting rich? I mean, once a few people get very rich, it will always be harder for anyone else to do so, because wealth easily creates more wealth.'

Ken shrugs, nods . . . fair point . . . seems to agree. For all the outward poise, he's just one more confused human stuck on the face of this earth. He takes a sigh, summarises, 'This country's different to the way it used to be.'

Day 130 – St Augustin Pass – 13,354 Miles

I packed up my bed, pushed my bike towards town, through the shell of Deming Truck Terminal, its empty arches, tumbleweed . . . the name of a bankrupt establishment painted in blue letters, a yellow roof on a skeleton of girders.

With tubes replaced and tyre inflated I lumbered on. No thirst for the road, the undertaking, the whole concept of records already so boring and remote. The wind and the dry, desert air had altered my features come that point, almost a week since I first rode into Sonora. My skin felt stretched, as if wrapped tighter than normal against my face. My nostrils cracked, lips almost useless . . . I couldn't have smiled much even if I'd had cause to do so. My mouth had grown smaller, where the lips were thinnest they'd hardened, as if only the skin of my face. Where the lips grew full, the small creases had turned to dry ravines, the blood just below the surface and raspberry-coloured sores marking the space between them. I tried to keep my lips still as I spoke to people and then I saw a sign: '*Prison Facilities – Please do not pick up hitchhikers*' . . . I smiled, and as I did so my lips tore, pulled open and began to bleed.

Riding north after dark, outside the city of Las Cruces, there came a creaking of metal on a service road joining Highway 70. I looked down and saw a bicycle, two wheels completely obscured by baggage, a turtle of a machine, an entire life crawling along the highway's edge. He had belongings hanging from the handlebars, a duvet rolled up, tied to a shopping basket strapped over the front wheel. Above the back wheel were laundry bags held down with ropes and string, tied back together where they'd snapped. From beneath the baggage the lower portion of the wheels were trundling along, the bicycle ridden by a duffle coat with a beard and bushels of hair, two eyes buried among it all. The man was lumbering, shoulders shifting side to side as he and his home made their way north. I call down. He looks up. A large smile, happy to have found something by surprise, he starts shifting his shoulders quicker, pedals hard and comes gradually alongside.

'Where you going?'

He pants, catches breath, pulls level . . . quieter . . . 'Alamogordo.'

I smile . . . 'Me too.'

'Want to ride together?' he asks, nervously happy, like he's asking for a date. 'You riding over Organ, over Saint Augustin Pass?'

'I don't know. I'm riding Highway 70, straight ahead.'

'There you have it, my friend. That's the road to Organ!'

He asks where I'm from, bursts with excitement at the mention of London. He's Mike . . . Mike from Montana. We shake hands, fingers back to front, balancing handlebars as we reach across to one another. I look at his face, through the beard, the mouth obscured, only a hole where I guess he's smiling, beard climbing over cheekbones, hair falling low down his forehead . . . a masquerade ball of the highway, a narrow strip with his eyes on show. I remember those eyes, child's eyes, excitable, joyful, wide open and hungry. It's easy to overcook eyes, get carried away, talk of sparkles and baubles and all that, but not with Mike. In those eyes, peering from a beard, a homeless man riding a bicycle through the New Mexico night, there was such peace. I look at his bike . . . wide tyres, plastic pedals, large frame, a mountain bike called *'Avalanche'*. The more I look, the more bags I see. He's wearing jeans and a pair of work boots beneath his duffle coat, a padlock and chain dangling from his bicycle frame, clanking against the metal as he pedals. Mike sees me looking at his bike, hurries his sentences as he pants.

'Picked this one up for 300 bucks about 4,000 miles ago. The last one was done for. This . . . she don't look like much, but everything works really smooth. I gotta say I love her.'

We ride together, hill rising, Mike rattling beside me like the Ghost of Christmas Past, chain hitting frame and he in his duffle coat turning a good pace. I ask where he's riding. Mike pedals fast, panting between words.

'I just go where it's warm for the winter, or to where there's work. Been doing it three years now since I left Montana . . . *man!* . . . nothing like you, but I've ridden thousands of miles.'

'Why did you leave?'

'Don't know . . . guess I just got too comfortable there. I'm a regular guy, really . . . still got my family, sister and Mum up in

Montana. Used to work in a whole foods shop, assistant man-ager. Then one day, my old girl, she cleared out and left me. We'd been together five years . . . She was older than me, in her forties. I'm only 32 now.' Mike smiles, teeth through beard. 'We didn't fight or nothing. One day she just says she's going. I went back to work, but I didn't want to be there, it all seemed so point-less . . . I always loved riding a bicycle, eventually decided to start doing it.'

I paused, couldn't relate to that, to anything so impromptu, uncalculated. I asked something, some stupid question, the sort of thing I was more used to being asked myself, but it just falls out . . . 'How did you decide where to go first?'

'I had a friend out in Montana, a really remote part of Montana. He's got a home in a creek, between two ridges where a river runs. I stayed with him a while. He's got everything, man . . . got his shelter between the rocks, got his fire pit, got a line for drying clothes even, and you just go right down to the river for cooking water and washing. I tell you . . . he's got just *everything*.'

You can't imagine how it felt, just how it sounded, that affir-mation of sanity on Highway 70. After all those people at the university, with their colour-coordinated stationery and ever-smaller personal computers, after life in London, sitting around Mayfair, outside the Cartier shop on Bond Street, the electronic boutiques down the road, department stores with their six-berth toasters and electric toothbrushes, the consumer troops collecting badges and labels to adorn lives that could never possibly have '*everything*' because it would always want for something. After all that, you don't know how beautiful it was to find Mike, a homeless man with his bicycle, describing a creek in Montana with a wash-ing line and a river and a fire pit as a place that had '*everything*'. That was tender, I can tell you that felt right, and it wasn't gratui-tous either, wasn't romanticism on my part, a glorification of somebody else's hardship . . . oh no . . . Mike was fine, I'm happy to guarantee to you that he leads a happier life than you, or I . . . or almost everybody else you've ever met in one of these existences we like to think fulfilling.

After a while we sit down on a kerb, my bicycle on its stand, Mike's on its side upon the road. It's late, sometime past 10. He reaches inside his jacket, brings out a paper bag from McDonald's, offers a jam tart. We eat together, crumbs falling down our fronts as I ask what he does for money, he sticks out his lips.

'You know . . . work here, work there. Last year, in Las Cruces, I worked a week shovelling gravel, really hard-going but I got $300 for it . . . that was why I came back here, to see if there was more work.'

'Was there?'

Mike shakes his head. 'Perhaps I'll try at the Air Force base in Alamogordo. Sometimes they need help putting up fences.'

'Is that what you do, just go from job to job?'

'Pretty much, until it finishes or I get tired and want to move on. I don't need much money . . . people give me stuff all the time, Jesus looks after me. That stuff from McDonald's . . . I just went in there at the end of the day and they said they'd throw it in the trash if they didn't give it away. I was happy to pay for it, but they said it was better if I just took it.'

I return to God, the question unnatural to me. 'You found Jesus on the road?'

'Pretty much . . . I mean, I don't really go to church, but when somebody gives me food, that's Jesus, and meeting you, that is too. I like looking at the sky at night, and when I can see the stars . . . I imagine Jesus is looking after me. When I can see the stars at night . . . I know everything is fine.'

It's not often that I can listen to sentences like that, that I get so carried away in a moment to find myself caught up by the mystical sentiments that people use to make their lives meaningful. I don't know why it's so seldom that I let my guard down, who it is I expect to laugh at me. The highway was deserted, Mike's stars out above the desert, the two of us sitting beside one another. Mike with his beard and duffle coat, me in my knee-warmers, our lives briefly colliding there in New Mexico. The sound of his voice was so different from his face and his clothes, it was still young, higher pitch, coherent and hopeful in a face that had dropped out of society . . . skin blotched a little pink, that mass of beard. Without that voice and those eyes he could have been an old man. Mike stands, walks over to his bicycle, takes out a jumper with a big hood, pulls it over his head.

'I got this when I started riding . . . rode 5,000 miles and wore this jumper every night. I wrote the names of all the states I've been to . . .' He turns, points to black marker pen scrawled across the back. 'Montana, Washington, Idaho, Utah, Colorado, Arizona . . . I was in Texas, but they ain't so friendly to cyclists, I went to the cities, looked for work in Dallas, Houston.' Mike reflects, 'I don't know that I like cities so much . . . people always seem nicer in the country.'

We both smile agreement, Mike picks up a stick and pokes it at the road. Time's passing, it must be almost midnight . . . I suppose I've still got a record to break. I turn and smile, make excuses for myself.

'I should probably get going to make the top of the Pass . . . you want to ride?'

He laughs. 'Not me. I'll probably watch the sky a bit, I'm almost ready to sleep.' And he pauses. Unease. He sucks moustache, lets out, 'What's London like?'

Scratching my head, I wave a palm at the desert. 'Not a lot like this.'

'You like it there?'

'Not a lot . . . it's OK. There's a lot of money there, it's everywhere, everybody's all caught up with it. People don't have time for one another.'

'I'd love to go there. I'd love to see it . . . to see St Paul's. *What's it like?*'

'Yeah, St Paul's is pretty beautiful, the stone is so white, I love the white stone next to the blue sky . . . especially when it's cold in winter.'

'I read a lot, a lot of crime novels. Some of them are set in London, they're my favourite. It sounds like a different world there, everything must be so old.' Mike pauses, thinks, and then a flicker . . . he realises something, jumps to his feet. 'London Bridge! I saw London Bridge . . . they moved it to Lake Havasu City in Arizona. I went and saw it! To think some guy bought it and moved it across the Atlantic. It's crazy . . . seeing it in Arizona and imagining it used to be in London!'

I laughed. 'Yeah, I heard that . . . there are a couple of the keystones from the original bridge, they keep them on the South Bank with a little plaque.'

'*Wow!* I'd love to go and see it . . . *just once!*'

'But you won't see any stars in London, maybe one or two. The light from the city blocks them out . . . it'll be harder for Jesus to find you in London.' I pause, think . . . look at Mike, standing there, the names of his states written on his jumper in marker pen. 'You think you'll always ride like this?'

'I guess so . . . until I decide to stop. I'll probably spend some more time at the creek in Montana. I still go and visit my family now and then.'

'What do they think?'

Mike shrugs, arms hanging at his sides. 'They know I'm happiest like this.'

He laughs, sighs, shrugs again, sticks out his hand. We shake hands, holding tight. I look for words, something to say . . . and *'good to meet you'* is all that comes. We're not prepared for it, this world of ours doesn't prepare you for Mike. Even me, counting myself outside this whole rat race as I do, still I couldn't comprehend Mike, failed to understand him. Standing there in the desert, with a man who possessed nothing, absolutely nothing but his own sense of complete wellbeing. After all I'd been put through, after school and the exams, reading the papers, the talks from parents, teachers and passing acquaintances . . . after all that, I'll tell you what urge takes you, when you're confronted with Mike from Montana. You'll want to talk to him, you'll want to help him think about what he can do next, consider how he could maybe start afresh, not be homeless anymore, get fixed up again. You think about what he could do to improve the situation, a training course he might enrol in, perhaps he could become a bike mechanic, *anything* . . . anything that could help him get something to his name beyond a bicycle and a beard. Mike from Montana . . . with nothing to call his own and no need to do so either. He terrifies you, stands us on edge, demonstrates the problem is not the person standing there with the duffle coat and the beard who knows exactly what he's up to, the problem is the one in the knee-warmers who hasn't a clue, who will always need more than that with which he is presented. Mike's beaten it, he doesn't need to *do* anything because he just *is* . . . he exists and there is nothing left to say because Mike from Montana is fine, is at peace . . . it's me who has fear inside, anxiety and angst. Mike should be talking to me, trying to help me, to show me a direction with which I might feel better about things. Mike's fine . . . the problem is us . . . is those he left behind.

Waving over my shoulder, I rode away, the lone silhouette of Mike soon swallowed by the night, waving back at me until he was lost from sight. I waved until he vanished, wanted him to know that I wasn't just going to turn around and get on with my own life, that I wouldn't forget him. I took to the hill, rode through the small settlement of Organ. An abandoned caravan, the Star-Spangled Banner pulling at its flagpole with a chiming of metal rings. I rode hard, span my legs against the hill, giant orbits that banked around the rockface. As I rode upwards I thought about it all, threw myself towards the stars, stars that trembled up there like popcorn in a frying pan. I thought of myself, of my record-breaking rivals and all the rest of us self-promoters, with our bankcards, our little plastic rectangles embossed with names, numbers and circuitry that can make it OK again, make it all go away and remedy our every melodrama.

That was only the beginning, what passed for adventure itself, life on the road. Forget about what we planned to do with it once we returned home, once we tried to create *accessible and yet stimulating* accounts of our stories, a way of bringing our experiences to a wider audience, inviting others to share a little in the adventure. That was us . . . with '*adventure*' never more than a sentence from our names, a bunch of other hyperbole thrown in for good measure, the fearless and the heart-stopping and the life-affirming, all those words to be tossed around. And then there was Mike, standing in his beard, jeans and work boots, a duvet tied to the back of his bicycle, wearing a jumper with the names of his states scrawled upon it in a marker pen. There was us . . . and then there was Mike . . . living that thing of which we could only talk.

Day 131 – Oil Country – 13,422 Miles

Next day, Wednesday, 28 October . . . I suppose the wind was blowing, coming off the Pacific and rushing straight for me. In cycling they say there's no such thing as tailwinds, only headwinds and good days. That was a good day, a very good day.

By noon I'd covered 50 miles to Roswell, a grid of rectangles with a water tower and no quirk to be had. A signpost welcomes you to town, followed by two road signs with logos for the same fried chicken business in both directions. Freedom of choice in modern America . . . whether you turn left or right, there's always fried chicken. I rode east, the Rockies long gone and so too the tiny lips of mountain trailing from them. The wind hurried past, the two of us rushing for the Atlantic and me required only to stare ahead for an effortless 30mph. Flashing out of New Mexico into Texas, a signpost greets you at the state line . . . 'The Lone Star State'.

I'd had bad feelings about Texas. For a long time I'd harboured a vague resentment of the place, some idea that it was obnoxious, brusque, arrogant. Down the Pacific Coast the liberals had sneered at it, told me not to go there . . . said Texans only cared about Texas, didn't give a damn about the rest of the world, proud of their isolation and intolerance. The landscape changed, grew fertile . . . sands turned to soil, ploughed and tilled, or left deserted but for the picked stems on which the cotton had grown, swabs strewn over the ground. The size of it all is what hits hardest . . . Texas alone the same size as all Spain and Portugal. Metal gates barred the driveways of the ranches, the sign at the bottom of one of those driveways . . . 'Ranch house – 11 miles'.

Bronco. A small diner with red leather cushions on the stools and around the stalls, floor to ceiling with black and white photography from yesterday's events. There are motorcars and racing drivers with wreathes around their necks, men standing with their horses, men standing with their oil wells, a man standing with his woman, pretty in skirt and heels, with silver bracelets on her wrists and flowers in her hair. I unfolded my maps, poured over them . . . looked for roads, at place names, counted the miles to

my coming waypoints. To Austin, New Orleans, Jacksonville . . .
I didn't know. I knew I needed to ride more miles than naturally
existed between Edisto and me, but I was never sure of exactly
where to find them. I spent so much time looking at maps without
any resolution ever coming from it . . . up until the last I was
making it up as I went along. I thought about the coming night,
the total miles that I might cover by the day's end. If the time was
only 5.17pm and I'd anoth— *'Excuse me, sir.'* . . . I look up, lower
my map. A man is looking at me from the table opposite, smiling,
his palm half raised in some gesture between apology and a waiting question.

'I couldn't help but notice your bicycle out front . . . and your
accent too. You wouldn't mind me asking where you're from,
would you?'

Say what you will about Texans, they may not care much about
the rest of the world, but they certainly place an emphasis on good
manners within their own state.

'Not at all, I'm from London.'

'From London? I thought you sounded British. Are you riding
cross-country?'

'Well . . . I'm riding across the country . . . so I suppose so.'

We talked a while. He asked why I was doing it, nodding kindly
as I gave my spiel. An accountant, he worked with construction
projects in Las Vegas, disliked the nature of the work, the superfi-
cial ways of the city. As my food arrived, he smoothed his hands
over his knees and stood to leave, smiled, bade me enjoy my meal.
Picking up his briefcase, he set a tweed hat upon his head, fastened
the buckle on a long jacket, looked down at me.

'It's been a real pleasure meeting you.' He said it slowly, nodding
his head as he did so. He extended his hand, but only after he'd
finished the sentence, as if not to dilute one gesture with the other.
We shook hands, said goodnight.

Soon after I set to follow him out the door. I asked one of the
three women from the kitchen, wiping down a table in the far corner, for the bill.

'There's no need, that gentleman you were talking to paid your
bill.'

What does she mean, he's paid my bill.

'He paid your bill,' she repeats.

Still I don't understand . . . 'All of it?'

'*All of it.*' She laughs.

* * *

I regained my bicycle, the day a little over 100 miles, the time just
after 6pm and the wind still sending me east. Spots of rain began
to fall, to fly past me into the distance. The road was deserted, the
wind striking against the earth, throwing up bursts of dust that
pelted the side of my face. Coils of electricity cable swung slowly
from power lines, their hinges cold and squealing. I sailed through
towns, puddles of yellow light in the gutters, collecting beneath
railway bridges as though a heavy rain had already fallen. It was
coming, that night must have been the start of it, the peeling away
of my mind as from the earth there came a steady groan . . . an
aching, a screaming struggle as all went spinning, ever spinning.
The grasshoppers, nodding donkeys, pump-jacks . . . the metal
slaves that pump the crude, the oil that made Houston that vulgar
sprawl to the south. Overhead the pylons hummed, sweeping
down with the electricity that turns the axles ever onwards. They
cried, deep and tremulous they cried . . . heavy, gulping sobs . . .
weeping, wheezing and heaving from the bowels of the earth and
into the night. I rode by, listening to them whimper and mourn, to
them spin and creak as they plunged, hit bottom and *ker-chunk*,
ker-chunk, and *ker-chunk* . . . drawing breath to sob some more.

They told stories, sad stories, gasping for air before plunging back down into dreams that turned sour. They had wanted to be a gallery . . . a studio, museum, a stage, a hospital trolley, a seesaw. They'd said yes, they needed the money. Just for a while, just for the money . . . just for a while they agreed. Those poles and axles had been sunk into the ground, anchored, bolted, set to work. The money had been good. Thick and slow, it coursed in them, through them, black gold blackening. The years had passed, passed kindly at $50 a barrel, 200,000 barrels a day: $89 and a quarter of a million barrels. They'd waited for one last year, one last glut of cash before they did what they'd always wanted, at last followed their dreams. A skyrocket went up . . . $110 a barrel and a quarter of a million barrels a day . . . $140 a barrel and they'd squeezed an extra 10,000 barrels of capacity. The money was spectacular, crazy money to be had, never-work-again sort of money . . . a couple of months and they'd be set for good. A couple of months spinning, pumping, blackening, blackened. It all stank. The bowels of the earth release gas like any other, they flared it all along the night sky, the flame rattling with the wind, fluttering, raised banners of the battlefield. It stank of rotten cabbage stewed with old eggs, sulphur . . . sulphur and worse besides. The oil flowed, splashed, and along with the fumes of the burning smoke it stuck against the rigs, their coats of paint once a cheerful yellow. The yellow blackened, drooped, died all heavy-headed. They never got out. Dead sunflowers plunged onwards until a newer model of pump-jack arrived and the old were pulled out. The rigs of years gone by are retired at the Texan roadside, a coat of iron oxide and black oil for their troubles. Severed limbs of metal . . . an arm here, a ballast there. Mile after mile, piles of hoists and cables sat rusting in the cemeteries of oil country.

As night deepened, cotton replaced oil across the land, and in floodlit hangars giant bales of white waited, stacked-up the size of buses. The clouds broke briefly, and from the sky there fell . . . snow. In Texas it started to snow, only a few flakes, but on my upturned palm as I pedalled along, unmistakably snow was falling from above. Lamesa neared . . . toes disappearing to cold as 200 miles came and went, 230 soon following the same way. Come 4am my head was asleep. I'd ceased to think, stopped processing the world accurately. Brain had gone to bed, left Body to swim, fend for itself. I couldn't manage any more . . . 235 miles and I didn't care enough.

The world around was shimmering, not just the wet asphalt in the lights, the reflection of the signals on the level crossings . . . the fields too were moving. All of it: the warehouses, pump-jacks and parked-up tractors . . . the tall, thin combine harvesters with long, cotton-picking teeth. It all went drifting up and down, dribbling as my legs fell away, stopped working from the bottom up. From the road to a field I climbed, brown earth swallowing my shoes, spilling over my ankles. There I rolled out my mat . . . pulled on Long Johns, extra socks, another sweater. I drew the hood of my sleeping bag over my head, fastened tight, only an opening through which to breathe. Closed my eyes, ceased to exist.

Day 133 – Cross Plains – 13,781 Miles

As I left the Interstate and moved south for Austin, an unexpected challenge emerged, in the form of paying for my own meals. While I would sit among maps and wet clothes, the steam of a bowl of chilli warming in my nostrils, Texans made it their business to secretly take care of my bill on the way out of every diner in which I opened my British mouth. Three meals and two hundred miles had passed before I beat them to it and managed to pay my own way.

The state was turning green by then, quieter roads, stores and small-town filling stations instead of the corporations of the Interstate. Fields of pasture emerged, cows standing in the shade of trees, hooves in the muddy banks of a brook as the sun came out and the world warmed. A grey pickup passes by, a Stetson hat silhouetted in the windscreen, the hat rotating to take a closer look at me. The truck passes, continues 100 metres down the road . . . brake lights come on. Driver pulls in. A door opens. I watch, curious as I pedal closer. The man stands beside his vehicle, raises his hand. Stop! He's ageing, greying hair in a ponytail, a look of American Indian to him, expressionless face. It's hard to make out his purpose until he opens his mouth. He cocks a thumb at the back of the truck. 'Need a ride? We'll put your bike in the back.' Laughing, I explain I'm happy riding. He smiles at me as you would a simpleton. Tilts head, tips hat. 'You know best, ride safe now.'

Horses watched from behind picket fences as I checked the map, blades of grass tickling my calves. A truck pulls in, gleaming white. She winds down the window, leans out, a pair of sunglasses and a smile, arms folded over the door. She removes her sunglasses . . . American eyes, sparkling with dream, a big grin stuck on her face. 'Howdy . . . You need a ride somewhere? We can put your bike in the back.'

It was strange, to find myself suddenly outside that mist of fear, never far away almost everywhere else in America. Already I was a convert to Texas, the Californian liberals were all wrong, and which bohemian pacifist would have guessed a loaded gun in every glove box seemed to have brought about the most cheerful and good-natured state in the union? Life felt good, rolling through shadows cast by boughs of live oak, 15 miles to the Cross Plains junction as I stand up on the pedals to make my way into an incline. The road goes gently rising as I dance, spin, pulling pedals around and around and suddenly I'm falling. Falling through the air . . . crashing back to bike, landing on the frame as foot comes unclipped from pedal.

It happens every so often, your cleat loses its hold, and the force with which you typically pull serves to tear free your leg, disturb the balance and send you tumbling. It's too incidental to mention, and so I've never mentioned it before now. I lift back up from the cross frame, my knee with an ache from where it hit the steel on the way through. I look down. That was a sorry sight . . . I promise you it couldn't have looked much more untoward. Pedal still on foot, cleat happily in place, pedal in loyal attendance . . . leg waits confusedly in midair for its next instruction. It was the crank, the crank was the issue, the topmost part of the crank was still on the pedal that was still on the foot. An ugly smile of snapped, solid metal was reflecting the sunlight where it should have connected my pedal to my bike.

Dismounting, I looked at my foot with the pedal on it. Looked at my bicycle without its pedal, again at my foot with the pedal on it. Unequivocal. The pedal was on my foot and my bicycle was missing a pedal. The crank had snapped. Ordinarily I'd be happier not to bother you with the details, ride a bicycle and never write a word about the thing . . . but that was a fairly significant thing to have happened. I knelt beside my bicycle, stood next to my bicycle, squatted beside my bicycle. From each and every angle the scene had every bit the look of quiet disaster about it. In my head I hear a conversation, those typically cavalier remarks with my friends in the bike shop, back on Lamb's Conduit Street, 48 hours before setting out for Rouen. The words burned in my mind, *Just put a cheap crank on it. It'll be fine, it's only a piece of metal.* And there I was . . . 15 miles from Cross Plains, Texas. The best part of 300 miles from the nearest bike shop and, lo, we'd been right all along . . . it was only a piece of metal, the problem was that now it was two pieces of metal. Folding my arms, I laughed. *Why not, eh?* . . . A pretty good one. I check the sky for answers, fluffy clouds roll through blue. I had to admit that was funny, really well done, positively Greek . . . exactly the sort of trick that being a god must be all about. One pedal, he'll have to ride his bicycle with one leg, we'll make him humble, real humble. I got back on my bicycle . . . what else was I supposed to do?

I headed into the 15 miles for Cross Plains, pedalling with my left leg circling round and round, right leg hovering out and then dipping in at the top of the pedal stroke, pushing the broken shard into a new rotation as my left leg heaved and drove. I put my back into it, my entire body plunging downwards, arms pulling with all available force, thrusting down, rising up. It was like rowing, rowing a bicycle, gripping the handlebars and pulling my body forwards. Leaning back, pulling forwards, leaning back, pulling forwards. Throat grunted away and eyes set straight ahead, unblinking. I tried not to dwell too long upon the absurdity of the moment, and yet . . . what an idiot, what a plain buffoon! Rowing through Texas on his one-legged bicycle in pursuit of a world record. In rowing a one-legged bicycle through the Texan backwaters, I was all set to secure the triumph of my ideals and make the world a better place. It was hard not to see the funny side.

After ten miles I had started to refine my technique, master my art . . . better at rowing a bicycle than I'd ever expected to become. A small pickup pulled alongside, old and battered, cans of paint and splattered overalls jumping around the rear with a stepladder. The window wound down, out leans a young man with red hair, brown paint all over his face as I row along. He calls out, 'You doin' that for exercise or d'you want a ride?' I decline, rowing as I talk, thank him but I'm almost there. Not as difficult as it looks really, just a case of getting enough momentum in the downward motion to start coming back up again after. *You see?*

The crossroads are a perfect split north, south, east and west . . .

Cross Plains. Outside a hangar are a line of gleaming cars, fresh paintwork polished, the sun reflecting up and down the curves of the body. A sign above the door: '*McReady's Rods and Rides*'. I've no idea what a rod or a ride is, but the cars look promising. I hobble up on one plimsoll and one cycling shoe, I shuffle in.

The scene is illuminated beneath strip lighting, the rotor blades of fans and funnels of extractors upon the ceiling. A military jeep elevated on a ramp, a mustang with a hole where its engine should be. The walls are covered in spanners and hammers, posters and insignias, manufacturers of engine oils, political slogans . . . '*Glory be to God!*', '*Born Free, Taxed to Death!*' I see pipes and tubes, lengths of silver bumpers and bodywork, a welding mask resting on a gas cylinder.

Heads look round from armchairs in a further room . . . one young, one old. The younger man pushes himself out of the chair, stands up, smooths down his jeans, adjusting the peak of his baseball cap over his glasses. He runs a hand through his goatee, walking towards where I stand in a cycling shoe and plimsoll, knee-warmers around my legs. He's stocky, small eyes behind the lenses of the spectacles, relaxed in his manner of speaking as he asks if he can help. I stand there in knee-warmers and odd shoes. *Where to start?*

'Well, it's a bit strange . . .'

'*Holy shit!* Where'd you get that accent from?'

'I'm from England . . . I'm cycling through the US, heading for Boston.'

'For *Boston*! *Whoa!* You're a long way from Boston.'

'Yes, yes, I know . . . I've just had some problems recently.'

'Problems . . . what kinda problems? And what's your name?'

Joel McReady introduces himself as we shake hands and he smiles, looks me straight and heartfelt in the eye . . . just like a Kazakh, just like a Texan. I tell him about the crank, the pedal unattached, the 15 miles with one leg. He laughs, loud and happy, slaps the idiot across his shoulder.

* * *

The elder man had stood up by the time we'd wheeled the bicycle back in. A tall man, a leather hat with a Confederate badge in metal on the front, Joel introduces him as James. He steps slowly, walks with a cane . . . a contented smile moves on his lips as he paces the workshop and picks a guitar from a bench. Sitting back, James begins to play chords, and Joel observes the snapped crank. From where he leans over my bicycle, Joel makes a noise of concern . . . *'That don't look like steel to me.'*

He takes a magnet from a bench, places it on the crank. It falls.

'Yep . . . it's alloy . . . I'm sorry, I don't have kit to weld alloys, ain't no bicycle shops round here either . . . but we must be able to do something, fix you up somehow.'

James speaks over his guitar . . . 'You really ride that fifteen miles with one leg?' I nod, he nods back, deliberating. 'That's a hell of an impressive thing you did there . . . I don't know many people could ride a bicycle fifteen miles with *two* legs.'

James walks over, leans on his cane. They look at my broken crank as Joel stoops down, strokes his chin, and together they resolve to drill into the remaining crank, make a splint. Joel starts looking around the workshop, James straightens up, resumes a prior conversation.

'. . . so John Wesley Harding shot a black guy, then after the war was finished the Union sent down soldiers to catch him . . . course he shot them too.' James spoke methodically, leaning on his cane, words like patient footsteps . . . 'Think you were thinkin' o' Jesse James . . . course they both wound up shot in the back of the head. That's always the way with these great gunfighters . . . nobody could beat 'em, so one time they just had someone walk up behind and do it the coward's way.'

James went on storytelling as Joel pulled on a heavy glove, picked up tongs, took a welding flame to metal and adjusted dials on a cylinder until the torch was roaring well, fierce and blue. He turned the metal, heating the centre until it glowed red, then white, and began to droop at either end. James stood, leaning on his cane, hat tipped forwards as he watched Joel hammering at the splint, curling it into a horseshoe, the temperature fading white to red, and then cold grey. Joel takes my pedal, his horseshoe splint, the topmost portion of the crank. He places pedal and crank inside the splint, pieces it together again. Looking at him, I asked hopefully, *'Think it'll work?'* I remember Joel's words in reply, more a maxim than a response, a way of life as much as an answer. He looked up from where he knelt, a smile over his face, gleam in the eye as he said *'I'll do it . . . I ain't afraid!'* Curls of metal shavings wound outwards, Joel drilling down into the pedal, talking as he worked.

'So . . . tell me . . . over in Britain, do you guys think us Texans are just a bunch of nasty rednecks?' I ponder, Joel goes on talking anyway. 'I mean, there are some pretty behind the times . . . Over in Comanche, next town along, they've got a plaque at the town hall with the name of the last black man hanged on it.' He looked up, shook his head, drew his face into a look of disgust. 'I mean, it's all shit, all that racism crap . . . you get some real idiots. But we ain't all rednecks . . . the South's about having time of day, about the music, about lookin' out for one another.' Joel turned. 'Hey James, where does that name come from again . . . *"redneck"* . . . where's that come from? You told me once.'

James straightened on his cane, sucked his tongue around his mouth a moment, held his wide jaw in a large hand, spoke a little louder than before.

'If I remember right . . . it originated over in Tennessee, in the coalmines. And I think the workers there, they formed a union to protest against poor working conditions and pay, course in those days it was illegal to form unions, and so the bosses sent men in to break it up. When the fighting started, the miners tied red bandannas around their necks, so they knew who to shoot at.' James paused, thoughtful. 'So really, the fact that "*redneck*" became a derogatory term was really quite unjust, like making an insult out of a political statement . . . but that goes without saying, that's the story of the South. We're always made to look a bunch of fools who hate blacks and don't know their ass from their elbow.'

Two hours after I'd arrived, Joel fastened my crank and my pedal back together, James played his guitar as I gave the handiwork a push. It held.

'Thank you, Joel . . . what can I pay you?'

Joel pulls a face, insulted. 'Don't you be stupid . . . I'm happy to help out. You take my address, send me a postcard when you're back in London.' He smiled . . . 'Tell 'em not all Texans are mean rednecks!'

Day 133 – Zephyr – 13,871 Miles

Still wearing one plimsoll and one cycling shoe, but able to put a little pressure upon the right-hand pedal, I was riding a bicycle again. It was gone 6pm when I set out for Austin, wanting only to kill the ride, to cycle all night and make the following day only a formality of arriving in the city and a bike shop. The sky watched me, Orion's Belt full in the centre of a clear firmament as I moved south, rushing over the bridge that spans Lake Brownwood, the faint land cut by rivers and streams, hills all about and the road running between them to the sound of gurgling water. I pedalled on, heaving with my left leg, helping with my right, splint holding strong, pedal still intact. I rode through Brownwood, through Zephyr, completed 100 miles for the day, 120 . . . grew impatient . . . started riding more orthodox, pushing further on the right pedal, applying more pressure, going faster. It worked for a time. For a time my speed grew, night passing more quickly; 2am had been and gone, 3am going the same way as there comes a movement beneath my right foot, a giving way, a creaking and a rattling. I look down, see screws missing from my splint, others working loose. I screw them back in, resume my one-legged discipline, row a little through the night.

By then all patience had deserted me. The lack of sleep, the anxiety of the crank, frustration . . . I just want it over. I push down. It snaps. Things fall apart. Crank falls free of cradle . . . pedal clatters from beneath my foot and onto the road. I sigh, stop, pick it up, return to my bicycle and start to row. Almost full, the moon casts a strong shadow, so that up ahead I see a demented silhouette, rowing strong into a night that eventually fades to a morning blue. After 150 miles everything was over, Body ready to follow the crank and fall apart. I row 10 final miles, the sun still not prepared to show its face above the horizon, end the darkness and help keep me going.

* * *

The sunrise failed to come. I slept, awoke to only a well-lit version of the same scenario. Roads quiet, hemmed in by trees, 10 miles of rowing and next morning the idiocy of the situation was already too much. I flash down a hill. Trees part on a wooden garage, planks missing from the walls and tiles from the roof. I got from my bike, peered in . . . the bare chassis of a car, nothing on it but rust and some tools. Just an old shed, the smell of creosote in the wood, engine oil, cobwebs. Outside the place was piled high with railway sleepers and disused pulleys, trestles, an old welding rig, all the collections of a hoarder. It didn't look like much, the whole place run down, and then inside . . . something remarkable was suspended from the ceiling beams.

Hanging from lengths of chain, like prisoners in a tower, were two bicycles. Not the regular sort either . . . not supermarket bikes sold for 100 dollars and never ridden. These were classics, real maidens. Hanging from the beams of a shed in Lampasas, Texas, were a pair of *LeMond* bicycles . . . dropped handlebars, shifters on the downtube, leather toe straps. The real deal . . . genuine road bicycles. In one plimsoll and one cycling shoe, I make my way down crumbling steps and knock at the front door. A woman appears, looks at me through the glass, stares at me, confused. 'What do you want?' she mouths, vague enquiry upon her face. 'I've a problem with my bicycle.' I point at the garage. 'Could I borrow some tools, please?' She's suspicious, mistrusting . . . 'Wait for my husband, wait at the shed.' A curtain pulls across the glass.

Twenty minutes pass, hope fades, I might as well keep rowing. There's a rustling from through the bush. Branches jump, part . . . 'Can I help you?' comes ahead of his appearance. There appears a short man with thin, red hair, orange eyebrows, a wispy beard on his chin, sparse over dimpled cheeks and above his lip. Spectacles cover tiny eyes, thin frames resting on an aquiline nose. He's dressed in a polo shirt, tucked tight inside jeans so that it accentuates a drooping chest and round paunch.

I straighten up, look polite, as formal as my footwear allows. 'I think I spoke with your wife.' I gesture to the bicycle. 'I've got some mechanical problems.'

Together we look down at my crank, squatted at the roadside as I explain the break. He strokes his chin, just as Joel had done, pulling on his chin as if answers might wait there. I mention the bicycles hanging from the ceiling, ask if he rides.

'Not anymore, not for a long time.' He sighs. 'I used to like it. My old man and I . . . we used to go out riding together.' He turns to me, lets go his chin, tired eyes, age in them. 'We fought a lot when I was younger, riding bikes was something we did to patch things up . . .' Pauses. 'Up until my old man got hit by a truck . . . died a week later. I kinda figured then that there wasn't much point riding to keep fit, not if it wound up killing you dead in a week.' He gives a quiet laugh . . . 'I'm Rusty by the way.' He sticks out his hand.

We shake hands, Rusty looking me in the eye, just as Joel had done the day before, no formality or procedure about it.

'What you doin' here on a bicycle, Julian?'

'Riding around the world.' I shrug.

Rusty laughs, the whole idea beyond peculiar. Telling Rusty I am trying to ride 18,000 miles faster than anybody else is not so different to telling one of those Californian redwoods the same thing.

'That's an interesting thought,' he says, dusting off his hands. 'I think maybe I've got an old crank somewhere in the garage, I cleared up in there five years ago, but it wouldn't be like me to have thrown it out.'

We go inside the shed, into the cobwebs and creosote, the bare chassis of Rusty's latest car. He starts climbing up a shelf the height of the wall, hands and feet between jars of hinges, screws, bolts and cans of paint.

He thinks aloud, talking about the crank . . . 'Must have been about '94 we bought it . . . Dad had the accident soon after and we never fitted it.' Rusty climbs back down the shelf, starts pulling drawers, the sound of wood rolling over runners. 'I've been in this town best part of thirty years now. From Boston originally . . . I was married up there when I met a woman from Texas, divorced and followed her down here . . .' He goes on opening drawers, his life falling out with the dust and cobwebs. 'Always thought I'd go back there, back to Massachusetts to see out my days.'

'Will you?'

'Doubt it. I've adjusted to life down here now, can't stand the rat race back in Boston. My brother and his family . . . he's still there, still working. Already had one heart attack. He's five years younger than me as well.' Rusty looks at me, smiles as he opens a cupboard door and disappears.

'I suppose your wife being from Texas is reason enough to stay?'

I listen to Rusty, muffled by the cupboard. 'I guess . . . This one's my third wife, though . . . divorced the one I moved here for. We only lasted about three years.'

'Do you think this one's the one?'

Rusty emerges, looks at me, pulls thumbs against belt. 'We don't get on so well . . . she in there is three-quarters invalid . . .' He pulls a tea chest from under his workbench, disappears. 'To tell the truth . . . she takes a lot of looking after.'

'You think you'll divorce again?'

'Oh no, no need . . . there ain't much longer to go in this world now.'

I scratch my head, silence settles. *Not much longer to go in this world?* What's he mean? Rusty calls from inside the tea chest.

'Here it is! I knew I wouldn't have thrown it out.' He holds it up. 'You're welcome to it.'

Rusty passes it over, adjusts his hat. Perfectly gleaming silver, unblemished, svelte and written along the face are the words *'Dura Ace'*.

My eyes go big. 'You're sure? This is really good kit! Let me give you something for it, if it fits.'

'Don't you worry about it, it was just gonna sit in that chest forever if you hadn't come along. My old man would be happy to have it used.'

We go back to my bicycle. I line up the new crank. It fits. Rusty goes back to the shed, comes back with just the right tool to complete the repair. I go dizzy . . . giddy with good luck, blessed all over my face.

'You're in high cotton!' Rusty chuckles.

'What's that mean?' I ask, confused.

'*Huh?* Does what mean?'

'What you just said about cotton . . .'

He laughs again, ponders. 'Guess you wouldn't know an expression like that if you've never picked cotton . . . you hold the flower, see . . . pull the cotton from the plant. Nowadays it's all machinery, but in old times it was hard work, all day long in the fields. If the cotton plants were small –' Rusty leans forwards, puts the back of his hand to the small of his back – 'you had to really bend over . . . but if the cotton's high, it's easier. Means you're lucky, I guess. We've got lots of expressions like that here in Texas, lots more than up in the north.'

Rusty tutored me Texan as I removed the crank, tells me stupid people couldn't hit water if they fell out of a boat, how some people were so ugly they have to sneak up on the mirror. I listen and, in one of his pauses, I interrupt . . .

'Rusty, what did you mean about there not being long left in this world?'

Rusty sucks cheeks. 'See . . . I'm a Christian . . . part of the Seventh-Day Adventist Church.' He inhales . . . 'The Bible says we're in the last days now.'

'So what do you believe . . . that the world's going to end?'

'We don't look at it like that . . .' He laughs . . . 'More that paradise is coming.'

'I saw Waco nearby on my map, is that the same Waco where

they held a siege with the religious people in a farmhouse?' I press ... 'Where the government went in with tanks and blew everybody up?'

Rusty nods. 'That's Waco, siege at Mount Carmel with David Koresh, 1994.'

'Your church is different?'

'Oh yeah, that was a cult. They thought Koresh was the Messiah ... he said he'd defend them as the Apocalypse came.' Rusty threw up his arms, more animated. 'But those guys had guns and rocket launchers, and Jesus doesn't need guns and rocket launchers to defeat people, he just lifts up his arms and they drop right down.' Rusty chuckles ... 'What would Jesus need a gun for?'

'So you don't own a gun?'

'*No!* I don't own a gun, why would I need a gun unless I wanted to hurt somebody?'

'I agree, but not many Americans seem to think like that. Didn't President Bush make it legal to carry guns in churches?'

'President Bush ... how should I put it ... wasn't a very good example of a Christian. I mean, it's right there in the Bible. Ten Commandments ... thou shalt not kill. And what does he go and do?' Rusty throws up his arms. 'He goes off starting wars all over the place!'

'I agree, and what about things the Bible says on homosexuals, abortions?'

'I can still love people who do wrong, they're children of God too ... we're all sinners, see? God will cast his own judgement soon and I hope they repent before he does.' Rusty stops, shrugs. 'I believe what I believe ... "*Occupy 'til I come*" ... that's what Jesus said ... "*Occupy 'til I come*", so that's what I do, I just occupy myself. I try and be good to people, try and help people that come along needing help. I fix up my hotrods at the weekends ... Y'know, just occupying myself 'til paradise comes.'

Day 135 – Confederacy – 14,255 Miles

The dew of the morning soaked my clothes, my sleeping bag, shoes. I sat on the forecourt of a petrol station in Bastrop, sun warming the belongings spread across my bicycle. Shoes on handlebars, everything drying in the bright rays, water lifting from the sleeping bag before my eyes. Barefoot, I sat staring at it all.

A rusty car pulled up, patched with different colours where the metal had worn bare and been covered in a protective paint. I know how I looked right then, the dejected expression becoming common on my face, without thirst for the task at hand, only an acceptance of the need to finish the bargain into which I'd entered. A man got out from the car, slamming the door shut in a way that shook the remainder of the vehicle. A black man with a short moustache, he spoke with a thick accent of the South. His jeans were torn at the knees, shirt splashed with oil, a waistcoat with large, square pockets sewn to the outside, polythene bags and cables spilling from them. He looked me up and down, nodded, clenched his fist at his side and said to me, a voice in some sort of solidarity, '*I been where you are, brother.*' Somehow I doubted it, doubted he'd ever misjudged his flight back to Europe in a circumnavigation by bicycle, but I nod back with a solemn face, drawn lips, silently acknowledge his support. Clench my fist.

Fatigued by the heat of the day, I rode lazily beneath temperatures I thought to have left behind. Lunchtime comes. Body requests vitamins, fresh fruit and vegetables. On offer is a seven-dollar all-you-can-eat pizza buffet. Miserably I ate, ate, ate again . . . ate a final time, masochistic food . . . I don't want to go into details, hurting myself with each mouthful, value for money, all I want is enough calories to get me back to Europe without need of another meal in America. Wiping the remains from my

266

mouth, I walk towards the counter, an all-you-can-eat woman standing behind it. Her head is above the till's numerical display, sucking cheeks into her mouth, violet eye-shadow, hoops in her ears, hair scraped back and slapped down with adhesive, body peering around either side of the counter. An aura of perfume, pools of sweat on the cotton of armpits, ripples of sweat where the cotton is trapped between forearms and elbow.

'Where you riding to?'

'Boston.' I'm not enthusiastic, want to leave, to leave Giddings, leave Texas, forget about the food and get out of there without a conversation.

'*Oh, my!* Is that accent from *England*?'

'Yes . . . I got it in England.'

She's business-like in response, palms flat against the till, matter-of-fact, level gaze . . . 'I find that accent very sexual in a man.'

After the meal I could have done without that, stomach unsettled and sorry for itself, and then my poor ears obliged to hear such things as that.

'I'll have to tell the guys back home to get themselves over here.'

'You should do that.' She smiles a little, a small opening of her face, the human inside struggling to get out.

From the bottom of my pocket, my hand emerges with six grubby dollars in it, torn and fraying. I went back in for the seventh dollar. She shakes her head, shakes her face, her cheeks, she shakes her earrings, a Doberman-shaking of the head.

'You guys . . . riding like that all day. You keep it.'

I hold out my dollar hand as we make eye contact . . . brief, fleeting, the sort of duration that demonstrates how rarely we look into one another's eyes when we speak, because most exchanges finish without even the first hint that we're talking to another being and not just one more social actor like ourselves. I saw her then, read her mind and saw her thoughts . . . her compassion, her sadness for me so young, and from England too, now stuck travelling on some bicycle. I thought of what I'd said about '*the guys back home*' and that they should come to America. She didn't realise I was referring to individuals with jobs and degrees, she thought I meant a group of men that I spent my days with, huddling around a bonfire in an oil drum and looking for cardboard boxes to sleep on. I thought of Mike from Montana, what he'd said about being given food at McDonald's, I thought of the man that morning, his words . . . '*I been where you are, brother.*' She went on looking at me. And I realise . . . They all think I'm homeless.

* * *

The day got no better . . . legs floundering, everything still fatigued from sleep deprivation and my rowing the night to Austin. Texas was pretty, so very pretty with its hills and creeks and tumbling streams, twinkling xylophones in a dreamlike space under some trance of sunlight. I made myself stay seated, pedalling . . . but I didn't care, the obligation to hurry for the sake of those numerical targets engendered such a resentment in me. I had no motivation, nor could I find it in numbers and dates and miles. I was deferring, every day, deferring, *tomorrow* always to be the start of it . . . the day on which I would wake and mean business.

* * *

I rode east, made for Louisiana, passing great lakes with the water a mirror to the sky, the surface pierced by cypress trees rising from beneath. Clusters of leaves, red through green, stood from the forest, went reflected against that blue glass. Wildlife returned to the roads . . . the crushed shell of the tortoise, black leather feet flattened against the asphalt, a splintered shield at its back. The armadillo too, interlocking plates of armour snaking all the way down the spine of the tail, tiny feet with four claws and bristles of hair sprouting from tough, pink flesh. The creature was cracked open, smashed right down the centre as if it was nothing more complicated than a broken dinner plate. Inside nothing remained, no flesh nor muscle, innard nor organ . . . the whole thing had disappeared, scrubbed clean and not even a smell of death remaining. Fewer than 50 metres down the road and there was the scavenger . . . lying dead, the turkey vulture, disturbed just as its work was complete. I could see it finishing the scraps, alerted by the sound of the engine. Head turns, wings spread, flying upwards, but without time to climb above the windscreen. The impact had preserved it perfectly . . . good, clean kill. Thick plumage of black feathers, a real shine to them, good diet. The bird had gone down just before I came along, lay in the centre of the road, framed between the yellow lines. One wing pointing upwards, Polonius-style, 'I am slain' on his bald face, tough and grey, one eye still watching the audience.

Day 136 – Cajun – 14,317 Miles

Alexandria arrives . . . *thump* . . . falls like a report on American wealth distribution. Litter on streets . . . deserted, lifeless but for a few people walking to work. A police car moves slowly along the road. There are old docks, warehouses boasting new developments on billboards, refurbished apartments . . . '*waterfront living*' writ enthusiastic in as many places as possible. The properties deteriorate, Alexandria goes from bad to worse. Windowpanes cracking, doors falling open, smoke of fires scorching soot against paint. The bodywork of cars becomes dented, driveways shorter, the bags of rubbish at the end of those driveways larger. They split . . . empty bottles and cardboard packaging, leftover rice and chicken bones on the pavement. Across one picket fence is the tape of a police cordon, house spilling onto the street: broken furniture, sprawled clothes, a settee, cushions slashed and torn, the whole thing falling through a hole in the porch.

At a petrol station I stop to refill water bottles, buy food, my final slice of Alexandria. A small gathering is already assembled on the forecourt, a dozen men just circulating listlessly or squatting in the dust, perhaps around 11am. It's 5 November, Thursday, and no job to go to. One battered car is filling up at the pump with $9.50 of petrol . . . $9.80, $9.92, $9.95, $9.99, $10.00 of petrol and not a cent more. I'll cut to the chase with this little scene of mine, come right out and say it rather than go about things the subtle way and be called a racist anyway. Right now I'm sticking out like a sore, pink thumb as everyone is black, each and every person black, their lives looking like little more than killing time outside a petrol station. It's not all bad . . . the man who budgets precisely $10 for petrol is also black, as is the patron, but in truth the over-whelming majority look pretty down-and-out. You can tell by the squatting. They're good at it and, in the developed world, good squatting technique is a sure sign of social exclusion, people with nowhere of their own to sit down . . . excellent balance, perfectly stable, forearms on knees. A man approaches the driver with his $10 of petrol, shows him something from his pocket before being unceremoniously told to '*fuck off!*' as the driver pushes by and into the shop.

Full of compassion and social justice, I remove anything of value from my pannier, half-watching the men remonstrating with one another. The shop door opens, owner storms out with a roar. '*Stop troubling ma customers!*' From afar there comes a distraction, commotion starts. All dressed in burlesque, two women arrive, ladies in the loosest sense of the word. They roll in, breasts and necklaces rolling as I double-take at society bottoming out in front of me. Two prostitutes come wobbling in on high heels and wide hips, giant orbits of necklace, cocktail dresses five years too small, one green, one pink, fabric pulled too tight over bodies too big, the colour of the dye giving way to white elastic stretched too far.

The shop is dimly lit and cramped. Shopkeeper is friendly, cheerful. 'Where you ridin' ta, boy? I'm sorry about them outside . . . they ain't bad guys, just troubled.' I give a nod, return outside, where one man stands over my bicycle, the others cavorting around the women. He's tall, well-built, older guy . . . has tight curls of grey hair, red eyes, yellow husks developing on the cornea. I've never heard an accent so thick as that, spoken from the throat, lips barely moving, syllables grunted and flat, words with tails clipped.

'Where y'fra'?'

'London.'

'Londo' . . . where'that?'

'England.'

'Where'that?'

I sort of shrug, point northeast. 'About 6,000 miles that way.'

He considers, looks at my bike, looks at me, has a thought.

'Near China?'

Day 138 – Atchafalaya – 14,438 Miles

Headed for the Mississippi River, 3pm and only 40 miles ridden. It comes . . . One more going down . . . that rupture, that explosion. *Bang!* Another spoke. Just 40 miles, another 100 needed before the day would have been a good distance. Body is reluctant, up above and Brain is repulsed by this giant Quixotic turd, this hair-brained monstrosity, my bank balance the only reason for hurrying in the name of that record.

* * *

'I don't mind helping nobody . . .' They're his words when I pull in at the garage and ask for a pump. I'm tired, resignation written all over my face as I start replacing spokes. He walks towards me and out of the corner of one eye I see boots in gravel . . . 'You want a place to stay? I don't mind giving nobody a shower and a meal and a bed for the night.' But I haven't ridden enough. Brain says I haven't ridden enough, got to keep going. Such a kind offer but I must keep going. Soul calls veto, leaves Brain as furious as he is impotent. Body follows the order, moves lips . . . 'Thank you, that would be really kind.'

I reach crossroads, cross train tracks, follow directions. I can see it now, down the trail, 15 minutes down the trail, no obvious house. Eventually it comes. A pickup truck pulled in . . . one caravan, two caravans, three caravans and a dried-up bayou. The leaves are falling all about, fluttering downwards as I look in at the clearing and there, beneath the small lean-to, sit a gathering of men in picnic chairs, on benches, on paint cans and water butts, each with a beer. Ryan Lemoine Junior walks up to me, his vest and his open shirt, jeans and boots, his right eye that constantly squints and twitches, tongue that clicks in the corner of his mouth as he looks there for a word stuck between his teeth, squinting with his eyes and his stretched face, the cigarette always smoking. He shakes my hand with one hand and passes a beer with the other . . . they give me a stool and down I sit. There, right there in Louisiana, in the clearing with the trailers.

They're all looking at me, three generations of Lemoine men. Ryan squints and clicks as he introduces Grandpa, an elderly thing

272

by the name of Arnouville. Paul Arnouville, he sits in a rocking chair from which he seldom lifts, a face like a crocodile. Heavy-lidded eyes that blink slow, rise and fall and do not once move from their gaze at me and me alone. Two legs planted fast, one hand planted on the arm of the rocking chair, the other on the head of a walking stick standing straight in the dirt. He's got a collar, wide open, and you can hear his chest as it struggles to breathe, lungs clogged with age, his white hair all about the place and a set expression in his eyes . . . eyes that set right upon me, that look into only me. I see it, those eyes they have suspicion in them. I must look strange all right, with my shorts and knee-warmers and bicycle, carbon fibre soles of my cycling shoes that make me walk so rigid and mechanically.

We sit together, five of us, all gathered before the house, beneath the oak and beyond the bayou. Paul Arnouville still suspicious as Ryan introduces me.

'This is Julian.'

'Julian?'

'Julian.'

'Where's he from?'

'He's from London.

'*London?* What state's that?'

'London, England.'

Paul Arnouville raises his head. Slowly up, slowly down . . . that was all.

That was what they called me thereafter . . . Julian London, in that clearing where the place from which you come is half of that which defines you.

A pickup pulls into the driveway, out steps still more white hair, a cigarette, a moustache covering the top lip and then at each side of his mouth sticking straight down like a pitchfork towards the Louisiana earth. He coughs with all his might, coughs out a globule of cancer, hocks it into his mouth and spits it to the ground. White hair swept back on his crown, hairline receding . . . a yellow shirt, open collar, white hair from his chest, drainpipe jeans and huge, lolloping boots of brown leather. Ryan Lemoine Senior slopes towards us. We shake hands and he meets Julian London, takes a beer, all of us sitting together in the gathering evening. The first woman comes home . . . fat falling off her, a round face, black spectacles and two eyes peering from behind, like lumps of coal inside a snowman. She's huge, real huge, wears a summer dress big enough to block out the sun, it's like the mainsail of a boat and covered in gerberas. Ankles squeeze from a pair of tiny shoes. Marjory Lemoine comes over all delighted . . . 'From London? . . . Our Miss Irene, she went to London . . . did you ever meet a Miss Irene when you was in London?'

* * *

We walk through fields, Ryan showing me to the bayou, dry and full of leaves, waiting for the river to rise. 'Real peaceful out here,' he murmurs, squints and clicks through speech, his crew-cut hair, the vein in his temple and tendons in the side of his long neck. He tells me about alligators in the summertime, calls them just *'gators'* . . . coming right up to the house to be beaten back with a broom head. He explains how you hear them from afar, how you hear them *hiss* at you . . . and as he tells me, Ryan Lemoine makes the *hiss-hiss* of a *gator*, just as he'll go on to make the *waa-waa* sound of a police siren when he tells his stories from the city of New Orleans. Ryan talks of hunting, of squirrel and boar, squirrel with not so much meat, but good sport. 'You come back sometime and we'll hunt some squirrel for ya . . .' The door to a small hut stands open, the smell of hessian sacks and cobwebs. A single bulb hangs from a flex in the ceiling, one intrepid moth determined to get at the incandescent filament.

Ryan Senior is there with a beer and a litter of pups yapping at his feet, biting at the tails of the white moustache that slips over each end of his mouth. He leans into them, picks them up and pats them, one at a time, a dozen of them but he knows each by name. Making sentimental faces, he leans down close to kiss them.

'Some folk drown 'em but I could never do that to any animal . . . oh no!' Ryan Senior tells me, his blue eyes looking straight at me, distracted from his dogs a moment. He gathers magnitude. 'This here, it's ma home . . . and I ain't got much but what I got you can call ya own. You can make yaself at home here. I won't take nothin' from ya and, if ya want medicine, I can give it ya . . . 'k?'

I didn't know what medicine I might have needed, nor what he meant in saying he'd take nothing from me, but the gist was that Ryan Lemoine Senior was one more man with almost nothing in the world but happy to share it. I put my hand on my chest, thanked him, thanked him again before a silence settled, only the sound of the cicadas coming from outside. I was sitting atop some sack, some old sack with faded words printed on the side. Slapping it, I ask what's inside.

'Pecans,' he said, though in a way I could never really write. '*P'kans*' was more like it, and I can still hear that sound.

'They buy 'em,' he added. 'They buy *p'kans* . . . three-and-half dollars a pound.'

'How much is that?' I asked, pointing to my seat.

' 'bout 40 pounds. I go out and pick 'em after work.' Ryan Senior smiles. 'The money comes useful, that bag's worth about a hundred bucks.'

That was a sizable sack on which I sat. I should say it again . . . that was a big sack, a lot of *p'kans* inside . . . not budging, stuck there fast like the politics of the United States of America, the world's richest nation, land of opportunity. Capitol Hill, Martha's Vineyard and down in Louisiana, a man will pick half his wiry bodyweight in pecans for just a hundred bucks, winds up pretty pleased with the trade too. Don't mistake me, the Lemoines are no worse off for this life of theirs . . . but whether that makes it anything like fair is a different question.

Marjory Lemoine, with a spoon that could paddle a canoe, piled up the plates to different heights of liver, bacon, rice and lettuce dressed with cream. We sit down at the table together, a tray of hot fat spitting to a standstill beside us. Ryan Junior and Senior scarcely eat, wolf it down and are smoking cigarettes on the terrace the moment the plate is clean.

One other man has been kicking around since I first arrived, yet to say a word but always leaning with a laid-back authority on every doorway. Marjory introduces Martin. He is wearing a baseball cap with the peak pointing upwards, an ageing face with quietus to it, simple eyes, really simple eyes, the kind that don't conceal much of what goes on in the head, a head with not much going on. Martin eats slowly, always looking around, grunting, pointing to somebody, something, grunting. He tries to get my attention, a pointed finger on the tabletop, points to something I can't guess at in the corner of the room, grunts again, harder.

Marjory Lemoine instructs him leave off, apologises and explains he is deaf and mute, shunted between foster families all his life . . . 'When his last family cleared off three years back, I said he ought come live with us.' Marjory just reports it, tells me what happened. That's it, that's all; there's no fishing, no sentiment laid on, no self-congratulation. Marjory Lemoine is not looking for medals, honours or remuneration as a careworker, she just says how they took in deaf, mute Martin as matter-of-fact as if she'd taken in washing when the raincloud broke. That's the South, and you come to understand the signs outside trailer park villages . . . big letters, beneath the name of the park: *'Just ordinary folk looking out for one another'*.

'Trailer Trash', that's them . . . trailer trash, fit only to belittle, demean and take cheap shots at. The media, the liberals, the right-eous of the West who talk so much about morality we think ourselves moral, while hicks and trailer trash take in the deaf, mute and soft-headed Martin when his foster family clear off.

After dinner, I follow the family to the terrace, matches spark-ing as each of them lights up a cigarette. Ryan talks about his divorce from a woman in New Orleans, of his gambling addiction and how this six months is his longest abstinence in four years. He tells me how casinos never have clocks or windows, to ensure their punters lose track of time. 'That doesn't seem fair,' I say sadly, before listening to Ryan's response . . . 'I don't know, guess every-body's got to make a profit somehow.'

An old lady, the wife of Paul Arnouville, points up above us. 'Nice to have this back.' I follow her arm up to the roof, ask what she means. Ryan tells me of a hurricane called Katrina, which blew the roof off a year ago, the family only just finding enough money to repair it. I give a noise of recognition, tell them I'd heard about Katrina. Ryan Senior speaks, surprised, through his cigarette, a man in a Louisiana trailer who doesn't understand that his roof blowing off was a detail in an international media commodity. 'They was talking about Katrina . . . in London?'

Conversation changes direction, the mood lightens and Arnou-ville's wife cries out, 'Tell a joke!' The words shriek from her sharp, yellow face, her shoulders covered in a matching cardigan. Ryan begins with playful reluctance. Happy to be persuaded, he tells a joke about dumb Southerners like them, jokes they've all heard before but are happy hearing again. With the punchline, laughter flies and the whole terrace rocks. Old Mrs Arnouville has her face contract tight with joy, eyes puckering as she starts hissing and holding her sides. Laughter subsides, crackles, then bursts to a coughing fit, the terrace itself starts coughing on its rafters, lungs bellowing up in revenge, Lemoines and Arnouvilles taking long heaves on cigarettes to settle down the bronchi. The terrace rocks, laughs and wheezes, Ryan smiling gently to himself as there comes a shout . . . Arnouville again, her sharp face and yellow cardigan, crying from the corner. 'Tell one about the niggers!'

Ryan's tone cools. 'We don't call 'em "niggers" no more, Grandma, we call 'em black people.' He looks at me. 'But there are lots of jokes 'bout black people round these parts. Some people say they're just lazy and only want handouts from government . . .'

'It ain't no lie!' pipes up Arnouville in her cardigan and her wrinkled face. 'Back when I was young, there was this thing called segregation, you see, and all of it was separate . . . separate buses, separate schools, you name it . . . and it all worked a damn sight better too, I'll tell you that much! And now, now these blacks they think they own the place, they walk around, livin' the easy life.'

'Aw now, Grandma, I'm sure some black folk are out to earn an honest living.' Ryan tries to soothe the old cardigan with its sharp face. Unconvinced, she stifles a sarcastic laugh, demands her joke.

Ryan sighs, begins . . . 'Well, down here in the South we have three different types of nigger . . . you got the *Randabak*, the *Motesa* and the *Wemachek*. *Randabak*, he's a real hardworking nigger . . . he follows behind the garbage truck, slapping the truck, throwing in the trashcans and all the while shouting, "Round the back, round the back!" Then you got the *Motesa*, now he's a real polite nigger, always working for white people, and he's always saying nothing but "More tea, sir? More tea, sir?"' The terrace beams more and more as Ryan reels them out. 'Then you got the *Wemachek* . . . see . . . he a real lazy nigger, never worked a day, and he's always there, first thing at the social security office, and he just says, "Where's ma cheque? Where's ma cheque?"'

And the whole terrace splits with laughter . . . *Whoosh, brilliant!* Fat arms fly up in the air and moustaches stand to attention, cardigans gripped tight about waists so sides don't peel to burst with glee. Even deaf, mute Martin with faulty ears that didn't hear a word, even Martin's struck, starts bobbing up and down and holding his mouth as they all laugh harder until finally one person hits the wall and has to cough . . . and then another, and then everybody is coughing and laughing and then just coughing. Stone-faced, I sit on the terrace as the Lemoines and the Arnouvilles cough, splutter and then soothe it all with a cigarette.

'You get it?' Ryan notices I didn't laugh. 'You see, he's saying, "Where-is-ma-cheque?" and he's asking, "Would you like more-tea-sir?"'

But it's no good, I just can't laugh at a racist joke. Try as I might, I just wind up in a grimace. With all that said though, there's a final word here . . . about the Lemoines and the Arnouvilles, living in deepest Louisiana, where Ryan Lemoine Senior has picked twenty kilos of pecans that autumn . . . twenty damn kilos, half his scrawny bodyweight, bending down to each nut in order to make a hundred bucks and go on living in a trailer with the rest of his family, a generation in each direction, and a dozen yapping dogs with squashed faces and respiratory problems. Twenty kilos of pecans to go on living on the breadline in the richest country on earth, where all you have to do is turn on a television set to see everything you haven't got and just how easy some other bastard has it. The Lemoines, the Arnouvilles . . . even that old dragon in the yellow cardigan, you don't meet better people than that. Only pawns in their game . . . racist as sin, but when you're a signed-up, bought-and-paid-for member of Underclass, where you've no ambition in life beyond continuing to be poor, and where your sense of entitlement runs no further than the right to be hood-winked and bent over double for somebody else's gain . . . When you're destined to live a life so primitive . . . well, it's not hard to imagine seeing a tribe with more pigment, different lineage and voices as a people different, especially when that separate tribe is thrown into the same crummy strata of society you'd been told 50 years earlier you could call your own. Go to Washington DC, go to New York and to London . . . that's where you'll find the ones who are responsible.

* * *

Before evening was out, Marjory Lemoine handed me pen and paper, had me write my address in London. When I returned home, 7 December . . . sure enough, waiting for me was a card from Louisiana, a picture of a globe with dolls linking arms all around it. Marjory Lemoine, there in blue biro . . . 'Write to us sometime, let us know you got home safe.'

Day 142 – Panhandle – 14,877 Miles

Shortly after that, it changed . . . things fell apart, grew strange. I'd known it before I stopped that night, that night in Hamburg with the Lemoines, the beers on the terrace. I'd known then it was to be the last such night, that I had to get faster, my sauntering at an end at last. Next day I set off, passed over the Atchafalaya River at Simmesport, where Mrs Arnouville warned of blacks, drug addicts beneath the bridge.

Into the canals and levees upon that river I went, pursued by a need for some haste best left unconsidered. My bicycle steers north, and together we cross the Mississippi, coal barges shunting slowly in either direction along that legendary river, my fourth and final. Danube, Volga, Yangtze, Mississippi, my final great river. After that I suppose I retreated from the world outside, withdrew and started knocking away the days . . . a tunnel vision settling upon me, the conversations over.

* * *

A hurricane was coming, but don't be alarmed . . . that's only the politics of America. I see it now, you tell people there's a hurricane on its way, and by the time your hurricane proves a non-starter, transpires to be just a little wind and rain, come then Christmas is in the offing and new distractions are on their way. For three days and 400 miles, every last person, not one of them could stop talking about it . . . made it their personal business to terrify me with the prospect of winds that would rip a bike from underneath me, strike me down with flying sheets of corrugated iron.

In my head I see the thing, spinning out over the Gulf of Mexico, every cloud in the southeast pulled into its orbit and rushing out to meet with it. All the time my legs circled slowly against its headwind, the wind flattening trees over the Black Water Saloon, shut up and abandoned on the Mississippi border. My mind begins to blur. I see the engines of freight trains firing up to speed, wheels throwing sparks as the rails intersect and then, without even realising it, in the blink of an eye, Alabama is all but behind me. I spin away, ricochet into Mobile Bay . . . the road sinking, rolling down towards the centre of the earth and the middle of the night. Sky vanishes, a wall above, a tunnel . . . strip lighting, white light, almost blue like the lights that kill flies in cheap restaurants. I buzz down into the tunnel. It coils, white walls of tile, morgue . . . that warm, stagnant air and those tiled walls. Somehow familiar, that air. *Where am I?* Where have I found myself, to be in a place so familiar beneath the Bay of Mobile and, yes . . . that's it! It's the Tube, the London Underground . . . a little piece of home beneath the waters of Mobile Bay as the road rises back up and the smell abates. I'm thrown back into the night, over causeways that skate the surface of the estuary, over the delta that spits me into Florida, *'the only thing we have to fear is fear itself'* ringing in my ears.

If some hurricane was going to hit me, it had better do it hard. Don't doubt I was going to hit the bastard back, right back into the Gulf of Mexico, spinning off into the Atlantic. *Yallah, yallah!* I muttered my oaths even as that rear wheel once more started giving up the ghost. Two spokes, perhaps three had already blown up, wanted no more to do with the whole joke as I rode 71 miles into that final day of storm. It's not spectacular, not in numerical terms . . . if I reached 10mph then it was fast. So devastating to remember how slowly I crawled, yet I scarcely stopped even once. All day I watched, looking over my right shoulder . . . the sky a solid boulder, falling to crush the earth as I hurried into the Panhandle of Florida at 10mph, the waves crashing upon the sea, upon the sand, exploding on piers and quaysides.

East Coast

Day 145 – Brooker – 15,241 Miles

Lying on my back, a hard picnic table beneath me . . . I look up at the Florida sky, just as I'd once looked up from a Chinaman's bench in a Malaysian garage. South Carolina and the Busbees were nearing. I'd spoken to Danty by phone, given it two days, two days more and I would meet with him and Nita, go to the house at Edisto. There I'd rest a day, but in order to use that day to its full potential I had to arrive late one night, sleep in a bed, rest a day, sleep in a bed and then set off. To me a rest day meant two sleeps, anything less and I wasn't interested.

By 7pm, I'd ridden 100 miles, sky scarcely dark, some nine hours earlier than my recent bedtimes, but I couldn't carry on. I'd splashed all day long, trudged more exhausted than ever. It always went that way, five big days and then a crash; 180, 130, 130, hurricane . . . 220 miles sunk down into Tallahassee and then flat. The town of Brooker comes and I fall asleep. Body pulled wool right over Brain's eyes, good and proper. Convinced Brain a five-hour nap would lead to riding steadily at 20mph next day. Hook, line and sinker, Brain took it. Press release issued: 'After lengthy negotiations, it has been decided we should stop and sleep for five hours in order that afterwards we ride steadily at 20mph all day tomorrow.'

Midnight came. Alarm strikes up the band . . . that synthesised, electronic birdsong, unfailingly cheery, entirely oblivious to my

pain, completely insensitive to the rain and the only five hours'
sleep. The way that alarm goes off you'd think something wonderful was happening, no mere bleeping, not for the twenty-first
century. The damn alarm thinks I've learned to fly, thinks there
are amaryllis blossoming . . . I hit the thing. Sleep. Ten minutes
and the alarm goes off, just as optimistic. Sleep. Ten minutes. Body
won't let go of sleep, just another hour. I reset the alarm. Alarm
goes off . . . unperturbed, just as cheerful . . . perhaps just two
more hours. At 5am, I wake up beneath a damp shelter, a disused
signpost leaning against the wall of Greater Bell Methodist
Church. Eyes open, read the schedule for worship services. I'm
riding.

By then I had to do it, had to dig in. The greatest motivation I
found anywhere in the world was not to be late for people prepared to go out on a limb for me. There's no extreme psychological
depths, no driving ambition, no personal torment and no superhuman resolve comparable to my desire not to inconvenience
decent folk. 5am and I had the best part of 200 miles to ride
before a respectable time, an hour that would not force the Busbees to stay up beyond civilised bedtime. The truth was that all
day I knew it would be impossible. Even with a 5am start, it would
require until early next morning for 200 miles to be up. I suppose
I knew it then, but perhaps there was a chance . . . that same old
hope for a rocketing tailwind. Preparing to try my hand at failing
in the impossible, heading north of Jacksonville the road signs
confirmed it. '*Savannah – 120 miles*'. The computer on my handlebars reads 50 miles at 9am. My map reads Edisto 100 miles beyond
Savannah. What all that meant, in short, was that I'd overcooked
it. The maths were wrong, stacked against me. I'd gone too far
south in search of miles . . . I shouldn't have slept, I shouldn't
have slept so long. At noon I called Danty, somewhere just over
the Georgia state line. '*Danty . . . I can't do it.*' Laughter down the

phone, he brushes it right off . . . 'You keep going! Perhaps we can pick you up at a roadside somewhere near the Edisto junction. Just keep going!'

That became the story of the day. I'd call Danty, tell him it was no good, that it couldn't be done, and he'd just tell me to keep going and we'd see what happened. I didn't stop, only two twenty-minute refuelling sessions . . . chocolate, bananas, peanut butter straight into the tank. My wheel was the other feature, built in California, in Encinitas . . . that day and night in Georgia I killed it, murdered the thing. All week it had caused trouble, spokes breaking, spokes replaced, spokes breaking. For days it had been apparent the wheel would not hold up back to Europe, come that time it seemed it wouldn't last even as far as New York. Caution thrown to the wind, there was no time to waste nursing my wheel as I'd done beforehand, spinning easier gears, avoiding cranking out big pedalstrokes. The rim protested, gave way . . . that rim performed out-and-out mutiny. Spokes broke, of course they did, that much was nothing new, but that day it was the rim itself that went. Eyelets burst right through, genuine explosions as my pedalstrokes pulled a chain, pulled a sprocket, a sprocket that pulled a hub, and a hub bolted by 32 spokes to a rim that was in turn supposed to pull along. The rim wasn't interested. If previously the spokes had been the breaking point, what happened then was the spoke remained intact but pulled a chunk clean out of the rim. *Bang!* It makes such a din . . . a bazooka . . . a real racket when pedalling starts pulling your wheel apart, tearing holes in the aluminium. Right after one of the loudest bangs, I stopped and bent beneath my wheel, peered in. There it was, the spoke intact, floating electrified in the air, shivering on the breeze above an exit wound, the hole where once it had been. Shards of jagged metal, bucked teeth where spoke left wheel . . . and nothing in the world I could do about it.

Then 6pm comes, Nita Busbee tells me Danty is out hunting deer, call back in an hour; 7pm and I speak to Danty driving to the abattoir to pick up venison . . . 'just keep going, we'll see what happens'; 10pm and I'm in, let me see now . . . a town called Darien. Danty announces it, 'Keep on for Savannah, we're leaving South Carolina, we'll come meet you . . . Highway 84 from the west, Highway 17 from the south.'

A bed waiting, a shower, my rest day and the knowledge it would all be OK . . . a healthy bicycle beneath me and I could have destroyed that road, torn strips out of the tarmac. Yet what I had was so far from a healthy bicycle, spoke after spoke going down. I made it north, made it to within 10 miles of the appointed spot, but by then it was no good. As 180 miles reared up, eight spokes had either broken at the spoke or pulled from the rim. My rim looked as though landmines had been placed there to stop unwanted visitors, a cycling horror story. The wheel couldn't handle it . . . dead-and-buried at last, rolling so far out of line and off-centre that the tyre hit the frame in each revolution. Torn in two, half the wheel pulled home towards Encinitas, the other wanted to visit Europe. It hit . . . *it hit, it hit, it hit* . . . the tyre wearing away, smoothing bald, wheels refusing to turn any faster, turns slowing, ever more encumbered. I could have done it, could have kept on beating through the pedal strokes, as full of adrenaline as I was, but adrenaline does strange things to a mind. Adrenaline will power into the open road with the wheel scarcely turning, thriving upon only itself, unconcerned that only 10mph are being ridden. I call Danty . . . 2am, they're waiting at the junction, 10 miles north. I call Danty, apologise one last time. He chuckles, 'That's all right, don't you worry about it now . . . We're on our way.'

Day 147 – Edisto – 15,436 Miles

White sheets, sunlight hits. Really white sheets, like arctic wastes, tundra stretching as far as I could see. That pillow it is so plump behind my head, the duvet so heavy, the mattress pulling down upon my body, joints massaged by clean cotton. I look . . . call out into the vast white. No reply. Just me. Arms and legs point all four corners. Nowhere to cycle, 10am and I'm still in bed, right on schedule. It's all going to plan.

We sit together, talking for quickly passing hours, the Atlantic rolling next to me, just as the Pacific had done three weeks earlier. Danty praises Nita's cooking. She snaps back, playful . . . 'If I die first, he'll have to find himself a new wife pretty fast or he'll starve to death!' Danty gives something between a smile and shudder, a little laugh, as if to dismiss the possibility that such a scenario could ever occur. He takes off his glasses, gives the lenses a wipe . . . 'Well, I'd hope that I'd die first . . . because I wouldn't want to be married to anyone but you, Nita Busbee.'

Four decades the Busbees have been married, a marital fairy-tale: first loves, starry-eyed, straight out of the blocks and it turns out perfect. Four decades on and you'd think it was the day after their wedding. They talk about their children. Nita speaks up . . . 'Danty, he can never say no to them. Danty Busbee doesn't know how to say no to anybody!' She talks about the daughter who studied business but now cuts hair in her salon in Los Angeles, the son who works in environmental legislation. They talk of how '*modern*' their children are, of all the fights growing up . . . and then Danty says something remarkable. '*We learned a lot from our children.*' The line pierces my ear, scalds right in. You want to know how rare a thing that is, how many parents I've ever heard saying how much they learned from their children, suggesting wisdom can run up out of youth, not only down out of age? I've never heard any other adult say as much, don't ever expect to again.

Danty talks politics, not dogmatic, just speaks his heart . . . 'I'd like to pay more taxes for a better society, pay a little more, so as the money could help people with less than we've been fortunate enough to find ourselves with.' That statement was the least American thing I heard in my two months there. He goes on, 'Too many people are just . . . they're just . . .' and he looks around for the word and then puts '*consumed*' on the table with his palm. 'They're just consumed with *gimme, gimme, gimme*.' As he says it, he makes to pull in piles of coins across the table. 'Take my partner, my partner at my law firm . . . a good man, a good man, but he just doesn't get it, and no matter how many times we talk about it, he still doesn't get it. Black people . . . if you talk to this guy about black people, he'll say that, in their position, what he'd do is get a dead-end job, work all hours to save all of his money, pay to do a college course so that he could get a qualification and then a better job . . .' Danty places his palms down. 'And every time, *every time* he says it . . . I have to tell him that he knows his ancestors in this country owned shops . . .' He opens one palm. 'And that black people know their ancestors were slaves . . .' He opens the other. 'How could that be a comparable starting position in society?'

Danty Busbee is almost 60 years old, a white man born in South Carolina, growing up with segregation around him, a state where, even 150 years later, people still call the Civil War '*the War of Northern Aggression*'. Danty grew up South . . . you hear it in his voice, jaunty, musical tones as he speaks, his storytelling calm and joyful. He grew up in Confederacy and yet, despite that . . . no, that's not it . . . *because* of that, he actually talks about an issue like the black people of America with more heart and empathy, more sensitivity and straightforward common sense than most liberal chatterers who learned their opinions by heart and now regurgitate them for any dinner table that'll listen. Danty Busbee is the political ideal, a human with progressive thinking that comes not as a lifestyle choice or even a logical idea, but as a result of genuinely understanding how it feels to be a human in the first place, of living each day by such spirit.

Day 148 – Savannah – 15,436 Miles

Next morning I'm standing in my bedroom, packing a pannier as Danty comes in. He is wearing his regular chinos, short-sleeved shirt tucked in, his white hair and high hairline. He pushes his spectacles up his nose, sort of mumbling something before he starts saying it. He walks towards me.

'It's been very nice having you . . . a real pleasure. This is a little something from Nita and me, we like you a lot . . . it's just something to make life a bit easier for you. Nothing much, not enough to go out partying . . . but here you go.'

A wrap of green presidents came out towards me and *oh no!*

'No . . . *Danty, I can't!* I couldn't . . . you've been so kind, so generous. I don't want to take you for granted . . . don't want to take liberties . . .'

Danty insists, presses the presidents towards me . . . 'Don't you be silly now! We don't feel that way, you didn't ask for anything . . .' Those were his very words, and he was right . . . I hadn't asked for anything, hadn't expected a thing, and I am still so very grateful. I tried to refuse, but I was so broke . . . so very broke, and Danty wanted to give me that hundred dollars. So I took it.

We drove to Savannah, a two-hour drive just for me, on account of a bike shop and the return to that junction. It had been a day and a half with the Busbees . . . 36 hours as a human being, and I knew exactly what was coming, what lay in store. I was forlorn . . . had enjoyed those hours so much, all of it waiting to shatter before my very eyes, from human being back to destitute imbecile with some athletic achievement like a stick up his ass. What was it needed? Let me see . . . 1,200 miles still to go before my flight out of Boston, nine days to ride them, eight days with a final rest day in New York taken into account. All that left 150 miles every day . . . for eight days.

As evening neared, we returned to collect my wheel, my legs aching from a day of Savannah. I'm no good at walking any more . . . to this day I'm still a useless walker, what with all that couriering in London and then the 18,000 . . . my muscles have forgotten how to do anything else. Back in the shop I sat with Nita on a bench in the corner, watched a mechanic finishing my wheel. Danty stood at the counter, talking to the owner of the shop. And I saw it coming. It wasn't like Doug Schultz in Los Angeles, straight out of nowhere . . . I knew what Danty was about to do. Tone quietens, fingers point . . . the wheel in the workshop, the till on the counter. I saw it happening, saw what was coming. The shop owner starts ringing up a total, numbers emerging at right angles . . . $95, $145 . . . in white-green light on that old display screen. I heave up to my feet, up to the counter as Danty draws his wallet from his pocket and I knew I should've leapt the moment I got a whiff of what was going on.

'Danty . . . *Danty! You can't, you just can't!* You've already been so generous,' I murmur, trying for firm but grateful. 'I don't think I'd feel comfortable with you paying for the wheel.'

'*I hear ya . . . oh, I hear ya!* But don't you worry about it . . . *really don't* . . . we want to do this. This is just our little contribution to get you rolling again.'

'But, Danty, really . . . it's very kind of you . . . but I just can't accept it.'

'You're not accepting anything here . . . don't you worry about it.'

* * *

I don't know what to say. I've expressed my thanks, both then and a thousand times since, increasingly guilty for all that I've received in return for only words. I sent my presents over to South Carolina, bought and posted the things as soon as I'd earned a little money back in London. I've poured out my gratitude and love for Danty and Nita Busbee, yet there's no adequate response to such generosity, not beyond showing whatever thanks you can at the time, and then endeavouring to visit your own kindness upon those in need when you happen upon them.

I'm still searching for a sufficient tribute to just how much all that generosity meant to me, from all those different people. The unnamed Kazakhs, Tartars, Chinese, the Moirs in Singapore, Ray in New Zealand, the couple with the $20 driving through Big Sur, Doug Schultz in Los Angeles, Erik in Encinitas, Rusty in Texas, still others you're yet to meet, others the damn editors killed off . . . and then the Busbees . . . again and again . . . the Busbees. My ride, my record-breaking 18,000 . . . I could've done it without them all. I'm not going to hash out some old trite here. I *could* have turned those pedals anyway, could've borrowed still more borrowed money. I could've done the whole thing alone and without help . . . but had I done so, well . . . the feat would've been harder and still more pointless, the whole fiasco hardly worth bothering with. Those kindnesses mean so much more than any large number of miles or dumb total of days. I set out from Rouen with my half-baked ideology against a loveless politics . . . and you can believe me if you wish or doubt me too, it makes no difference to me now . . . but I set out on that deranged quest with an agenda that meant everything to me in spite of how little it meant to everybody else, and each time I received such kindness as that, it gave me my reason, furnished my convictions, my meaning of life and my reason for trying. With all other words superfluous, these few are precise. It's all about the people . . . it has to be.

Day 150 – The Carolinas – 15,612 Miles

Away from the equator and the warmth of the sun, I rode deep into autumn. I would sit and watch the leaves . . . gold, red, brown and already dead upon the branches. Curling back on themselves like cleaved hearts, I watched them, white veins of deadened sap all ready to return to earth. That final moment came, came silently . . . some slight movement of wind shook the air, and the air shook the stem of the leaf, dry and lifeless so that it cracked in the silence and parachuted down, rocking back and forth like a crib on its way to a final resting.

As I watched the leaves fall and the sun retreat, the days grew shorter, bringing forward the darkness each evening. Bayous returned all around the skirts of the cypress trees, growing out the waters and then reflected in that still mirror, growing down towards the bottom as the tops of the trees weft black and pale in the early-morning mists. Cotton was everywhere, bud after bud bursting from inside the barbs of their cases, sticking like marshmallows on the end of sticks. The dew and the low cloud of late afternoon both sat in droplets upon those balls of cotton, pluming in a star from the cask that held them.

The first spoke broke. *Bang!* Straight out of nowhere. That's all you need to know really, all that matters. I was riding north, South Carolina ebbing towards North . . . Jamestown, Johnsonville,

Whiteville. I rounded a high-winding corner where a house stood alone, a chain-link fence surrounding its grounds, a roof of corrugated tin, dogs . . . dogs . . . five of them, no . . . *six*! All over the world, dogs had chased me, barking and yapping, and there they were again in North Carolina, six dogs, running at the chain-link fence that kept them off the road. They hit the fence with a cymbal crashing . . . unperturbed they run its length, teeth flashing . . . a gate . . . an open gate and the dogs are all out on the road. No playful mutts either, no Labrador with a pink tongue and a golden coat . . . these dogs are the kind that their owners put on treadmills with images of horror in front of them, dogs encouraged to attack and then fed when they do. They pile out of the gate . . . six of the things and, one in particular, one at the head of them all . . . small and white, bull terrier, disgustingly ugly, really foul as far as creatures go. Two feet tall, one foot wide and pink gums falling out the side of its face, saliva trickling the length of its teeth and onto the tarmac below. I'm going slow, always slow things right down when pursued by dogs; the best option is giving them nothing to chase. Foolproof, worked every time that one did, just slow it down. Chasing dogs are one thing, biting dogs a different matter entirely. Confronted with biting dogs and slowing down is poor counsel. There I was, at a canter . . . my six dogs in tow, that white bull terrier in particular, a smile of pink gums in the thick of the action underneath my flank. I look down at it, it looks up at me.

Something was amiss. I felt it in my gut that time . . . interspecies communication was going strong. Looking down at the thing, somehow closer than normal, it looked to have gotten itself into a position from which to bite rather than just bark. I pedal faster, Body and legs are unsure what to do, consider a kick. Sitting safe distance . . . Brain overrules it. Legs continue onwards, everything a little uncertain apart from that damn bull terrier, moving beyond the point at which dozens of dogs before it had started a retreat. From where I sat, that stinking creature looked every bit like it was about to bite me and then . . . there it was, suspended in the air and suddenly looking every bit like it was biting me, and dammit, but it *was* biting me . . . it was biting me! As if I didn't have enough on my plate without a bull terrier biting at my calves.

'*IT FUCKING BIT ME!*' . . . that's what I shout, a perfect description of the situation as it had happened, entirely for the benefit of personal verification and five other dogs. It stops biting me . . . I'm still pedalling, my leg feels like it has been pinched between finger and thumb of an angry god. The muscle felt bruised, aching at its core but barely a tear to the flesh and just a dot of blood. I pedal on, dogs still at it . . . the bull terrier, that god-awful creature, still barking at my pedalling legs that had never posed any threat to its chain-link fence and the grotty shack it guarded. I get off my bike, five dogs and the bull terrier around my ankles, noses and its disgusting snout right under both of my calves, a banquet right in front of them . . . and me, limping slowly away, pushing my bicycle to the top of the hill.

Day 153 – Mason–Dixon – 15,883 Miles

Another spoke . . . *Bang!* I'll replace the two at lunchtime. Another spoke . . . *Bang!* Three spokes in three days with a so-called brand-new wheel. I unload my bicycle, upturn it, sit down on a pannier bag and go about addressing my wheel, the worst-built wheel in all history, little more than a toy. A hopscotch of spokes, some of them stainless steel, some galvanised steel . . . a real mess, that's all there is to say.

The Carolinas moved behind me, washed away. I passed Rocky Mount, passed Roanoke Rapids. Virginia, I reached Virginia . . .

homing in on the Mason–Dixon line, nearing the Union. *Bang!* Another spoke . . . Yankee territory. The dead of night rising . . . 2am, 3am, no margin to fall behind in my 150s. It was the Interstate, Interstate 95 . . . you're not supposed to ride them on a bicycle but at three in the morning there's nobody to stop you. I was tired of going in and out of towns on the smaller roads, there was nothing there for me any longer. I wanted Interstate . . . straight road, well-lit, signs counting down remaining miles. My head tries to stay awake, wants comfort, wants so many things it can't possibly have.

Day 154 – Chesapeake – 15,977 Miles

The morning comes with my alarm, obliviously cheerful. I sleep until 9am, make my way to the beginning of the bridge . . . the mouth of Chesapeake Bay, where the French Navy defeated the British and so helped the United States on its way to independence, cutting out the middle-man . . . autonomous exploitation, the most efficient form.

I didn't see it coming, didn't realise it would be so huge. What came next was an addition to the catalogue, my portfolio of epic rides . . . the showpiece battles that won the war. Into Shanghai with 200 miles, 400 in those 48 hours into Singapore, 235 in the Texan night . . . 19 November and a Thursday morning with the plan to be in New York on Friday evening: 330 miles in a day and a half. Ten miles each hour would do it . . . doesn't sound so fast, does it?

A man by the name of Elliot Kalmus had read about me on the Internet, sent an email offering any help I might need in New York. The bicycle, a bed for a night, companionship for the ride out of the city, anything and I should let him know. I'd called

Elliot from Edisto, thanked him for the offer of help with the bicycle, fine at the time, and accepted his offer to ride out of New York together. He told me then, on the phone in Edisto, of a ferry that sailed from the town of Belford on the New Jersey shore, directly into the harbour at Manhattan. It cut out heavy traffic, the tunnels and roads into the city, and the last boat to sail at 8pm Friday. At around 11am, Thursday morning, I pulled my panniers from the service vehicle that had driven me the five miles of Chesapeake Bridge and loaded them onto the shore.

It was lacklustre, that's how I remember it . . . a headwind in the morning, dying as the day wore on, my legs no better even after it had blown over. I hurried, no great speed and yet so much haste inside my head. The cities waited for me ahead . . . a century to Salisbury . . . then 60 to Dover, 50 to Wilmington, the bridge into New Jersey and a final 100 to Belford. I wanted 200 miles that first day, in order to leave just a 100-mile formality for Friday daytime. Riding like that, the signposts can come to be such (*Bang!* . . . another spoke) monumental occasions. Forget Christmas, forget birthdays, there's no anticipation, excitement or disappointment quite like a signpost. Ten miles south of Salisbury and you get the first sign for Dover, that's a thrill, I can tell you. I set about making plans for my arrival in Dover, right on schedule. An hour later and you're still leaving Salisbury and Dover remains three hard hours away. The first signpost that mentioned Wilmington . . . *121 miles* . . . was a real joy. I prepared the rostrum for my success, and in the hysteria of that moment I would lose all sight of the fact that those 120 miles would take until beyond the crack of dawn. Sometimes the signpost would just omit the city I was waiting for entirely. It felt like being stabbed in the back, being told nobody cares where I'm going, told Wilmington isn't so important after all.

Virginia, Maryland, Delaware. All day and night, I rode through each of those cold, dark states before the sun next came to rise. I tried to distract my mind, stay awake as I cycled through Odessa, Delaware, just as I'd cycled through Odessa in the Ukraine. I cycled through Smyrna, Delaware . . . Smyrna the Greek name for the Turkish city of Izmir, where my father was born on the Ides of March in 1947. And, as I swam through the Delaware night, I could see him, the afternoon sun through the rainclouds and net curtain at the kitchen window, a rainbow spread across the sky as he opens first his arms and then that baritone of his. With a partisan choir from the bottom of his lungs, he booms . . . *'because life is beautiful!'*

The rains started again, dark and wet. The first drops zipped and pattered, landing as if the road were a drum skin. Streetlights shimmer, the lollipop of the traffic lights moving up and down the tarmac, alternating red to green, blurring and waving in the puddles. The road illuminated into the furthest distance, repeated and glistening on wet asphalt. I look up, see lines drawn across the night sky . . . strong, parallel lines running horizontal, line after line pulled across the night and notes landing there fast. Up from the road and down from the trees and cosmos, impaling themselves upon those bars . . . hoops, sticks, minims, quavers and crotchets, all of them harpoon themselves onto my bars of the most horrendous music, bum note after note, falling and leaping from out of the gutters. Violins quiver in the background, a collapsing tenement, a broken stylus. I know how I looked that morning as the sun came up, that sun slow as ever. A solitary streetlamp above me, signposts for Baltimore to the west, my head scooped inside its hood, a furrow in my brow as if a tally of days had been etched there, four vertical lines with a strike through the centre. And then my eyes. Bags beneath the eyes were nothing new, but that day, peering uncertainly into the camera, the bags had really made themselves comfortable, had started cultivating wrinkles, bags beneath the bags. My eyes . . . but they look so sad, all vulnerable and lost they seem, and yet I know that was not the truth of it. That photograph it lies, for I remember my soul right then . . . and, for all my bodily sufferings, I know that I was at peace, and now, as I walk the streets of London without a tally on my brow or purse of fatigue beneath my eyes, it's now that I feel sadnesses . . . it's here that I feel lost.

Day 155 – Garden State – 16,258 Miles

The sun shone. Delaware Memorial Bridge, a mile and a half of suspension bridge, four lanes east and four west. I made a break for it, no interest in stopping just for the police to tell me to find a detour. I made a break for it, raced across . . . found myself in Deepwater. Deepwater, New Jersey. It was perfect.

New Jersey, they call it the Garden State, and when you arrive in mid-November like that you know why. The sun up high, trails of white cloud through that deep blue, shallow furrows of dry earth across ploughed fields. Along the horizon stood trees already lost to winter, stripped almost bare by wind and chill, so that their trunks and branches created only a wall of cold stone, set here and there with the survivors of autumn and summer, leaves remaining in the midst of that stone, a splash of green, bunches of blood orange, pockets of colour set like gemstones in a rockface.

I rode on, elated. Home straight. For all the world, if I was not a specimen of pure happiness that morning, nought but mirth and (*Bang!* . . . another spoke) contentment . . . nothing more. In my head it was all but over, the hardest part done with. I'd triumphed, ridden so hard and so consistently that I then had only 100 miles in 12 hours for New York. In New York I would rest a day, leaving almost two complete days to ride less than 250 miles to Boston.

After Boston, back in darling Europe, I would reel in my glittering prize, the end of my travails rounded off with a week of days at 120 miles. As I stood removing waterproofs, a woman watched me from inside her car, beckoned me to the window. Middle-aged, cardigan, spectacles . . . no idea what she could want. Down goes the window, out comes a hand, a hand with $10 in it. She speaks with a smile . . . 'I want you to take this . . . you've achieved something really special here today.' And I'm speechless.

What came next was such tragedy . . . Othello with Desdemona's handkerchief, so avoidable, really classic stuff. The New Jersey morning shines on down, the bicycle rolls free and I hear it whisper to the road . . . 'perdition catch my soul but I do love thee, and when I love thee not . . . then chaos has come again'. Between that seer and I, things were being set up for a fall . . . heartbreaking . . . it's really heartbreaking to see just how wrong I was, so blissfully unawares, clueless as to what lay in store for me, the pig's ear and ham-fisted mess I was yet to make of it all.

* * *

Sometime after dusk I made it, riding solidly, wired . . . I didn't trust myself with a nap, didn't trust the Atlantic not to throw up a headwind and snatch my triumph from me. Another 110 miles went down, 330 since that spot outside Norfolk where I last awoke.

Arriving at the harbour, I asked an attendant when the last boat was. I hugged him as he told me there was an hour before it docked. Upon the quay, the night so clear, across the waters I watched New York glowing, nothing but light, the night sky turned white. Eventually the boat docked, disembarked by suits and briefcases and people dressed for power, dressed in ways such as I'd not seen since London. With my bicycle I stumbled aboard, footsteps so tired and hesitant as the heels and pointed toes strode purposefully past.

I missed it, missed it all. That hard-on ... Manhattan ... Céline's hard-on, standing erect and bolt upright on the horizon, one long shaft shooting at the night. As soon as I boarded that boat I was asleep. I found a seat, lay my head upon a pillow of my hands and *Whack!* ... an explosion. *Kaboom!* Knocked-out loaded ... a sleep to end all sleeps. The Statue of Liberty skulked past, joined the prestigious list of sights around the world either I slept through or bypassed altogether. I didn't see New York rise above me, didn't see a thing until I felt a voice calling from afar ... 'Mister! Hey, Mister!' ... chest shaking, the voice closer as eyes open. I leap back out of the ground, the skipper's nose right in front of me. 'You're here ... it's time to wake up!'

Day 156 – Lower East Side – 16,352 Miles

West 108th and Broadway was where I was headed first, that's where Milap lived, a friend from university who they'd somehow let in at Columbia. In all the world, Milap was the only person I met that I actually knew.

Broadway ... lights of the theatre, crowds dolled up for the weekend. Gents in long jackets and girls in short skirts, stilettos, all of them standing on corners together, pulling one another with nobody sure which way they're going. The bright lights become gradually less bright, dimming on the road up to Harlem. At 108th I stand beside a buzzer ... minutes pass, doors opening and then, bolts, bolts, bolts. A latch scratches, bolts. Fitting bolts in New York City, my word but that must be a good earner. They know a thing or two about bolts in that place, a human Fort Knox, everyone locked away in their own square metres ... you keep to yourself.

Milap sits across from me in an armchair, leaning forwards,

elbows on knees . . . a couple of wide eyes ask questions, ready to listen. I've forgotten everything. Forgotten how to speak and what to say, forgotten my personality. Turfan, Oregon, Steppe. Where did it get to? Who was I before all that happened, how did I behave and what did people make of me? I ponder what to say, ponder whether or not I was lonely before this moment. It gets worse, it'll get much worse than this . . . just you wait for London, my boy, that's what confusion really feels like. It's 330 miles since proper sleep, almost 48 hours since I last awoke from anything more restful than that concussion on the boat. The phone rings, a flatmate . . . Mary from North Carolina, asking our plans. Already in a bar, she shouts loudly . . . 'There's something really going down on the Lower East Side tonight!' It sounds dramatic, ominous. I ask what's going down: 'Has something serious happened?' but no . . . that's just how people speak here. That's the way that you say you're having fun on the Lower East Side of Manhattan, when the country is only three centuries old and everything's still exciting. That's how you speak, living in the centre of the universe that is New York City on Friday night. Milap looks at me . . . '*Do you want to go out?*'

We hit the street . . . you don't just walk on the things, not in New York City. It's all well and good back home, back in the sticks from whence you sprung, the provinces . . . but not in New York . . . you don't just walk around like the same small-town schmuck you always were. We hit the streets, head off to ride the subway . . . so much better than just taking a train. As the rats scuttle below the sleepers and still air, Milap and I catch up, find out where we've got to in the race that we were entered into at birth, that struggle to get a little esteem, some respect and recognition, a few more units of currency away from the decimal point in this world of ours. A subway cart rattles in. We get on, we're lowered down the tunnel, rocking side by side in our bucket seats. Ten days . . . it's 10 days until the end of my 18,000 . . . two weeks before I have to figure out another way of justifying my existence again. I felt it then, felt the weight of that burden growing about my shoulders, my legs . . . but no, not yet, not yet with this, dread can wait . . . right now there's no world outside of New York City.

We bound from the subway, black-and-white, silent film from the silver screen . . . that place where destinies are forged, where we are shown just what we can be, just how much larger than life it is we can become. We're Hyperions the lot of us, emperors all over the face of the earth, educated on a silver screen and then left to flounder in reality, left with all of our off-kilter blemishes, all those retorts thought up too late, those wisecracks overeager and poorly timed, flaccid cocks between our legs, breasts too small, lop-sided, spots on the chin and flaking scalp across your shoulders. In short, we're fucked, fucked by our own expectations. But not that night, not that first night in New York City . . . riding in on the bicycle after 330 miles and no sleep. That's up to it, that's big enough, that's legend . . . the sort of stuff you can tell people with head held high, arriving in the centre of the universe and emerging from out of the subway. Together we live the dream, spring from the tiles of the subway morgue, up into the lights of the Lower East Side as Milap calls out. The screen-door slams and there she is . . . Mary's dress waves, she strides our way . . . Mary from North Carolina, in heels and blonde curls, a hand offered with the fingers deftly dipped, a hand to be taken rather than shaken, the smile of a Southern girl.

The basement bars spill over, catalogue crowds all *shooting-the-shit* for New York where anywhere else in the world they'd have just been talking. We walk down the street, straight out of a movie poster, purpose in that step, with Mary in the middle in dress and curls . . . three abreast. My word but we make that street our own, marvellous cinematography, into the bar with all love of life and just who it is we are. Down the steps we go, into the pit . . . orange lighting, warm air, like being slipped beneath an electric grill. We remove jackets, we talk . . . *no* . . . I forget . . . we *shoot-the-shit* with friends of Mary's, young guys, software developer and banker. The software developer he's bored by his job, doesn't want to talk about it. The banker coughs when Milap asks his . . . 'I'm a speculator' . . . and out comes laughter, like a bucket of water thrown in the face. The developer hits his back, 'Tell the truth, admit it! You're a banker!' The banker throws his head away, theatrical protest. '*No! Nooo!*' he wails, defiant. 'I work for a Swiss NGO, we're called UBS . . . we haven't made a profit in 13 years!' And we all burst into laughter, order drinks and *shoot-the-shit*, one of those shouted, half-caught conversations, the volume too loud and nobody saying a thing worth hearing anyway, like walking down a corridor in the dark when you can't see exactly where you're going but nevertheless know approximately where to tread. You feel your way through misheard proclamations and jokes you didn't get, reacting to the noises . . . nodding, laughing, stepping gingerly, hoping not to trip and fall flat . . . reveal you've no idea what the fuck anyone's been talking about. A round of drinks is called, the only thing we understand. We toast, clashing glass, cheers and dancing, hesitant dancing . . . nobody wants to dance, only Mary in her dress, shaking moves between rebuffed men all scrabbling like magpies to silver . . . Athenians at Melos, an onslaught as Mary bats eyes, moves hips and we all just stand, drinking, shouting half-conversation between long swallows of drink.

Those metropolitan bars, the First World, Second and Third too, where the young and aspiring go to shout snatched words at one another, subterranean bunkers where music throbs and communication withers. We stand alone, all of us lined up and isolated in stationary promenades. It's not important . . . we're not here to communicate, this generation of mine, we're individuals, every last one of us an individual, no care in the world for interaction, we're display pieces, mannequins for the poise and garments and drinks that will make us who we are. What use is an interaction once you're nothing but an individual anyway? *But enough!* Enough of this pondering . . . *Another round! Another round!* I get to the bar, deep in overdraft but, who cares, it's my one civic duty in this community of ours.

From above his manicured beard the barman clocks me. He wears silver loud around his neck, shaped stubble disappearing up towards his short hair, diamonds in his lobes, sideward baseball cap, conceited eyes that settle on me lazily, as if forced there, as if they had to look at me in spite of just how disinteresting a subject I cut. I order the round. Four drinks ringing up thirty-six bucks precisely. I hand over two twenties . . . forty bucks . . . surplus four dollars. You know what he said to me? You know what that conceited, bearded swine with the lopsided baseball cap said as I hand over forty dollars for four drinks?

'You good for change?'

I straighten up, all English . . . what's he getting at? 'Pardon?'

He repeats . . . 'You good for change?'

'Huh?' quizzical . . . 'Sorry, what do you mean?'

His eyes roll a high arc . . . 'Do you want your change?'

Did I want my change? Of course I wanted my change, that '*change*' was the best part of five bucks! Yes . . . or no . . . whatever the answer was supposed to be. I wasn't *good for change*, I needed that change, *Give it back!* He gave me my $4, placed curses on the bills pressed back into my hands, pure hatred for me, foreign filth . . . a cheapskate and a bastard. Shaking his head in disgust, his eyes narrowed, really put out, insulted to be faced by such a prick as me.

Day 157 – Hudson – 16,353 Miles

Elliot Kalmus came with morning. Damn but I needed help with my bicycle! It was that rear wheel, that godawful rear wheel. Four or five burst spokes, the thing well on its way to shrapnel all over again. It's 8am and Elliot arrives on the doorstep, works at a bike shop back across the Hudson in New Jersey. He takes my ruined wheel, says he'll drive back with the thing rebuilt after work.

The streets sleepwalked beneath me that day. I wandered across the city, nursing my head back to health, talking with Milap about life in New York, reflecting on my coming life in London. Two more weeks with a purpose, an answer to that infernal '*what do you do?*' question . . . two weeks and I'd be drifting again.

Elliot returned with evening, the wheel rebuilt as promised, spokes replaced. He didn't ask for money, wouldn't accept any. Elliot Kalmus drove into New York that morning to collect my wheel, drove it to New Jersey to have the thing rebuilt, and in return for his troubles wanted to take me out for dinner. All those kindnesses, six months so riddled with generosity. I don't know what I did to deserve all that.

We talked next morning's ride, the town of Nyack a destination at the heart of Elliot's plan. Nyack is a cycling hive beside the Hudson, home to The Runcible Spoon café, where I'm told all self-respecting rides ought to culminate. A lovely evening, great conversation but, with 12 days to Rouen . . . I should cut to the chase. The blueprint runs thus: Early next morning we cross the George Washington Bridge, north to Nyack, where Elliot would turn back and I'd head east through to Boston. When Elliot first explained the plan I'd agreed reluctantly, but second time around, over the course of dinner . . . impolite or otherwise, I had to say something.

'I'm sure it's *nicer*, more relaxed than the drag along coast, through the industry. I'd love to ride up the Hudson, but the direct route to Boston is maybe 230 miles . . . via Nyack it must be around 300. I'm not sure I can do it.'

That wasn't true. In fact I was almost sure I *couldn't*. I knew then it would end in tears, that it was too much. I put my dilemma to Elliot. Unperturbed, a man of the most gentle natures, he didn't see the circumstances in which riding with the traffic of the coast could possibly compare to the scenic route up the Hudson Valley. He batted away my reservations.

* * *

Morning came all too quickly, pulled me up from the settee. Even then I knew I needed help, needed miraculous tailwinds, that it was all but impossible. I said goodbye to Milap, he waved as I pedalled away to meet Elliot, a handful of blocks north, and together we rode out under the wrought-iron rafters of the George Washington Bridge. The weather was perfect that morning, a cobalt sky all empty of excuses or shadows, bright and keen the sun shone down on my undoing. Looking at New York from that bridge, you see how Rome must once have appeared to a peasant coming in from the provinces, the way it towers above heights any normal person ever has cause to look, constructions big enough to make us feel triumphant by proxy alone. I looked upon all those towers of Babel, saw why we no longer try to reach God. Those towers have grown tall enough now, tall enough that we need not bother with heaven and whatever might wait there. Our society has its meaning now and it's in New York, with the Hudson flowing in beneath a misty sun.

Packs of cyclists were heading along the river, Elliot initially carefree at my shoulder as we rolled over hills, talked cycling. By the time we reached Nyack at noon, he'd caught my concern. I think he knew it even then, knew what had happened and what would become of me. His brow had split, folds in his forehead as we arrived at The Runcible Spoon café. Other cyclists were sitting there already, squeezed inside their Lycra, sipping coffees as they eyed me suspiciously through the carbon-fibre frames of road bicycles leaning against kerbstones. It's tribal, there's a hierarchy to everything in this world and cycling is no exception. No matter how much you know about the Tour de France, no matter how integral cycling might be to your very soul, if you show up in front of road cyclists without Lycra around your thighs, a chamois on your crotch and dropped handlebars on your bike, they reserve the right to judge you. Even at the best of times . . . I've slim patience for them. A cyclist cocks his thumb, Elliot is dressed like one of their number, a roadie. The cyclist speaks to him instead of me, a translator.

'Where's he riding to, with all that?'

'Boston.'

'You're riding to *Boston*?'

'Yes.'

'When do you hope to make it there by?'

'I've got a flight to catch so I have to make it by four, tomorrow afternoon.'

'By four tomorrow afternoon . . . it's midday now! You're going to ride to Boston *in a day*?' His face broke into a smile, then a laugh.

'I suppose I have to.'

'You're going to ride to Boston *in a day*?'

I groaned . . . 'Can you *please* stop saying that?'

* * *

Elliot and I said our goodbyes, embraced, said our *great to meet yous* and good lucks. I gave my profuse thanks and was gone. He contacted me soon after my return, those first woebegone weeks back in London, said he felt responsible for the Hudson debacle, for leading me north out of the city. He said it broke his heart to hear how his wheel let me down. I told him not to worry about it, that I could never have been anything but grateful for all his help. Whatever went wrong for the sake of my record meant nothing in comparison to the worth of just meeting him. I told him that, and I knew I meant it too, but the whole thing was still too raw. I meant it, and yet I did not then feel it in my heart. There was no resentment, not in the least, but in so many ways that ride left me so sad, left so many new demons it took years to recover from.

* * *

North up the Hudson I stormed, through the grey stone walls of the valley, the long, golden grasses that grow beneath the rocks and in the riverbanks. Grey and gold is how it lives on in my imagination, with cold, dark waters thrashing like a river of ink through the middle. For all that it went wrong, that memory of Hudson in autumn is one I wouldn't like to be without. The road climbs high up the valley walls . . . it makes you sweat, corkscrew climbs and switchbacks to race back down. I hammered the thing, thrust north towards the first bridge that would allow me to cross the river and start east towards Boston, towards Europe. I gave no thought to my new wheel. All morning I'd powered into hills, the thing feeling rigid, trustworthy. I ploughed up the valley wall, heading for the bridge at Bear Mountain. There it came. I'll say it short and quick, just as it happened. I was all too accustomed to that sound by then, always from nowhere, without warning or announcement. It's only right that it should happen like that once more. *Bang!* Another spoke. I rode on, hoped it was just misfortune, only a maverick in one of the 32. *Hoped*. I had no time to nurse that wheel . . . it had to be abused, to have power forced through it for 24 hours and 250 waiting miles.

I gave it nine hours before the game was up. I wasn't going to do it, not that night. My stars were crossed, thumbscrews tightening and everything against me as I rode into Connecticut, evening settling as I neared Danbury in a funk, sides splitting, face gurning with anxiety. I took to Interstate . . . there's no time for the legitimate route through the Taconic Mountains. It was rush hour, heavy traffic, my bicycle conspicuous on the hard shoulder, white lights flashing across my flank. White lights, white lights, horns and then finally a solid white light sending forth a long shadow. A blue siren . . . a damn siren. *Bicyclist! . . . pull over!*

I pull over, dismount my bike and start walking towards the bonnet of the police car, a megaphone . . . *Stop! Stay where you are!* I stay where I am and out he comes, striding towards me with short legs and club-arms. He's scowling as he comes my way . . . shaved head, chewing gum, bulging eyes . . . one of those hooligans they give a uniform. Officer turns to me, eyeballing, eyeballs like billiard balls, halfway from his skull, roaring hate . . . 'Don't walk towards a police car! You might be armed! You want to get shot?' Why yes, that was it . . . I wanted to get shot. Siren on his face, he snaps, 'Why are you cycling on the Interstate?' I stutter up to speed . . . 'There's no other way, the law says I can . . . when there's no other route.'

'There are other routes,' he shouts. 'Get off here . . . drop south or go north.'

'I'm sorry . . . I have to be in Boston at 4pm tomorrow. The Interstate is the only way. *Please* . . . just three more junctions . . . it's safer than country roads anyway.'

He straightens, stiffens, asks for my passport . . . the same way they always did, as if they'd every right to see it, as if I was guilty of something. I sigh, fetch my passport. He leafs pages, finds the right page, looks at the wrong stamp . . . 'This isn't valid, what are you doing here?' He's destroying his gum, a contorted face, chewing his gum as if he hated it, as if it were the bit that his superiors gave him to bite upon as a means of controlling his anger. I take back the passport, point to the correct stamp. He nods, sheepish . . . orders me push the bike up to the exit we stand beside.

Resigned, off I go. But there's one last thing, a Parthian shot. Chewing on his gum, a mean smile spreads over his face, bulging eyes shining blue from sirens. Smug from thin lips, he gives a final sentence. '*You give your country a bad name . . .*' All hell . . . but that was rich, coming from him. I felt exactly the same way about him and yet somehow, somehow it hurt, cut to the quick. In that moment at the roadside it was all too much, with the flight to Boston unravelling before me, the cold miles waiting with only a dozen hard decisions and one gargantuan failure. I gulp . . . 'Excuse me?' He repeats, goads. '*You're a bad citizen*, you give your country a *bad* name.'

Night lowering by the second, hard-pressed by a predicament not quite comely, failing to make the world a better place, I couldn't stomach being called a bad citizen as well. I choked, that's what happened, I actually choked . . . it was too much. I felt his words in my soul, swallowed hard, almost fought back tears in launching a defence . . .

'I'm not a bad citizen, I care about people . . . about society and about justice. I believe in what is good in this world . . . *an-and* . . . I might be riding on the Interstate because I have to get to Boston before four o'clock tomorrow, but that doesn't mean I give my country a bad name . . . and equally . . .' I wasn't finished yet, still gagging on the wound of his words but plucking away regardless. 'If the role of the police is to help people in need, to convey a good image on behalf of the country that they represent . . . then, without meaning to be impolite, I could argue that you also give your country a bad name ...' I gulp ... 'For you haven't tried at all to help me.'

That got him, socked the bastard right in the face. Even hooligans don't like making people cry, that creaking in the voice as the taps are turned on and the waterworks bubble. He swallowed hard, the eyes receded, turned human. I touched the heart of a thug with that one, right at the Connecticut roadside. He chews his gum a little slower, softens ... 'My hands are tied, take the road towards Brookfield Centre.'

* * *

That put me into countryside, a road sloping up and down the hills rather than engineering a level route through them. I know, I know ... it's exactly as it should be, *'hills are the heart of cycling'*. I'm sure I must be on record as saying that somewhere, somewhere else though ... not there. What I needed was a flat drag, straight as a die. A runway all the way to Boston was all that I could handle and instead I got the Taconics through rural Connecticut. I've seen bigger, don't mistake me, they're hardly formidable ... but still quite sufficient where climbing a little more than you'd like is concerned.

A shadow of myself sits on a kerb, beneath a large white church, the village of Bridgewater among dark and wooded lanes. I'm fading, disappearing ... swigging from a bottle of corn syrup as if it were liquor, trying not to retch as it coagulated at my gag-reflex. The night was well advanced by then, swirling mists to trap the cold, the air thick with droplets of almost ice. The cold, yes, that was it ... the cold was coming for me at last. Perhaps it had reached ten o'clock, maybe a little past the hour and I was stricken, panicked. The airline ... I would call the airline ... I had to, nothing else for it. I would reschedule the flight, put it back a couple of days. I would ride a longer route to Boston, head north for Canada and shorten the European return to accommodate the extra miles I'd find. I call the airline. No answer. Office closed.

Day 159 – Nutmeg State – 16,549 Miles

Bridgewater, Roxbury, east to Southbury . . . slow progress, the night is gathering, smothering my efforts to fight the foregone conclusion. I edged towards dots and arrows I'd once drawn so simply as a route across my map. At Southbury a part of me gave up. I threw off the idea of the diagonal route, couldn't handle those ups and downs. It was a mistake, looking back now, scrutinising the scene of my undoing. I was all but over the Taconics by the time Southbury came into sight. It would have levelled out soon after, but that's nothing but hindsight now, sitting here so stoic and serene . . . Spartacus himself, all comfortable at his desk, but sleep-deprived, part hung-over and staring down the barrel of a 1,000-dollar airfare . . . I made the wrong call . . . I headed south, plunged down to the coast, away from Boston. Having shunned the flat coast and ridden over the Taconic Mountains to get out of New York, I then headed for the flat coast as an alternative to the flat marshes of inland Connecticut, lengthened my route for a road no easier than the one all set to open before me.

At 2am, gathering a head of steam and it was constant numbers by then, the numbers were going mad, an electrical storm of times, distances and infinite conjecture . . . white noise from ear to ear, like one of those computer systems they teach to play chess, a billion scenarios mapped out and ready to manifest themselves. Eventuality after eventuality scrolled through my brain, leaving still slender hopes of success not yet extinguished. It would be my greatest triumph to date, my greatest triumph to date, my greatest triumph to date.

Towards New London I crawled, old London the scene of my less-than-glorious past, New London the scene of coming horrors. It must've been deep into the night by then, Brain spinning, an exit-strategy formulating. Trains were pulling into the station platform on my head, a train bound for Boston but the station of departure as yet unnamed. I fought with it, didn't want to take a train, didn't want to stack, to quit, throw in the towel . . . *I didn't want to be a failure, so help me.* I did it . . . I did it then for the first time. Such a cruel thing, such a mean trick to play.

I needed sleep. I'd reached that point at which resting a while would be quicker than continuing so hopelessly. I pushed myself from the road, a clearing of grass covered in brown leaves, a bed of leaves that would have seemed inviting had they not been sodden, each one wet to the last. I put my bicycle on its stand, zipped up my jacket, set an alarm for 45 minutes. And that was it. I lay down . . . rippling applause as my form crashed into the leaves . . . lay down as though that was the spot where I planned to die. With nothing between me and that cold, wet earth I fell to sleeping, neither mat nor sleeping bag to trap the warmth of my body, not that *warmth* was the right word for it by that time. Here's the thing though, here's the part that really makes me shudder. It was no negligence, no forgetfulness on my part that had me lie down so ill prepared. No hurry nor earnestness had me lose all of my wits . . . *oh no* . . . I lay down in the cold Connecticut night, and with no measures against that cold, precisely because I desired that I should have no inclination to lie there in sleep for a minute longer than the 45 I was allowing and could barely afford. I lay down, planning to wake in such horrendous cold that I would be compelled to climb back aboard my bike and retake the road. It was such a mean trick to play.

Near-frozen, I awoke, pedalled as hard as I could to muster some warmth and reach the bridge that spans the Connecticut River. You could never imagine the anguish I gave myself that day, the flagellations, staring at that signpost for Rhode Island and the city of Providence at a distance of 50 miles. Each day of my life I live with my failures . . . the disappointments are scored so keen I scarcely see my achievements. I stared at a signpost for the city of Providence . . . of Providence so beautifully named . . . just 50 miles from Providence. Providence would have been a dignified failure, the Americas culminating in a place called Providence, a little poetry to make up the shortfall in mileage. And yet standing beneath that signpost I was so unsure, unsure of whether or not I could make those 50 miles and also the train to Boston. That's right, the train to Boston . . . that's where this one winds up. Cycling there was already out of the question by then, had been for the previous 12 hours if I'd been a little more honest with myself. And so I walked into the train station at New London, a utilitarian affair of red brick, built like a crematorium. I walked in there and, get a load of this, this is a good one, I walked in there to *enquire* . . . that's right, to enquire about the times and cost of trains from New London to Boston. Would you believe it? The wool so far over my eyes I had myself believing I was only ascertaining the hypothetical particulars of that train journey. I took my place in the queue, waited . . . made my enquiry into the window and the microphone, a pair of large spectacles and pink lips sticking out at me, fingers twiddling the pearls of a necklace. I made my enquiries about costs and times and, hold your breath, wait for it . . . *well* . . . after all that it really wouldn't do not to get myself a ticket. One single to Boston, please.

* * *

And with that it was over. My Americas ended in New London, Connecticut. A city I'd never heard of before, a state I'd scarcely thought of. I sold myself short there, put myself on the scrapheap as far as my future is concerned too . . . really battered my stock as a motivational speaker in the making. I'll never be one of them now, a real pity but it's just not possible, not after choking like that, failing in the New London morning, boarding the Boston train and throwing it all away. They'll never invite me to a bank or a gala dinner now . . . never ask me to shoot my mouth off about adversity, give the good folk at the yacht club an adventure hard-on. I can't give the rousing speech about not quitting even when it seems impossible, a hypocrite is what they'd call me and quite right too. But wait . . . it wasn't all in vain, New London taught me one important lesson, I gleaned some wisdom from the mishaps that night, found a truth that has fortified me against all that has since occurred and is doubtless yet to come . . . *Ready?* Here it is, my one truth, my new motto . . . things go wrong, life goes wrong . . . it won't happen as you planned it, there will be no glory. Make the most of the hand you're dealt, it could be so much worse.

What do you think? Hardly motivational is it? Not in the twenty-first century, not with everyone brought up on dream-following and sky's the limit. I'm sorry, this isn't very dignified of me, all these histrionics have no place in the understated minimalism of modernity, storytelling and all. I'm not afraid to say that New London that day was the worst and most unfair thing that has ever happened to mankind . . . but that's just not what anybody wants to hear, not a bit of it, and I can't give them what they want either, try as I might . . . it's just not in there. *But listen to me, that's enough* . . . I'll stop now, go quietly, climbing aboard the train as I am, hush now . . . *hush!* . . . it's over. It's over.

Europe

Day 160 – Iberia – 16,638 Miles

I landed in Madrid, sleepwalked about the airport before catching a 45-minute flight to Lisbon that I'd spend the following 72 hours undoing by bicycle. More absurd heroics. There isn't time enough to tell you what had happened. The pink bedsheet my bike had been wrapped in aboard the flight: torn to pieces. The brake levers: mangled. The wheels: bent. Each and every Lisbon bike shop: closed on a three-hour lunch break, down in southern Europe, where folk are yet to realise that life is about work rather than dignity and simple pleasures.

Disconnecting broken brakes, down the cobbled hills of that city I went careering, a foot stuck in the wheel to slow my speed. Red lights, a stop sign . . . straight through them both, traffic parting with a brass band of horns. I weaved over bonnets, screaming tyres, screeching brakes and waved fists. Mouths gaped, my heart flashing before my eyes and *why, oh why*, didn't I pack my bicycle in a box? Lisbon was so pretty that sunny morning, plazas and fountains and castle walls, humungous stones cut before anyone had even thought of America, back when America was just a rock with buffalo and indigenous tribes left to their own devices. I've gotta say I liked being in Europe, that return to my rightful station, surrounded by things so much older, things that made me properly insignificant again. I crawled through time. From the airport that morning there had been nine days to reach my ridiculous quarry in Rouen. Nine days that morning . . . by the time I finished lunch, it was eight and a half days, with me still in Lisbon, still without brakes, and the shop closed for a three-hour lunch that began only an hour ago.

I got the daily plate at the restaurant, eight euros, two euros remaining in my hypothetical daily budget . . . whatever happened to that, lost somewhere in France on the second day. I stood eating at the bar, the brass rail below, suits and flat caps either side of me, elbow to elbow, noses hovering above plates, feet rested upon the brass rail. Shined shoes, beaten shoes, my grubby cycling shoes . . .

Back in the street there was still another hour to kill before the bike shops reopened. It died so slow, a laborious, screaming death as first I paced the pavement, then sat upon a bag of luggage, then paced again . . . my required daily average between Lisbon and Rouen growing by the minute. I sat cursing upon the doorstep, cursing myself, my idiocy, my enslavement to this idiotic challenge and still half an hour of lunch break to go. Twenty minutes to go, then ten . . . and then ten minutes late.

It was evening as I left Lisbon, following my nose north out of the city, criss-crossing my way between hills, stadiums, tower blocks, flight-path. The neighbourhoods changed, grew newer and taller, graffiti and footballs bouncing from walls, a smouldering pile of rubbish. The people changed . . . skins darken, turn gypsy, turn black. Headdresses are tied, baskets lifted onto heads, colourful skirts sweep to and fro, their lengths growing just like the stares that fell upon me, labouring up the hills, beneath the tower blocks and satellite dishes, the railings on first-floor windows.

A siren, flashing blue, rotates on the road before me, a loudspeaker crackled, shouts something about a *bicyclista*. I stop. The door opens and out steps a policeman, boots to his knees, trousers tucked in, truncheon at one hip, a pistol at the other, baseball cap on top of a long nose and a truly miserable expression. Three more faces are back in the car, packed in, staring out to get a look. He hits me in the face with Portuguese. I shrug. He speaks English . . .

'I know that the English are crazy . . . yes? But not stupid, not normally. This is a bad area . . . a *bad* area! *Can't you see?*' I look around, he goes on . . . 'Didn't you see the gypsies, the blacks? It is not safe for you here . . . follow us.'

Whatever my distaste for such slurs against the poor, and especially in the mouth of a police officer, after weeks of being stopped by police as a suspected deadbeat, it was nice to be mistaken for a respectable citizen again, with my own cause to fear the deadbeats. They drove beside me, real inconspicuous . . . four police officers with a blue flashing light rotating in the dark, poorly lit streets alternating blue and black. We crawled together up a large hill, the police and their discotheque, me and my orange bags . . . subtle as you like and with everybody watching. At the top they gave me directions, left me to look out at Portugal. Lisbon was over, shut behind as before me appeared the ill-kept beginnings of country-side. Wooden fences derelict and splintered, fields of high grasses blossoming with urban debris, paint cans and tarpaulins. The land ahead fell dark with shadows and, zipping up my jacket against the night, I plunged down to meet it.

Day 161 – Algarve – 16,731 Miles

What happened? I've grown hazy on the details, the precise numbers escape me now, they've left me in peace at last. By the quickest route as the crow flies, the distance between Lisbon and Rouen was perhaps a little more than 1,000 miles. For my 18,000, though . . . for this fool to have accomplished anything, I needed maybe a little less than 1,500. And so it began, across the bridge from Vila Franca de Xira, Body and Soul yearning for Rouen, to the northeast, so it was that I turned right and headed south, headed south to find my missing miles, riding hard . . . in the wrong direction.

It blurs, I hope you'll forgive me if it blurs hereafter. I lost my right mind, misplaced it somewhere, began to degenerate. Next morning I awoke in a ditch . . . that much stayed the same, I maintained a fine eye for a good ditch. It must have been early when my alarm roused me, its synthesised sounds as cheerful as ever. The quiet of the morning was heavy . . . no cars, the sound of leaves whispering to one another from high up on the branches, taking bets on which one was to fall next. They fluttered down towards me, dried edges scratching minutely on tarmac, on the metal of the crash barrier, the fabric of my sleeping bag, or else falling silent to the long grass. There was a heavy dew that morning, sunlight set upon the webs of spiders ranged through it, fingerprints everywhere, the scene a stitch-up . . . conspiracy, the whole state of affairs sabotaged by design, every last bit. The broken brakes, the cock-up beside the Hudson, still more to come . . . somebody had planned it so, fingerprints smudged all around my bedside in the ditch to prove it.

Awaking was the highpoint of the day. The clouds came in as I made my way south in the wrong direction, picking among the roads of rural Portugal. Those roads were real stinkers . . . relics, cobblestones, potholes and fissures the size of a bicycle, all perfectly suited to carthorses and wagons for the Algarve Tourist Board brochure. With perfect aplomb the drizzle began and I was left to simper, left to slip among those cobbles, water slowly dripping down the back of my neck. Nor was the land flat . . . or at least, that is to say it wasn't flat enough. I avoided every real hill on the surface of the earth and yet, when your concern for speed is so great, there is no such thing as flat, just as there is no tailwind that is not actually a sidewind with perhaps a slight frontward bias. Even the smallest undulations of that road through Portugal became mountains in my head. I cursed my way through the vineyards, through villages of stone houses, across the bridges spanning the lakes where Portugal meets Spain. My wheel broke – of course my wheel broke – it wouldn't have been the same had it not. I ploughed into those inclines of road, carrying the momentum of a descent and then *Bang!* Another spoke. Ruptured metal joining the wobble.

* * *

I rattled big days: 150, 150, 150, 150, 150 miles . . . five in succession, knocking them off the bat, one after the next, with an average three hours sleep. I still like the ideal, that back-against-the-wall sort of stuff . . . but even with that, I'm not so sure I was enjoying life much by then. I hit La Mancha . . . La Mancha hit me back with a force far greater than I had spirit to resist, Don Quixote illustrated in town centres and bars for 100 miles, riding with horse and lance through the windmills of La Mancha in the name of chivalry and ideals. I chased after him with my bicycle and panniers, just as hopeless, the end of my quest for a world bettered by circumnavigation.

My favourite moments came in the evenings, after dark, when I needed help finding the correct road out of town. I would ask directions, can still picture my favourite scene on returning to Europe. She was a woman of middle-aged appearance, hips that children had passed through, the paunch of menopause at her middle, handbag by her side, a coat sensible and shapeless, down to her thighs, a little fur at the collar. It was a dark street, nobody but the two of us in sight as she walked her little white dog. With a plastic bag in her hand she crouched to pick up shit from the rear-end of the thing, and I walked towards her with my beard, my unruly hair, face and unlit silhouette heading straight for her out of the darkness, stuttering words scarcely Spanish. I stopped, stood before her . . . and asked the road to Toledo. The thing I loved was that, with a stranger coming forward out of the night, standing over her, still she looked me directly in the face, wrinkles at the side of her eyes. Shrinking with old age, her hand inside a plastic bag full of dog shit, she just looked straight at me without fear, without any concern that I meant her harm, might desire for some peculiar reason to overpower her. She addressed the stranger from whom she had nothing to fear, told him the road to Toledo. That was what I loved most about being back in Europe after America . . . the fear had lifted, Europeans do not fantasise after the horrors strangers will visit upon us. I find it sad to think that something so basic seemed so tender, but it did.

Day 163 – Castille – 17,103 Miles

I never made it into Toledo itself, looked down on the city from outside instead. The city has a cathedral, slender spires and gothic airs illuminated by night . . . yet you scarcely notice it. On a hill-top, dwarfing everything, there you see the Alcázar, glowing in the night, a lip of blue sky above stone walls incandescent white. It was a Roman palace, built with four turrets and indomitable ramparts. From my hilltop above the town I yearned, looking down on that fairytale town, the chill wind still hankering for a piece of me . . . still trying to get into my bones as Toledo looked so warm, so civilised, full of love and fairytale. I saw first dates pouring wine, friends busking in plazas with their guitars, beside fountains that tinkle and fall like flipped coins upon the flagstones. Oh but

Toledo . . . Oh but the Alcázar . . . orchestras sliding into the sea, every joy man had ever known was happening inside the city walls that night, the Alcázar glowing up there and like that, with me on the outside, the world full of warmth and me alone, prohibited from attending by a self-inflicted fate. Never had I felt so excluded, so much like I was missing out, upon that hill with the Alcázar so pretty and enchanting across the valley. I turned away, got back to my bicycle.

Madrid came next day, my antipode . . . straight through the earth and back to Wellington. I skulked in with a flat tyre . . . found food. Food in Madrid, in the state I was, that wasn't a pleasant experience. Bankrupt, bankrupt and worse, that bill hurt like a hundred miles. A coffee and croissant, a pretty poor croissant at that . . . *tapas* and a basket of bread . . . *thump!* . . . smacked in the side, straight in the wallet. Not just that, not just the impoverishment, but the scorn too. *My word, the scorn!*

In fairness, I was bedraggled, stinking, half-shivering, the capillaries of my face beaten down, smashed to pieces, a face like a swollen beetroot, eyes above the bags. My clothes were dank and ill fitting in appearance, though that wasn't quite it . . . it was my body that was the problem. My body had become warped, hunkered, contorted. The clothes fit fine, but Body was wilting, limp here, protruding there. Not about to take me in their stride, the people stared, but just how those patrons stared . . . napkins dabbed scorn politely over every mouth in that little eatery off the Calle de Goya. The staff too, the staff were worse, disgusted that they should be expected to serve a customer such as I . . . unfit to wait their table and they expected to wait at mine. I went to the bathroom, washed hands, washed face, washed forearms up to my elbow. I walked back into the restaurant looking a little cleaner. Heads shake . . . *tut, tut, tut* . . . places like that hate you when you show up dirty and hate you more when you use the sink and soap to try to get a little cleaner. They want you dirty and they want you to stay dirty, but all of it as far away as possible, not in front of them.

* * *

Out of Madrid by the northeast, through the graffiti, the Latinos, Africans, gypsies and industrial zones, a road moving up towards a plateau on a mountainous horizon. I rode into the night, though morning, day and night had already come to mean so little to me by then. There were 24 hours in a day, a good many less than I needed, and less than a week to reach Rouen. Soon after, the days lost their relevance entirely, became only a countdown of hours and, though it was preferable, more convenient and warmer to ride during the eight daily hours of daylight, I was required to ride so much after dark that such became only a minor consideration. I would stop at approximately ten each night, before the restaurants closed, would drink an espresso, eat *tortilla* and start again. Taking off my gloves, I would blow into them, again and again until they were full with my warm air. I stuffed my hands quickly inside, bound them in and punched my fists together, rallied myself with something, I know not what.

Through the night I rode ferocious winds, thrashing into hills cut open for the road, pedalling as hard as I could on the head of the gale. As it tore over my ears, I struggled to keep pace . . . watched as it sent rain streaming past me, watched as the rain turned to snow and flakes danced away in the light of my head torch, flailing deeper towards the mines of Soria. It becomes all too cursory . . . place-to-place and scant on detail. Dear readers . . . but I neglect you . . . and yet I know not what else to say. This was how it happened, some unctuous haze punctuated by a few lasting impressions. Finally I awoke . . . awoke to the cold and to the wet, hurrying back aboard my bike so as to pedal hard and become warm again. The land turned sparse, thinned the same wintery grey as that sky above. Earth rose and fell, contours tipping this way and that, the road bouncing through the hills towards a horizon so far away, decorated by boulders with gorse thickets sprouting among them. Sporadic clusters of olive trees appeared, withered trunks all cracked and ageing, a barren land through which I wound, running for the city of Pamplona beneath the Pyrenees.

Day 164 – Basque – 17,321 Miles

As night returned, it began to hail, pellets shooting at me from the sky. The petrol station was empty beneath white light, to its side a brick building without windows . . . 'BAR' stamped on the night in neon. I walked to it, a heavy door braced with metal straps. It looked shut, all closed up despite the neon and the early hour. I pulled at that large handle and, as the hinges rolled back, so did pink light fall out into the hail.

The room was hot, heated well beyond normal temperatures, a row of round men slouched on high stools at the bar, cut like a cluster of top-heavy mushrooms, jackets kept on despite the heat. The room poured into my vision, set most notably of all by a shining pole, gleaming steel, proud within a spotlight. I let the door close again. Standing in the rain, the night all around, sky low . . . wind pulling at my collar, trying to take my neck in its jaws. The road ahead was empty, my stomach was empty . . . legs and willpower empty, all of it exhausted. I wanted food, knew of no good reason not to eat food in sight of a metal pole, in sight of strutting women in decorated bits and pieces. Not my taste, but who cares? Sure it might not have been a bar of the greatest repute, but it was still a bar and that was all I needed as the hail kept coming. I stood deliberating when the door opened, slow but wide it opened.

She's trussed up in gold leaf . . . a warm, pink light glows against a shining purse that just about holds back her vagina. The purse traces up to a belt behind her back, swaps flanks, ties around the neck, sweeps down to offer salvation for her nipples, the rest of her zeppelin breasts floating out into the cold night. Blink. Atop stilettos she stood, hail pummelling against her, teetering on heels, skin all bronze, black hair, big, dark eyes with a trace of human concern for this strange man left to the cold. She gave smiles . . . caring smiles that show some drop of crystal stuck to a tooth. Her name is Annie, and softly Annie tells me all I want to hear, 'Yes . . . yes señor, yes we have food.'

Annie encourages me over to the back door with a look of agreement . . . 'Yes, yes, there is food. Go! . . . the back door!' The door closes, the hail falls and I walk to the back door, listen as the bolts slide open to reveal Annie once again, ushering me inside. I follow down a dark corridor . . . Annie's buttocks held inside a golden orb of underwear that beckons like lanterns in the dark. Down the corridor of numbered rooms we go, small rooms, as many as possible squeezed down into that filing cabinet of sex. As I followed, so my reservations lost their reservations, piped up regarding this emerging situation and the availability of food.

I called her stop. Annie stopped, gloriously obedient she stands there sparkling, insouciant, leg cocked in a puddle of light. She leans against a wall, fidgets a stiletto, smiles the more. I ask about the food . . . she moves to me. The food . . . she'd promised food. I ask again about the food, she moves towards me further or perhaps I move towards her . . . it doesn't matter, by hook or crook we wind up real close in that corridor. For so long it had rained on me, rained and blown cold so that I was dressed for the weather . . . dripping wet in waterproof trousers and a head torch, half-man half-flannel as Annie purrs enquiries after my wellbeing, sidles towards me, tilts head down and eyes up. I look into them . . . eye-to-eye as I stammer some more about food . . . no idea who I'm trying to convince.

She pressed herself on me, sent one hand shuffling down between my legs, massaging at my cock, another tracing upwards to tickle beneath my chin. Lifting the corner of a mouth and the corner of an eyebrow, she showed me the crystal stuck on her tooth, purred at me . . . *What did I want? But what did señor want?*

'Yo gusta, yo gusta . . . I wan . . . I want . . . I wawa . . .' I wanted food, how hard could it be? *'Comer* . . . food . . .' I quivered . . . damn her but I was quivering, bona-fide pathetic. She massaged my faculties for decision, my waterproof cock in her manicured hand massaged, massaged, *mas-saged, ma-ssaged, massaged* . . . and all the time purring . . . *'Tu gusta? Tu gusta? . . . Hmmmm?'*

I stammered my picayune replies, the most stammering of Spanish, *'Yo gusta comer! Tu tiene raciones? Tu tiene bocadillos?'* And Annie, she just stood there, leaning all the more. *'Si? Si? Si?'* And dammit, but nobody need exhale so much and so deep as they *'si'* to such simple questions as mine. Little Annie just went right on massaging as if I hadn't said a word, as if I hadn't asserted, *'I want food!'*, as if I hadn't just enquired whether or not there were sandwiches in this establishment. She just went on massaging, me all full of the rights of women and a reluctance to condone the moral blight that is prostitution, and Little Annie not at all put out by any of that, making my supposed principles much harder than was necessary, massaging my poor hermit of a penis, fondling my neck as I stand there, dripping wet . . . dripping wet in a pair of water-proof trousers, a cycling cap, head torch and Annie massaging my groin. Finger in the air I stand there, stuttering and stumbling all over . . . 'Do you have food . . . sandwiches?' Little Annie, she goes right on massaging my cock as I repeat, pleading . . .

'*Sandwiches! Sandwiches!*' Sandwiches, let me tell you, is not a word to be repeated in indignation, all the less so when wearing a head torch . . . with Annie peering down at my belongings and looking up from her eyelid pillows.

My God, my God but I was buckling in Annie's hands then, ready to start talking prices, throw morality out the window along with the surviving financial discipline that — I ought not to lie to you — helped just as much as morals in my resistance. Just as Annie was about to claim my scalp and have me filed away in one of those rooms, so there came a commotion in the corridor. Two men come barrelling towards us, one short, the other gigantic, African and cut like some brass-forged, Beninese god, scars across his cheeks and '*Security*' on his forehead. The two of them come with a kerfuffle towards us. 'What do you want?' I sigh relief . . . such sweet interruption. I want food, only food. The Security knew some English, intimately acquainted with mankind. He gives his verdict: 'First you eat, then you fuck!' Scarred cheeks open wide as he laughs. The short man interjects, cottoning on to what's happening. 'What is the problem?' He shrugs palms towards Annie. 'Is Annie not very pretty?' Oh but Annie *was* very pretty, I assured him, that was not the problem . . . 'But I want food! Por favor, señor! Come!'

We walk to the kitchen, the four of us in convoy. The kitchen is heavy with the white of strip lighting, no more dim pinks to lull the senses. There were boxes of food, a whole row of them . . . box after box of salad, chicken wings, wholemeal pasta, rice, brown bread even. You need good sustenance if you're to spend all night screwing, swinging on a pole and feigning lust for men who lost their lives some quarter of a century ago. Annie and I ate together, a little date in the kitchen . . . she with legs crossed, the broadside of one splendid thigh, hung like a painting on the wall, me with my paper plate atop my knees, a plastic cup with orange squash in one hand. She's Brazilian, from a favela in Rio . . . eight years passed, her family still in the favela . . . she sends them money.

'How's Spain?'

Heavy shrugs and then, 'Spain is not agreeable or disagreeable.'

I specify, 'And Tafalla?'

'Tafalla is shit . . . one day I'll leave.'

I glance at my empty paper plate, the grease of cold chicken, unsure of what to say, how to avoid offending her. I might as well ask.

'The work?'

She's clinical about it . . . 'Work's OK, we girls get on well . . . a family. Brazilian, Spanish, Portuguese, Angolan, Moroccan.'

Annie asked after me, what my job was in London. We laughed together as my Spanish allowed me to say I was a postman. It felt nice to be a human again for a little while . . . sitting there with our picnic. She comes to sit astride me after I'd finished eating. I smile as I lift her off . . . she smiles back, and we hug. Goodbye kisses, two cheeks . . . polite as you like.

Day 165 – Aquitaine – 17,449 Miles

I headed for the tunnel, desperate to make France by the end of the night. France, the final country . . . France, where it all began. I took forbidden turnings, headed time after time towards the tunnel and away from the switchbacks. There was a man patrolling, pacing up and down in a fluorescent jacket outside the entrance, glowing soft, turbines suspended above the road, propellers turning lazily to move air into the mountain. The fluorescent jacket looks up with a start . . . sees a cyclist in the middle of the night. He calls out to me, raises a palm in the air, raises the palm towards me . . . *'It is prohibited! . . . Prohibited!'* . . . and he reaches out, grabs for my arm as I sail by, sorry to have to ignore him. A voice wailing in the night, he calls after me, the sound carrying away with the wind. Inside the tunnel turbines hover, turning slowly and passing echoes through the mountainside. The engines purred from afar, purred like Annie in my ear, growing louder and then fading away again. Red brake lights loitered, stained my vision as cars filed through the orange half-light, sped out into a black hole that opened on the night.

France came no different to Spain . . . I arrived with four and a half days to reach Rouen, some 700 miles still to ride. Hot chocolate was what kept me going, so delicate and soft, like a warm bed in my mouth, everywhere I went I drank it. From the foot of the Pyrenees I rode the Aquitaine coast, surfs crashing and a wind roaring inland. Each day it seemed the nights arrived more quickly, and always cold, so cold. Those nights in Aquitaine hurt me unforgivably, took me hostage and cut ribbons of my sensitivities. I rode through night, rode towards dawn, intention ever to remain in the saddle as the sun rose to warm me.

On it rained. My gloves, apparently waterproof, were not. I had overshoes, a sheaf into which I slipped my shoes, apparently waterproof . . . they were not. My jacket too, that was waterproof, apparently waterproof. I could never fathom whether the jacket leaked or if water was simply flowing down the drainpipe of my neck. Somehow I continued to sweat, haunted by the sticky remains of heat even as cold won out and danced across my skin. I clenched fists, watched water seep from the linings of my gloves, clutching tight so as not to let slip what warmth remained. I'd hold my hands together, palms facing, sharing the warmth, encouraging the escaping heat from one surface to travel towards the surface of the other hand. I rubbed them back and forth like cold, magicless lamps from which nothing would come. I took turns holding the back of one hand in the palm of the other, shuffling thumbs and fingers among themselves . . . everything to keep my hands and fingers moving, just so they hurt a little less.

And all the time I waited for the sun, unable to stop cycling for fear of the cold. It was at 2.30am that I gave up on that. All too exhausted . . . I had to stop, 2.30am written right there in my little book for the bureaucrats, the morning still too far away for me to meet with it, to conceive of passing so much time in such misery. I stopped to sleep, to disappear a couple of hours. It was still raining, scarcely so but spitting lightly nevertheless. I'll tell you where I slept, so far from glorious, it was behind one of those green metal boxes found at the end of a street, housing the circuits and connection points for the telephones in the small town of Sanguinet. Two hours I disappeared . . . it pains me just to write it, for that was no sound rest, what with the hum of electricity, the dripping of rain and cold ghosts still wrapped all about me. A dream came . . . a dream in which I was cycling, knees up-and-down but with something restraining me around my legs. With a start I awoke, awoke to see that I'd unzipped my sleeping bag in a dream all too much like life. At half-past four came the restart, I wrote that down too, my little book for the bureaucrats. It says so right here . . . at half-past four I climbed back to my bike, rode hard to get warm again, still so many hours waiting before daybreak.

Incessantly I looked to the east, the flat horizon and its thin, gangly pines. The sun rose, she must have done and, though the day grew lighter, no sun visited me, staring east with my unrequited longing for that orb of heat in the sky. How I wanted her to come to me, would have loved her then and forever. Jilted, I watched my heart's desire in a crowded sky so full of clouds. I saw her with those clouds and came to grow so jealous, consumed with longing as she cast shadows and only shadows upon me, shining her warmth against strangers in those thick banks of cloud. My face stretched away . . . pulled into a long, solemn slope with what felt like metres from forehead to jaw. From the distance I heard the scraping of a shovel against concrete. My mouth was dry, ever dry, lips wrinkled and breaking as my chin plummeted off the bottom of my face, rolled before me on the road, forming a ramp into which I pedalled. Endlessly, round and round I went . . . cycling into my chin, spread flat on the road before me as I rode on into my chin, into my chin, into my chin . . .

All the while the sky bore down upon me, gaping open, clouds strafed across the surface of that glaring eye, cut and turning above branches of contorted oak. The skies stared, flawless, impervious stares right through me, asking what I wanted of them, what passage it was I desired. They peered at me from through a monocle, tossed down my insignificance for contemplation, splashed it all over me just as they had done throughout those 18,000. And yet by then, with things so nearly over, my body so full and sated, fit to burst with discomfiture . . . then it became hard to tolerate the insignificance and still to persist in an undertaking I knew to be so empty, so futile and meaningless.

Determination was what it came down to . . . I'm terminally determined, have been called as much ever since I was old enough to exhibit a little of the stuff, one of those words that becomes applied so consistently to a personality that we can come to live by it, define ourselves by it, regard it a cornerstone of our existence and who we are. I was determined all right, riding home through France, out of the Aquitaine night and into an Aquitaine morning scarcely any better. I was determined and, yet, I saw then the true meaning of that word. My determination, I tell you now, was only the exhibition of unrelenting stupidity, a stubborn commitment to a thing pointless and achievable if only I had the desire to achieve it. Determination in the face of a meaningful challenge, one that will perhaps improve the lives of others, perhaps would be a noble thing, but determination in pursuit of seconds, minutes, kilometres?

You see, I knew all along that I could cycle the distance to the Cathedral of Rouen in time for 4 December. All along, I knew that I could do it . . . but I never found a good reason for *why* I should. I still remember now how cold it was. I know . . . I've told you once already, but forgive me, for truly . . . I became cold all over again. Like a haunch of venison out of the meat market at Smithfield, the cold poured off me as steam. I needed to defrost, to thaw, cold so deep beneath my skin, beneath my bones too, my entire body growing lifeless. I cycled on, that was all I ever did, just cycled on; compulsive pedalling had become an involuntary movement that was fast destroying my quality of life. And yet . . . I know that's not quite true. I wonder if I have not, perhaps, removed the beauty I know remained intact throughout. For if the past exists only as the form in which our mind accounts for it, as a negotiation, a slave to memory, and if a dream is only a form in which our mind recalls it, as a negotiation, a slave to memory . . . then I wonder, has that past of mine in Aquitaine, perhaps become only a dream anyway? I've no accurate memories of what it was I felt in those moments . . . I scarcely knew what was happening to begin with.

Day 167 – Maine et Loire – 17,667 Miles

Three hours later I awoke in a bus shelter, school children scarpering as the sleeping bag kicked, the time 7am by the tolling of the St Pompain church. I look groggily at my bicycle, staring, as if waiting for matters to improve, droplets of water hanging from the oil-dirtied chain and sprockets. Two and a half days to go, just shy of 400 miles remaining, Rouen within touching distance. Perhaps it was the closeness that was responsible for my undoing, I rode one more cold hundred and then slacked off, let my concentration lapse . . . I'll tell you about it.

It was as if it had all been planned in advance, as if they knew I was coming. I arrived in Angers, 100 miles delivering me to a bar for the evening. She came on me, I swear it . . . she came on me and with a cry too . . . '*THE CYCLIST!*' she called out, veritably screeched it to her friends, as if they'd been waiting for me there, as if she knew it all. She strode to me from out of the light in the bar doorway, marching as if to the defence of Verdun . . . long legs, strides . . . really long strides, on me in no time. I was taken off-guard, just time enough to look confused before Adrienne's in front of me, a finger levelled my way, pointing at my heart, that face of hers so close . . . so preciously close, like coins to a miser. I look into her tricolour face: soft red lips, pale skin like a tablecloth thrown over the blood vessels, a shade of blue, a shade of blue is just palpable on top of the eyelids. She snaps, her face in mine . . .

'Tonight you *will* rest! You cannot just ride, ride, *ride* . . . You cannot be only the sportsman all of the time . . . there are other things in this life!'

I still don't know how it was she came to say things so apt, how it was she knew so much. She kept right on, centimetres from my nose. '*You must relax, you must enjoy!*' Three-quarters drunk, she waved her arms wildly at each word, within a hundred seconds of our meeting she had refused all protest, explained that I wouldn't be leaving Angers, that two hundred more kilometres could wait until next day . . .

'You will stay at my 'ouse . . . tonight I will look after you. Tonight I will be nice to you and *tonight* . . .' she sang, '*tonight*, I will be *so* nice to you!'

That's what she said, I swear to you, word for darling word. The two of us just met, she announced it with a finger on my chest, her nose on mine and that face, that Tricolour face fluttering so close and purring with that accent . . . *that accent*, how it dripped . . . just how it dripped as among her assurances she began to place tiny, fleeting kisses on my dumbstruck lips. And my word . . . but her logic made such fine sense, and if it didn't feel right then . . . I'd been alone for what seemed so very long. My tongue gets shy. 'I *d-don't* know . . . I can't stay . . . *Rouen* . . . no time!'

'*NON!* . . . *Attent!* You cannot always be speed, speed, *speed!* Tonight, you must rest, *'ere in Angers you will rest and . . . you will stay at my 'ouse.*'

* * *

I showered. She gave me towels, the coarse variety adults keep folded in a warm cupboard. She walked into the bathroom as I washed, fully clothed she looked in at me naked, a clinical gaze, as if I were food on a plate. I watch an expression on her lips, set almost, and as if to say . . . *'will you satisfy me?'*, *'will you meet my expectations?'* She looked-on at me, entirely unselfconscious, and . . . would I satisfy her? Oh boy . . . if you don't already know the answer to that one. Just shy of my 18,000, a hamster in his rattling wheel, a fine chunk of world behind me, muscles pounding, head longing for Rouen and not Angers. *Would I satisfy her?* Already I was long dead . . . no use to anyone. I washed vigorously, like a patient cleaning before the operation. Adrienne had one of those brushes of the most unforgiving bristles. I tore it against my skin, hot water flooding the broken capillaries. I scrubbed. Right there in Angers was my first wash since New York. I haven't been omitting any details these 10 days past, haven't been washing without say-so, without letting you know . . . no, dear readers . . . there was simply no wash to report. Falling asleep in the rotting leaves of Connecticut, the damp earth under that bridge in Soria, stale air on the ferry across La Gironde, all riddled in my skin. Radiant, radiant filth . . . a benchmark and role model for dirt everywhere. I tore the bristles of that brush against my skin, went to work as if the thing were a plough, breaking the flesh where the skin is softest . . . pain is clean, as the sewage collects in the foot of the shower, grey with ribbons of black.

Once I had finished, the water was heavy with silt, skin and mud, no plug in sight to let it out. I call Adrienne, she comes, looks . . . 'orror . . . *But what 'ave you done?* Into a cupboard she goes, rubber gloves, huge and yellow on the ends of her arms. She crouches, reaches into the swamp, turns something and down it goes. Gurgling. Thick. Churning. It left the cubicle with its colour, white turned grey, as though a Louisiana bayou had run through that Angers bathroom. She was politely aghast, disgustedly impressed . . . *Mon dieu!* . . . She knelt, scrubbed at the grey as I took up a towel, dried, pulling that coarse fabric across my skin like sandpaper. With Adrienne scrubbing, turning the shower from grey back to white, so I scrubbed myself dry, towel moving white to grey. White is an awful colour for anything people would hope to see returned clean. Dark towels, I say . . . always offer the travelling cyclist dark towels. I dried my crotch, set to work down there, a few sores starting to bleed . . . scarlet on white. Adrienne noticed the blood on the towel before I did, gasped, *'But are you OK? But you are bleeding!'* I knew exactly what was bleeding, didn't want her looking at it . . . *'No, no,'* I insisted. *'It's OK, I'm all right . . . don't look!'*

She took me to bed . . . a large bed, an operating theatre. Took off her clothes, took out a set of prehensile fingers, blew out all of the candles. Darkness. She crawled up, kissing . . . throwing kisses like no tomorrow, like there's an election to be won and the cameras are out in force. She starts muttering . . . something about the French and making love and about the English and something not quite so romantic. I was punch-drunk by then, requiemed, hardly paying attention, good and ready to die right there in that bed, upon those clean sheets spotted with my blood.

I'll spare you details. She proceeded, went about establishing a foregone conclusion of me in no time at all. A real mantis of a woman, pride in her work . . . knows how to reduce a man to nothing and delights in so doing. By the time she found me it was too late. She didn't catch me quick enough . . . I was nothing, reduced already. I slept, but only after a fashion . . . either too hot or too cold, packed within unfamiliar surrounds, troubled by thoughts of what awaited in the daylight. I observed Adrienne's room, its framed photography of Paris, an easel casting a gallows-worth of shadows in the night, a dressing table with the accessories of her appearance upon it. She slept beside me, breathing gently, lying on her back and hardly moving. The night passed in fits and spurts. I woke to darkness, then to a purple, and then to the pale blue of first light.

My alarm brought me round in the end, obliviously cheerful as ever. It was seven in the morning . . . some 29 hours and 280 miles from the room of a stranger in Angers to a cathedral in Rouen. A thousand times I slapped my palm to my forehead.

Day 168 – Normandy – 17,768 Miles

It was the final complete day and, with sun rising in a blue sky, my spirits lifted higher. I dashed into central Angers, traffic at a standstill and my bicycle straight through the red light. To be honest, and I say it at a hush, for world records require adherence to traffic laws, it was probably more than one red light that I rode through during my 18,000. That day though, for the first time, it caused a siren. Alongside he comes, a motorbike: one motorbike and one siren. I see gauntlet pulled into fist, a fist except for one enormous, armoured finger, pointing first at me and then to the side of the road. After 17,800 miles . . . the police pull me over for jumping a red light. I dismount . . . motorbike pulls to a standstill beside me, two tall boots planted on the ground. He lifts a leg with a large boot on the end of it, slow motion, high over the bike. He stands in front of me, pulls up the face of his helmet with one of those gauntlets. There he is, all in blue, boots to his knees, gauntlets fit to wrestle minotaurs, mouth swallowed in his moustache, razor blades for cheekbones, a face unaccustomed to smiling and me and my bicycle reflecting back from the sheer lens of his sunglasses.

He hit me in the face with French, something about a red light. I respond in English: 'What seems to be the problem, officer?' I play dumb, dumb doesn't work, and so suddenly I realise what he's talking about, hand to forehead . . . *sacre bleu!* Struck down with guilt and so sorry for my mistake. *'Eighty euros!'* he snaps, that's all he has to say by way of accepting apologies, 80 euros and alarmingly forthright about it, not a lot of time for whys, wherefores or Anglo-French relations and sensitivity to an imbecile foreigner. 'But . . . but . . . Monsieur, I don't have eighty euros!' He changes tack. 'Passport!' He's still shouting, but that I can give him . . . I hand him my passport, just as I'd done to all those US officers who'd only wanted to look at the thing, flex their authority and set me on my way. He looks at it, starts writing details, a little time-consuming, but I'm happy to have my name written down on his paper, he can post me a letter to London for all I care. He finishes writing, tucks passport into pocket. Gives it a tap. The sunglasses point back at me, show me my reflection. 'Passport?' I stammer. 'Eighty euros!' he snaps. And I realise what's happening, I start up my protest . . . *Je n'avez pas! Je n'avez pas quatre-vingt euros!*

We go back and forth. 'Passport!' . . . 'Eighty euros!' . . . 'Passport!' . . . and then something terrible happens, for that face, that face so still began to change, and from through the moustache, encased within the hard lines of that jaw and those cheekbones, there came teeth, twitching at first but then barefaced teeth. The

officer smiles, opens his mouth into the most horrible and afflict-
ing of smiles, like the silver plate on a coffin: 'No eighty euros, no
passport.' He pats his pocket and makes to turn away. I catch hold
of his arm . . . 'No, no, no, no . . . please, please!' Some real pleading came over me . . . 80 euros was invaluable whereas my pride
could easily be recovered. *Je n'avez pas! Je n'avez pas! . . . World
Record! Un record du monde . . . Demain . . . Demain! Je n'avez pas
les temps!*', whatever that lot meant.

Old coffin-face he just repeats my fate, 'No eighty euros, no
passport!' The cunning rat, that was a police officer with five centuries of skulduggery behind him, not like those American coppers,
proud just to wear uniforms, request official documents and send
you on your way happy to have felt important. Oh no . . . that
French copper was a wily one, for in light of my pleading, his face
starts twitching again. His moustache twitches, me looking less
than assured in the reflection of his sunglasses. He comes upon a
second horrid smile and announces, words dropping . . . 'Twenty
euros . . .' He pauses. *'A present . . . un cadeau . . .'* He looks at me.
He grins. All our talk of corruption in the Third World . . . and on
day 168 it's a wretched Frenchman who shakes you down for a
bribe.

* * *

All day long I rode . . . rode headwinds, sidewinds, then a sidewind
I decided must have been a headwind. Finally, I just rode, for by
then there was nothing else for it. The skies stayed clear until evening neared, but as the wind died so clouds gathered. It started to
drizzle, and thereafter to rain. As the deluge began, I stopped in a
bus shelter on the edge of a town, upturned my bicycle.

The spokes were ruined. As the rain fell I set about them, tightening and loosening, the wheel spinning on the end of my nose.

Right now miles are secondary, right now I'm happy just to avoid the rainfall and discipline that damn wheel once and for all. I tighten, I loosen, the things creak. I know mechanics who'll laugh at me and that wheel . . . trust me, there's nothing so opinionated as a bicycle mechanic. And yet, out there on the road it was those same mechanics, time after time, who returned that wheel to me in the state I've told you. Night after night we rode together, with me looking transfixed through my turning legs. The wheel went wobbling fast on the downhill, wobbling slow on the up. Side to side it went, a fish on a riverbank, a bellydancer, an endless night-mare that simply wouldn't stop gyrating. It never left my mind. It scarcely left my vision but, after an hour beneath that shelter, the rains abating at last, I prepared to retake the road . . . the wheel straighter than at any point since New York.

Together we set out into the night, me and the wheel heading north for the city of Caen. Right now I remember that night so fondly, the stinging fatigue across the surface of my eyes was com-forting, the swaying of my head so gentle. It was a good life, whatever the tricks of my narration, the superlatives and dramatics I employ, don't let me deceive you . . . out there was as good a life as ever you could live.

I moved fast through forest and stars, a fair wind taking me to Caen before sun came back to the land. By the dead of night I arrived, police patrolling, friends walking home together through alleyways slicked wet. I crouched in a doorway . . . pizza, pastries, caffeinated drinks, all the usual going in before I set off again, veered east towards Rouen. I saw signposts for my quarry, nor-mally such a happy moment in reaching a destination . . . that night I hardly cared. Rouen was just another place. I rode until five next morning, 4 December, a little more than 100 miles to go, but my body resigned, head disinterested . . . swimming a bicycle to the end of the road.

I pulled into a field, lay down. That's what I did, I lay down . . . no sleeping bag, nothing. Wet clothes, one extra coat and I lay down. That Connecticut trick again . . . sleeping in a place and dress so cold that I would wake easily, not want to remain still once my alarm sounded. That night it didn't work . . . I was exhausted, exhausted but with caffeine berserk in each part of my brain. Not a jot of ease left in that body of mine, despite the titanic sleep welling inside me. I remember deciding it was too cold, lying there on the muddy earth . . . dead leaves sticking against the side of my face, head resting on a squashed plastic drinks bottle. Too cold directly on the cold earth and so, from the cold, cold ground, I reached to my bag and pulled down a packet of biscuits . . . cookies, to be precise . . . chocolate chip. I pulled them down and slipped the whole lot under my back . . . the plastic tray, shiny foil and all. I put a packet of biscuits beneath me and struggled towards sleep. Set my alarm for an hour later . . . got perhaps ten minutes of a dream-cursed sleep.

Day 169 – Cathedral – 18,049 Miles

Obliviously cheerful, the alarm grabbed me. I was frozen solid and frozen stiff, beyond the degree of any word that could convey just how terribly cold I'd become. Beneath the lightening sky I got . . . *sh-ivv-errri-nng* . . . to my feet, shivered towards my bicycle, and made to take it gingerly by the handlebars. My fingers though, my poor fingers, they'd slipped from me . . . all the colours of the rainbow as they passed away into some other place, red at the limits of where blood still reached, turning pink, yellow, green and then a cold, numb blue behind the fingernails. I breathed deep and, where I'd once watched the heat escape my body, that morning it was invisible . . . my heat no longer left me in clouds of hot air, for my body was no longer hot. The winter had taken me. My insides were cold, had succumbed to the same temperature as the world without.

I pulled on my gloves, I retook my saddle . . . made to pedal as hard and fast as I could until perhaps some warmth might be found. No good, for I was broken then . . . good only for shivering. I pedalled, shivered and pedalled a while, then just shivered. At Goustranville, I climbed off my bike to find a small café, restaurant, lodging, hotel . . . I don't know what it was. A woman of some years, grandmotherly in her spectacles, curled hair fresh from rollers, stood behind the bar, drying crockery with a tea towel. I asked for hot chocolate and perhaps some bread that . . . perhaps she wouldn't mind, I could eat with a little jam of my own.

She bade me a seat that I shivered towards. I sat there with a radiator in front of me, and yet it was no good . . . I'd grown so cold the world itself had begun shaking, so cold the planet on its very axis had come to tremble. The floor shook as that little grandmother wandered towards me with an entire, blessed bowl of hot chocolate. My word . . . I must've looked awful, so bedraggled, so scarred, bags with eyes atop them, mouth sucked dry, the world around me shaking. I heard her gentle voice express concern to a chef in the kitchen, aquiver as she pointed to me before covering her mouth with a trembling hand. I sat in that chair, promise I didn't move a muscle, and yet I tell you that chair was shaking as I reached out and took the bowl in my hands, poured hot chocolate down my throat. I'd love to speak of how that hot chocolate revived me, the way it soothed my pain, but it didn't; it was only a sensible action I undertook because I knew it to be advisable. The hot chocolate, with ripples shaking in the surface, did not taste of cocoa, and so I resolved to stir the cocoa lying at the bottom of the bowl. Hand calm and still, I reached towards the teaspoon beside me, steady as you like, and yet I tell you that spoon, that foul and humiliating spoon, began shaking, ringing and chiming against the saucer as it jumped and danced away from my steady grip and fell shaking to the trembling table. That old grandmother grew more concerned, and tenderly she placed her shaking hand on my still shoulder. I'd have liked to have had the presence or where-withal to thank her for her concern, but I was in no fit shape for anything when I left Goustranville that morning, relieved only that the world had stopped shaking.

* * *

Outside the sun was up. That's no figure of speech . . . I don't mean figuratively that day had arrived. No . . . at last, the sun was actually up. In a blue sky throbbed a full, unobstructed and unmistakable ball of burning gases. It wasn't exactly hot, nothing so extreme as that. I was still well wrapped up, but the world was dry, teetering on the verge of warm. By some great mercy, the weather was kind to me that last day. Thinking back, I don't know how I could have made it without that sunshine.

There was one problem. My gears, my infernal hub gear system, the shifter, the cables, the whole thing had been playing up for a while, chose day 169 to finally give up the ghost. My own fault really, only myself to blame, but I hadn't changed the cables, not once since London, and the whole thing was horribly seized, wouldn't budge from one gear to the next. There's no time for this now, no time to explain the mechanics of it all, my only option to select a single gear and motor in it. I opened it up, took a spanner to the gearbox, turned a bolt up to a big gear – 10 of 14 – one in which to plough through all remaining road, to blow however many spokes the wheel would let go, obliterating 100 more miles before the whole thing could die a death, condemned to the hell it deserved.

I didn't stop. 100 miles with full baggage and only one gear through the craggy hills, the sharp ups and downs of Normandy seemed so easy that day. I attacked, paid contemptuous respect and destroyed it. Merckx with panniers, damn but I enjoyed that last day! The weather kind at last, finally I had the opportunity to lay myself bare, to attack without being weakened the following day . . . there would be no following day. The open fields, the forested hills, the towns of Pont l'Évêque, Lisieux, I attacked throughout and, though a spoke or two exploded behind me, burst into earshot . . . I knew I didn't have to care. I stopped only once, late in the afternoon, 10 minutes for bananas, pastries and a shot of espresso, a final refuelling 20 miles from home, juggling my legs to stop them seizing.

I wish I could remember more clearly how it must have felt to have just 20 of 18,000 miles remaining . . . just 20 miles from an achievement that perhaps, I suppose, means more to me than I readily admit. Then 20 turned to 17, to 12 . . . banking against roundabouts at the crossroads of ploughed fields, telegraph poles marching between villages, a sky with dusk upon it as I went on motoring with merciless pedalstrokes, a calculated assassination of every remaining mile. Writing this now, I realise how magnificently unstoppable I felt that evening, possessed of such confidence, finally able to banish all doubt, within touching distance of ending that so-called suffering. It was never truly suffering, let me tell you . . . only ever an arduous joy, so quickly do hardships become the stuff of just stories and fond memories.

There was such surety, such surety I say . . . riding in and out of Elbeuf, that small town through which I'd passed a handful of times as a younger man. Such surety then, as I turned towards the river and made north for the city of Rouen. Such surety I tell you, the whole thing nearly at an end, all of it set and certain within my head as ten miles disappeared behind me and then five miles and then, and then . . . *and then* . . . *sweet Jesus* . . . such surety to crumble so swift. I was set upon by bewilderment, hallucinations pure and simple. I'll tell you what, tell you in no uncertain terms, that right there before my eyes was not the Cathedral of Rouen, not the Cathedral of Rouen on the skyline before me.

In front of me were two isosceles triangles, nicely illuminated, light against the dark, pointing to the heavens . . . but it was not, I repeat, the Cathedral of Rouen. For that was where it all had started, and that was where it was to end. And yet, surely it was not to end, it wasn't about to be over . . . I could not have left that spot for the east and returned to it from the west, with my bicycle and all of the world between. Could it have been . . . but surely not . . . only a flash in the pan of time?

Through an alleyway, narrow and empty, wet cobbles shone with promise under the night. I rolled slow, breathing light, breathing dreamlike. All around the air was soft, the stars so fine, as up ahead I saw the alley widen. The buildings opened, walls gave way to that square before the cathedral. I remember lights, bright lights, the stalls of a Christmas market, a carousel . . . I distinctly remember a carousel . . . and such bright lights. They were all there, all of them, waiting there with flags in such bright lights. The carousel turns, ponies and elephants on poles, beneath an awning of coloured lights, such bright lights, and all of them there. That fairground music rose up so loud, carousel circling, the fairground music so loud. A cheer went up . . . hands waving, a cheer, the fairground music so loud, so much light . . . *so much light!* They hung a wreath about my neck, all holly and ivy and mistletoe, hung it around my neck like the door-knocker on a Belgravia door at Advent, a bottle of something shoved in my hand. *A cheer!* Such bright light. And they were all there.

It was too much to reckon with. That first night, safely inside the farmhouse with a king-size bed made ready for me . . . I couldn't do it, got stage-fright. I stayed up late, staring alone into first the flames and then the embers. Alone, I slept before the fire, curled upon the settee with a blanket over me. Next morning, I woke early, halfway cold, my back aching, chill beneath my blanket, my knees curled upon the settee. I don't know why . . . but I felt comfortable that way.

JULIAN SAYARER cycled a half dozen times across Europe to his second nation of Turkey before breaking a world record for a circumnavigation by bicycle – riding 18,049 miles through 20 countries in 169 days. That extraordinary journey is the subject of this book. He is the winner of the Stanford Dolman Travel Writing Award for *Interstate* (2016), an account of hitchhiking through middle America, and is the author of *Messengers* (2016), *All at Sea* (2017), *Fifty Miles Wide* (2020) and *Iberia* (2021). Julian uses a background in political science to create a critically acclaimed travel-writing style – politics at roadsides. In this 12-mph view of the world in passing, his human stories and journeys document global issues for a broad audience. His writing has appeared in the *London Review of Books*, the *Guardian*, *Aeon Magazine*, among others, and in numerous cycling publications.